A CENTURY OF AGRICULTURAL GROWTH IN JAPAN

A CENTURY OF AGRICULTURAL GROWTH IN JAPAN

Its Relevance to Asian Development

YUJIRO HAYAMI

in association with
MASAKATSU AKINO
MASAHIKO SHINTANI
SABURO YAMADA

UNIVERSITY OF MINNESOTA PRESS
Minneapolis

UNIVERSITY OF TOKYO PRESS
Tokyo

© 1975
University of Tokyo Press
International Standard Book Number 0-8166-0748-6

Published in the United States of
America by the University of
Minnesota Press, Minneapolis, and
in Canada by Burns & MacEachern,
Don Mills, Ontario

Library of Congress Catalog Card Number 74-28912

Printed in Tokyo at Kenkyūsha Printing Company

Contents

List of Tables

List of Figures

Preface

What is the significance of agricultural development in Japan during a century of modern economic growth? Does the Japanese experience have any relevance to the problems that Asian farmers are now facing? These basic questions underlie the studies in this volume.

History is a mirror on which the image of the present comes into focus by comparison with similarities and differences of the past. In this volume we have tried to construct such a mirror, in the form of a positive economic analysis of the long-term growth of Japanese agriculture, that may facilitate a correct understanding of the nature and magnitude of the problems of agricultural development in Asia today.

The present volume represents a final report of a research project entitled "Science and Agricultural Progress: The Japanese Experience," which was conducted during the period 1972–1974. The project was supported by a generous grant from the Rockefeller Foundation to the University of Minnesota Economic Development Center. It was an extension of research conducted by the author with Vernon W. Ruttan at the University of Minnesota (the results were published in Hayami and Ruttan, *Agricultural Development: An International Perspective*, Johns Hopkins University Press, 1971).

Besides the author and the three associate authors, Masao Kikuchi and Keijiro Otsuka participated in the project. The six of us worked closely. Each step of research was examined carefully through group discussions. Thus, all of us contributed more or less to each chapter of the book. Major contributions of the associate authors to respective chapters are: Masakatsu Akino, Chapters 4, 6 and 7; Masahiko Shintani, Chapter 2; and Saburo Yamada, Chapters 2 and 5. However, part of the credit should also go to the two non-author participants in the project.

The book draws on a number of earlier studies by the authors extending back almost two decades (as acknowledged in the text). Especially, it draws heavily on the Hayami-Ruttan volume cited earlier and on Yujiro Hayami, *Nihon Nogyo no Hatten Katei* (The Process of Agricultural Development in Japan), (Tokyo: Sobunsha Press, 1973). The previously published results were, however, largely revised and reorganized for this volume.

It was Vernon Ruttan, the former director of the University of Minnesota Economic Development Center, who first stimulated the author to begin the project that resulted in this book. Without his encouragement the project would not have been undertaken and completed. Martin Abel, the present director of the center, has continued to provide the moral and logistical supports. I appreciate the professional interest of Sterling Wortman and R. K. Davidson of the Rockefeller Foundation in the substance of the study as well as the financial support of the Foundation. Randolph Barker, Shigeru Ishikawa, Kazushi Ohkawa, T. W. Schultz, and Mataji Umemura have been the secular source of our consultation. We have also benefited from comments and suggestions of Moses Abramovitz, Colin Clark, Robert Evenson, Zvi Griliches, Kenzo Henmi, Bruce Johnston, Dale Jorgenson, Simon Kuznets, Ryoshin Minami, James Nakamura, Takashi Negishi, Hugh Patrick, Willis Peterson, Gustav Ranis, Henry Rosovsky, Shujiro Sawada, Peter Timmer, Jeffrey Williamson, and Yasukichi Yasuba. Invaluable services on editorial and technical problems have been provided by Mrs. Barbara Miller, Miss Elizabeth Powers, and Tokei Kenkyu Kai (Institute of Statistical Research, Inc.). The fellowship grant to Masakatsu Akino from the Harvard University East-Asian Research Center has facilitated the final brush-up of the manuscript. Finally, my association with the International Rice Research Institute since last summer has provided me with a rare opportunity to reconsider the implications of the Japanese experience in light of the reality of the problems facing developing countries in Asia. For all these benefits, I express the deepest gratitude.

YUJIRO HAYAMI
Los Baños, Philippines
January 1975

A CENTURY OF AGRICULTURAL GROWTH IN JAPAN

Part 1 Chronology of Growth

MAP OF JAPAN

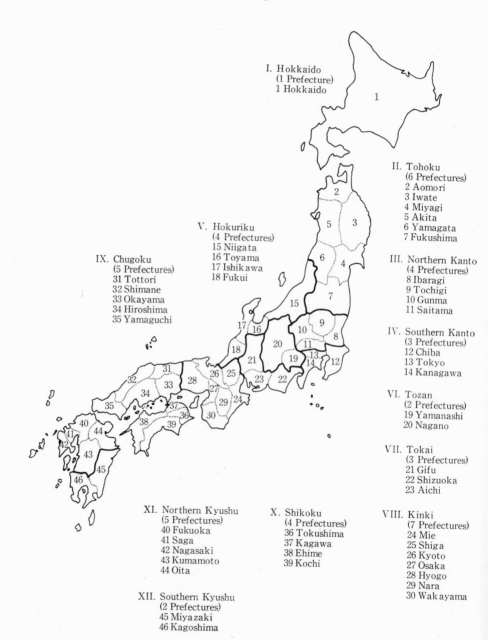

I. Hokkaido
(1 Prefecture)
1 Hokkaido

II. Tohoku
(6 Prefectures)
2 Aomori
3 Iwate
4 Miyagi
5 Akita
6 Yamagata
7 Fukushima

V. Hokuriku
(4 Prefectures)
15 Niigata
16 Toyama
17 Ishikawa
18 Fukui

IX. Chugoku
(5 Prefecturès)
31 Tottori
32 Shimane
33 Okayama
34 Hiroshima
35 Yamaguchi

III. Northern Kanto
(4 Prefectures)
8 Ibaragi
9 Tochigi
10 Gunma
11 Saitama

IV. Southern Kanto
(3 Prefectures)
12 Chiba
13 Tokyo
14 Kanagawa

VI. Tozan
(2 Prefectures)
19 Yamanashi
20 Nagano

VII. Tokai
(3 Prefectures)
21 Gifu
22 Shizuoka
23 Aichi

VIII. Kinki
(7 Prefectures)
24 Mie
25 Shiga
26 Kyoto
27 Osaka
28 Hyogo
29 Nara
30 Wakayama

XI. Northern Kyushu
(5 Prefectures)
40 Fukuoka
41 Saga
42 Nagasaki
43 Kumamoto
44 Oita

X. Shikoku
(4 Prefectures)
36 Tokushima
37 Kagawa
38 Ehime
39 Kochi

XII. Southern Kyushu
(2 Prefectures)
45 Miyazaki
46 Kagoshima

Chapter 1 Introduction

Within the century since the Meiji Restoration in 1868, Japan has emerged from a predominantly rural state to one of the most highly industrialized nations in the world (Table 1–1). In the process of structural transformation and economic growth the agricultural sector has played a critical role as a supplier of resources to the nonfarm sector and has provided a market for the products of urban industries.

Especially in the early periods, when there was no accumulated industrial capital, Japan was able to finance industrialization by mobilizing the surpluses of agriculture.[1] The major source of funds that enabled government programs to import modern plants and technology was the revenue from the land tax.[2] Landlords invested a substantial portion of income from rent in nonfarm economic activities, either directly or through financial intermediaries.

In addition, by the export of such primary commodities as silk and tea, foreign exchange needed in the early periods for the import of capital goods and technical know-how was accumulated. At the time of the Meiji Restoration in Japan the ratio of agricultural products in the total commodity export was nearly 80 percent, and the ratio did not decline to 50 percent until the twentieth century.[3]

Throughout the process of modern economic growth agriculture has been the source of the highly elastic supply of labor for industry. Until the spurt of postwar economic growth, beginning in the

Table 1-1. Indicators of Economic Growth and Structural Transformation

	Labor				Net Domestic Product	
	Primary[b]	Non-primary	Total	Ratio of Primary to Total	Primary[b]	Non-primary
	(1)	(2)	(3)	(1)/(3)	(4)	(5)
	·············1000 workers··············			%	··············million *yen*	
1880	16,408	5,462	21,870	75.0		
1885	16,424	5,883	22,307	73.6	1,619	2,557
1890	16,452	6,557	23,009	71.5	1,675	2,922
1895	16,511	7,213	23,724	69.6	1,744	3,561
1900	16,663	7,711	24,374	68.4	1,939	4,195
1905	16,767	8,212	24,979	67.1	2,126	4,679
1910	16,706	8,805	25,511	65.5	2,262	5,439
1915	16,146	10,188	26,334	61.3	2,589	6,395
1920	14,768	12,455	27.223	54.2	2,681	8,545
1925	14,264	13,889	28,153	50.7	2,672	9,848
1930	14,724	14,825	29,554	49.8	2,781	11,115
1935	14,606	16,570	31,176	46.9	2,985	13,843
1940	14,150	18,594	32,744	43.2	3,190	18,699
1945						
1950						
1955	16,274	24,414	40,688	40.0	4,633	19,283
1960	14,418	30,072	44,490	32.4	5,474	35,858
1965	12,144	35,488	47,632	25.5	6,531	58,840
1970	10,377	42,230	52,607	19.7	7,571	91,102

[a] Five-year averages centering the years shown.
[b] Agriculture, forestry, and fishing.

SOURCE : Labor force and national income data prepared for Kazushi

late 1950's, the outmigration of the labor force to urban occupations had not been large enough to reduce significantly the absolute size of the labor population in agriculture. Yet, the transfer of workers over and above the replacement population in the rural sector had been sufficient to keep the real wage rate stable in the urban sector, except for during the World War I boom.[4] Such an elastic labor supply to industry (which could well be approximated by the " unlimited supply " in the classical dual economy model of the Lewis-Fei and Ranis tradition)[5] prevented the rise in the wage cost in spite of the expanding demand for labor by urban enterprises, thereby providing a basis for the rapid in Japan[a]

(1934–1936 prices)	Net Domestic Product per Worker						Net
Total	Ratio of Primary to Total	Primary[b]	Non-primary	Total	Ratio of Primary to Non-primary	Total Population	Net Domestic Product per Capita
(6)	(4)/(6)	(7)	(8)	(9)	(7)/(8)	(10)	(6)/(10)
....	%	.... yen			%	1000 persons	yen
						36,701	
4,176	38.8	99	435	187	22.8	38,218	109
4,597	36.4	102	446	200	22.9	39,833	115
5,305	32.9	106	494	224	21.5	41,590	128
6,134	31.6	116	544	252	21.3	43,892	140
6,805	31.2	127	570	272	22.3	46,551	146
7,701	29.4	135	618	302	21.8	49,226	156
8,984	28.8	160	628	341	25.5	52,745	170
11,226	23.9	182	686	412	26.5	55,633	202
12,520	21.3	187	709	445	26.4	59,292	211
13,896	20.0	189	750	470	25.2	63,926	217
16,828	17.7	204	835	540	24.4	68,572	245
21,889	14.6	225	1,006	668	22.4	71,336	307
						74,640	
						83,058	
23,916	19.4	285	790	588	36.1	89,115	268
41,332	13.2	380	1,192	929	31.9	93,458	442
65,371	10.0	538	1,658	1,372	32.4	98,166	666
98,673	8.3	730	2,157	1,876	33.8	103,141	957

Ohkawa, Miyohei Shinohara, and Mataji Umemura, eds., *Estimates of Long-term Economic Statistics of Japan since 1868*, vols. 1 and 2 (Tokyo: Toyokeizaishimposha, forthcoming). Population data from Bank of Japan, *Hundred-Year Statistics of the Japanese Economy* (Tokyo, 1966), pp. 12–13.

accumulation of industrial profit.

A condition for the elastic supply of labor is the supply of food, the principal wage good, to the urban sector at stable prices. If the supply of food does not increase sufficiently to meet the demand of the growing urban population, food prices will rise sharply and push up the cost of living of urban workers. In the long run, the rise in the wage good prices will push up the money wage rate, resulting in a decline in the rate of profit, and, hence, contribute to the deceleration in the rate of capital formation.[6] Thus, an increase in the marketable surplus of food represents a necessary condition for structural transformation and economic growth.

Cheaper foodstuffs might be imported from abroad, but such a measure implies a serious drain on scarce foreign exchange. To recapitulate, in the course of modern economic growth in Japan, agriculture supported industrial development as a major source of resources. As a prerequisite, surpluses had to be created in the agricultural sector. Such institutions as the land tax and landlordism served to squeeze agricultural surpluses out to the nonagricultural sector. Despite such institutions, however, requirements for agricultural surpluses in the process of structural transformation could have not been met without an increase in agricultural productivity. It is the purpose of this book to identify the sources of productivity growth in agriculture that played such a critical role in the economic development of Japan.

A unique aspect of agricultural growth in modern Japan was that the sustained growth in productivity was achieved against the

Table 1-2. Comparison of Agricultural Productivities and Man/Land Ratios Between Japan and Selected Countries in Asia

	Agricultural Output per Male Farm Worker (wheat units per worker)	Agricultural Output per Hectare of Agricultural Land (wheat units per hectare)	Agricultural Land Area per Male Worker (hectares per worker)
Japan			
1878–1882	2.5	2.9	0.9
1898–1902	3.4	3.6	0.9
1933–1937	7.1	5.5	1.3
1957–1962	10.7	7.5	1.4
Asian, 1957–1962			
Ceylon	3.9	2.9	1.3
India	2.1	1.1	1.9
Pakistan	2.4		
Philippines	3.8	1.9	2.0

NOTE : *Agricultural output in wheat units:* Gross agricultural output net of intermediate products, such as seed and feed. Individual products are aggregated by the price ratios to the price of wheat per one metric ton.
Farm workers: Economically active male population in agriculture.
Agricultural land area: Includes permanent pasture land.
SOURCE : Yujiro Hayami and V. W. Ruttan, *Agricultural Development: An International Perspective* (Baltimore and London : Johns Hopkins University Press, 1971), pp. 70 and 328. Japan's time series are revised according to the revised data in the appendix of this book.

strong constraint of land resources without a drastic change occurring in the traditional structure of rural organization. Available data indicate that Meiji Japan inherited a very unfavorable man/land ratio from the feudal Tokugawa period, even when compared with the densely populated countries in South and Southeast Asia today (Table 1–2). The unfavorable endowment of land resources relative to labor was, however, compensated for by a higher land productivity, with the result that labor productivity in agriculture in Meiji Japan was at the level prevailing in Asia today.

From such a low initial level, the productivity of Japanese agriculture has grown and reached a level of agricultural output per male worker that exceeds the Asian standard by a wide margin. The long-term growth rates in output and productivity are comparable to those in such countries as the United States, which are favored by rich endowments of land resources.[7] A major com-

Table 1–3. Distribution of Farms by Size of Cultivated Land Area

Year	Number of Farms (1000)[a]						
	Less than 0.5 ha.	0.5–1 ha.	1–2 ha.	2–3 ha.	3–5 ha.	Larger than 5 ha.	Total
1908	2,016 (37.3)	1,764 (32.6)	1,055 (19.5)	348 (6.4)	163 (3.0)	62 (1.1)	5,408 (100.0)
1910	2,032 (37.5)	1,789 (33.0)	1,048 (19.3)	322 (5.9)	156 (2.9)	71 (1.3)	5,417 (100.0)
1920	1,935 (35.3)	1,829 (33.3)	1,133 (20.7)	341 (6.2)	154 (2.8)	92 (1.7)	5,485 (100.0)
1930	1,891 (34.3)	1,892 (34.3)	1,217 (22.1)	314 (5.7)	128 (2.3)	70 (1.3)	5,511 (100.0)
1940	1,796 (33.3)	1,768 (32.8)	1,322 (24.5)	309 (5.7)	119 (2.2)	76 (1.4)	5,390 (100.0)
1950	2,531 (41.0)	1,973 (32.0)	1,339 (21.7)	208 (3.4)	77 (1.2)	48 (0.8)	6,176 (100.0)
1960	2,320 (38.3)	1,923 (31.7)	1,430 (23.6)	233 (3.8)	91 (1.5)	60 (1.0)	6,057 (100.0)
1970	2,025 (38.0)	1,614 (30.2)	1,286 (24.1)	256 (4.8)	90 (1.7)	71 (1.3)	5,342 (100.0)

[a] Percentage distribution is shown in parentheses.
SOURCE: Institute of Developing Economies, *One Hundred Years of Agricultural Statistics in Japan* (Tokyo, 1969), p. 116; and Ministry of Agriculture and Forestry Statistical Research Division, *1970 World Census of Agriculture Report on Farmhouseholds and Population* (Tokyo, 1971).

ponent in the growth in the output per worker in Japanese agriculture was the increase in yield per unit of agricultural land area.
Meanwhile, there was little change in the structure of rural
organization in terms of a " unimodal " distribution of small-scale
family farms (Table 1–3). Technical improvements in agriculture
were clearly consistent with both the resource endowments and the
rural organization of Japan.

The Japanese experience, as outlined so far, is frequently
pointed to as a model of economic development for the developing
countries of Asia today.[8] Of course, we must strongly guard our-
selves against easy historical generalization and must be very
cautious about deriving " lessons " from past experiences. Also, we
should be reminded of the many dark sides of Japanese agricultural history. Because of the heavy burden of taxes and rent,
coupled with a lag in productivity growth in agriculture relative to
the nonfarm sector, the level of income and consumption of farm
households lagged behind urban households and resulted in serious
rural unrest, especially during the interwar period.

Yet, there is no denying that the process by which Japanese
agriculture sustained a long-term growth in productivity, in spite
of the severe constraint of land resources, suggests a possible
strategy for other Asian countries now groping for rapid economic
development under extremely strong population pressures upon
land.

Discussions on whether the Japanese experience is transferable,
or which aspects of the Japanese experience are transferable,
should be settled on the basis of positive economic analysis. This
book represents an attempt to add empirical evidence to such a
strategic question.

We approach the problem mainly from the side of real input-
output relations in agriculture within the framework of the partial
equilibrium analysis of Marshallian tradition.   A major focus is
placed on the evolution of the institutions that allocated resources
to produce the " high-payoff inputs," in the sense of Theodore
Schultz, necessary for transforming agriculture into a modern
dynamic sector.[9] In particular, we are concerned with the investments in social overhead capital, such as land infrastructure and
the agricultural-research system. In the organization of agriculture, characterized as in Japan by masses of small producers,

public support or group action to allocate resources for such public goods as irrigation and new technology represents a key to the growth in output and productivity. It is our major concern to investigate the process by which the development of critical infrastructure was induced by economic forces through dynamic interactions among farmers and public agents.

This book consists of four parts. In part I (chapters 2 and 3) we draw a chronology of agricultural development in modern Japan. In order to give a clear perspective on the quantitative aspects of agricultural growth, chapter 2 measures the long-term trends in output, inputs, productivities, and product and factor prices. Chapter 3 summarizes the process of the evolution of institutions for agricultural development in reference to the observed trends reported in the chapter 2.

In part II (chapters 4 and 5) we explore the sources of agricultural productivity growth through the analysis of aggregative data of the agricultural sector. Chapter 4 measures the contributions of various factors of production within the framework of the aggregate production function. Chapter 5 identifies the sources of significant changes in the major growth phases through the analysis of interregional diffusion of rice technology.

In part III (chapters 6 and 7) we analyze the process by which resources were allocated for the development of critical infrastructure. This infrastructure enabled the sustained growth of Japanese agriculture under the severe constraint of land resource. Chapter 6 demonstrates the contributions of the agricultural-research system by measuring the social returns to public investments in rice-breeding programs. Chapter 7 identifies the economic and social forces that induced investments in such improvements of land infrastructure as irrigation and drainage.

Finally, in part IV (chapter 8) we discuss the significance of the Japanese experience in drawing implications relevant to agricultural-development strategies in Asia today.

Notes to Chapter 1

[1] The hypothesis that there was a significant net flow of resources from the agricultural to the nonagricultural sector in the early period of modern economic growth in Japan was suggested by B. F. Johnston, "Agricultural Productivity and Economic Development in Japan," *Journal of Political Economy* 59 (December 1951):

498–513; and Kazushi Ohkawa and Henry Rosovsky, "The Role of Agriculture in Modern Japanese Economic Development," *Economic Development and Cultural Change* 9 (October 1960): 43–67. The comprehensive but somewhat preliminary study by Shigeru Ishikawa, *Economic Development in Asian Perspective* (Tokyo: Kinokuniya, 1967) supports this hypothesis. Partial supporting evidence includes the study of government finance by Gustav Ranis, "Financing of Japanese Economic Development," *Economic History Review* 11 (April 1959): 440–454; and the analysis of financial intermediaries by Yuzuru Kato, "Development of Long-Term Agricultural Credit," in *Agriculture and Economic Growth: Japan's Experience*, eds. Kazushi Ohkawa, B. F. Johnston, and Hiromitsu Kaneda (Tokyo: University of Tokyo Press, 1969), pp. 324–351.

[2] See Ranis, "Financing of Japanese Economic Development."

[3] Takekazu Ogura, ed., *Agricultural Development in Modern Japan* (Tokyo: Fuji Publishing Co., 1963), p. 24. Also, see Kenzo Henmi, "Primary Exports and Economic Development: The Case of Silk," in *Agriculture and Economic Growth*, eds. Ohkawa, Johnston, and Kaneda, pp. 303–323.

[4] Ryoshin Minami, "The Turning Point in the Japanese Economy," *Quarterly Journal of Economics* 82 (August 1968): 380–402.

[5] W. A. Lewis, "Economic Development with Unlimited Supplies of Labour," *Manchester School of Economics and Social Studies* 22 (May 1954): 139–191; and J. C. H. Fei and Gustav Ranis, *Development of the Labor Surplus Economy* (Homewood, Illinois: Richard D. Irwin, 1964).

[6] For a case study on the role of staple food prices in economic development, see the discussions on the role of rice as a principal wage good in Yujiro Hayami, "Rice Policy in Japan's Economic Development," *American Journal of Agricultural Economics* 54 (February 1972): 19–31.

[7] Yujiro Hayami and V. W. Ruttan, *Agricultural Development: An International Perspective* (Baltimore and London: Johns Hopkins University Press, 1971), pp. 111–135.

[8] Among others, see Johnston, "Agricultural Productivity and Economic Development"; and Ohkawa and Rosovsky, "The Role of Agriculture." Also, see B. F. Johnston, "The Japanese Model of Agricultural Development: Its Relevance to Developing Nations," in *Agriculture and Economic Growth*, eds., Ohkawa, Johnston, and Kaneda, pp. 58–102.

[9] T. W. Schultz, *Transforming Traditional Agriculture* (New Haven: Yale University Press, 1964).

Chapter 2 Trends in Output, Inputs, and Productivities[1]

As the first step in exploring the sources of long-term growth in Japanese agriculture, we will attempt in this chapter to measure the rates of change in agricultural output, inputs, and productivities for the period from approximately 1880 to 1970, almost the entire period of modern economic development in Japan. "Agriculture " is narrowly defined here as comprising the farm sector and does not include forestry and fishing.

The data on which it has been necessary to draw in conducting this study have substantial limitations. As is common for any historical statistics, both the reliability and the coverage of agricultural production statistics in Japan decline as we go back to the earlier periods of economic development.[2] Since there have been dramatic changes in relative prices and relative shares both among products and among inputs in the course of economic transformation, there is no way to escape index-number problems. In spite of efforts to improve our time-series data, substantial measurement errors undoubtedly still remain. Since much of the data are admittedly crude, analysis must be limited to the broadest trends in agricultural-growth experiences. In order to estimate the broad trends in long-term growth we have based our analysis on the data of five-year averages instead of annual observations.

Although we prepared quinquennial time-series data until 1970 (1968–1972 averages), the terminal observation generally used in this study is that of 1965 (1963–1967 averages). This is mainly because we wanted to avoid dealing with disturbances due to the extremely high level of rice price support in the late 1960's, which was followed by the paddy-field retirement program. There are signs that Japanese agriculture has entered into a new phase since the late 1960's, but the time-series are not long enough to ascertain the new phase within the framework of long-term growth analysis. For this reason we exclude the post-1965 period from the focus of analysis in this chapter. The nature of the agricultural problems of Japan in more recent years is discussed in detail in the next chapter.

The sources and the processing procedures of data used in this chapter are explained in the Appendix.

2-1   Trends in Agricultural Output

Growth in aggregate output

First we will follow the trends in aggregate agricultural output.

The " total output " primarily used in this study for the measurement of agricultural-growth rates is defined as " total production " in agriculture minus " agricultural intermediate products," aggregated by 1934–1936 average constant prices. The total production is the simple aggregate of all individual farm products; the sub-aggregates are (a) rice, (b) other field crops, (c) sericulture, and (d) livestock. The agricultural intermediate products include

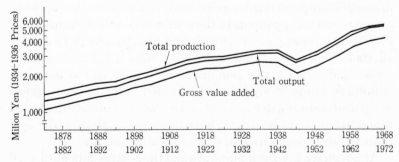

Figure 2–1. Trends in total production, total output, and gross value added in agriculture, 1934–1936 constant prices, five-year averages, semi-log scale.

SOURCE: Same as for Table 2–1.

Table 2-1.   Annual Compound Rates of Growth in Agriculture (%)*

		Total Production	Total Output	Gross Value Added
I	1880–1900	1.5	1.6	1.8
	(1880–1895)	(1.2)	(1.4)	(1.3)
II	1900–1920	1.9	2.0	1.9
	(1905–1920)	(1.9)	(2.0)	(1.9)
III	1920–1935	0.9	0.9	0.8
IV	1935–1945	−1.8	−1.9	−2.1
V	1945–1955	3.1	3.2	3.0
VI	1955–1965	3.3	3.6	3.2
	(1960–1970)	(2.2)	(2.4)	(1.9)
Prewar period :				
	1880–1935	1.5	1.6	1.6
Postwar period :				
	1945–1965	3.3	3.4	3.1
	(1945–1970)	(3.1)	(3.1)	(2.8)
Whole period :				
	1880–1965	1.5	1.6	1.5
	(1880–1970)	(1.5)	(1.6)	(1.5)

* Growth rates between five-year averages centering the years shown.
SOURCE :   Appendix Table A-1.

the agricultural products used as inputs for agricultural production, such as seeds and feeds (feeds processed by the nonfarm sector and imported from abroad are not included).

By subtracting " nonfarm current inputs " from total output, we obtain " gross value added " in agriculture (equivalent to " gross domestic product " in the terms of ordinary national-income accounting). " Nonfarm current inputs " are current inputs supplied to agriculture from the nonfarm sector, such as commercial fertilizers.

The time-series data of total production, total output, and gross value added in agriculture are plotted in Figure 2–1. Judging from the figure and the growth rates calculated in Table 2–1, these three series have the same major trends in common. Overall, agricultural output grew for the entire period 1880–1965 at the annual compound rate of about 1.5 percent. Three major phases are distinct: (a) relatively fast growth up to the 1910's, (b) relative stagnation in the interwar period, and (c) a spurt following World War II.

During the initial growth phase there is some evidence that the growth rate accelerated at the beginning of this century. In terms of total production and output the growth rates increased from 1880–1900 to 1900–1920 by 25 percent. The growth rates were particularly fast from the time of the Russo-Japanese War (1903–1904) to World War I (1914–1918). Though less clear, the acceleration in the growth rate of gross value added can also be observed.

The relatively rapid growth in the initial phase and the acceleration during the period from the Russo-Japanese War to World War I are, in general, parallel to the industrial growth.[3] This parallelism breaks down in the subsequent decades of the 1920's and 1930's. While industry continued to expand, agriculture entered into a stagnation phase. Growth rates in this period declined to one-half of those in the previous period in terms of total production and output, as well as of gross value added. Although there were signs in the mid-1930's that agricultural production had resumed rapid growth, increasing shortages in labor and other inputs for agriculture—due to military involvements in China followed by the Pacific War—caused a sharp decline in agricultural production.

After the devastation of World War II, Japanese agriculture recovered very rapidly and reached the prewar level by the end of the Korean War. It is generally agreed that the recovery was completed with the bumper crop of rice in 1955. The postwar spurt in agricultural growth was not simply a recovery phenomenon. Even after 1955 total production, output, and gross value added in agriculture continued to grow at annual rates higher than 3 percent, although there are signs of deceleration since the late 1950's.

From the above discussions we will adopt the approximate time breakdown into the six subperiods (I to VI) shown in Table 2–1. In the modern economic history of Japan, period I corresponds to the period of establishment of the physical and institutional infrastructure for industrial and economic development; period II to the initial spurt in industrialization (or take-off); period III to the post-World War I recession followed by the world-wide depression; period IV to the devastation due to World War II; period V to the recovery from the war; and period VI to the big spurt in postwar economic growth.

It has been observed that agricultural-growth trends in terms of

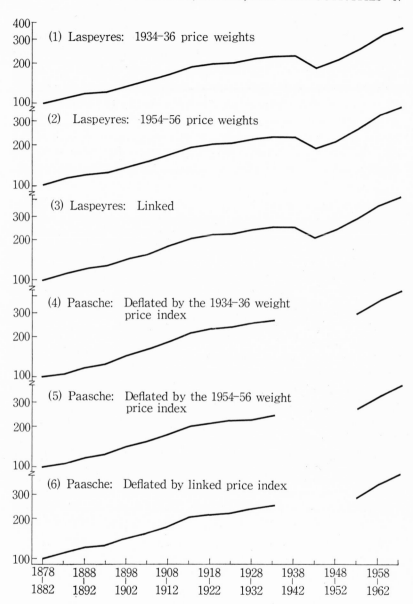

Figure 2–2. Comparison of trends in total output in agriculture by different index formulae, 1878–1872=100, five-year averages, semi-log
scale.

SOURCE: Same as for Table 2–2.

total production, total output, and gross value added are essentially the same. Henceforth, we will base our analysis on the series of total output. The gross value added could be more useful for intersectoral study, but it would not be appropriate for the analysis of growth in the agricultural sector per se because it excludes the nonfarm current inputs, especially fertilizers, which have been critical for Japanese agricultural development.

Our data of total output are aggregated by 1934–1936 constant prices. One may question if this might involve bias, typical to the quantity index of the Laspeyres type. However, a comparison with other output series using different aggregation procedures indicates that the choice of this particular method of aggregation does not significantly affect the conclusion concerning growth rates of agricultural output (see Figure 2–2 and Table 2–2).

Table 2-2.   Comparison of Annual Compound Rates of Growth in Total Output by Different Index Formulae (%)*

	I	II	III	IV	V
	1880– 1900	1900– 1920	1920– 1935	1945– 1955	1955– 1965
Laspeyres Index:					
(1) 1934–1936 price weights	1.6	2.0	0.9	3.2	3.6
(2) 1954–1956 price weights	1.7	2.0	0.8	3.4	3.5
(3) Linked[a]	1.8	2.2	0.9	3.4	3.6
Paasche Index:					
(4) Deflated by 1934–1936 weight price index	2.0	2.3	1.0		3.7
(5) Deflated by 1954–1956 weight price index	1.8	2.0	0.9		3.9
(6) Deflated by linked price index[b]	1.7	2.1	1.0		3.9

* Growth rates between five-year averages centering the years shown.
[a] Four quantity indices of price weights for 1874–1876, 1904–1906, 1934–1936, and 1954–1956 are linked in a chain by multiplying consecutively their average ratios at 1896–1898, 1918–1820, and 1944–1946.
[b] Four price indices of quantity weights for 1874–1876, 1904–1906, 1934–1936, and 1954–1956 are linked in a chain by multiplying consecutively their average ratios at 1896–1898, 1918–1920, and 1936.
SOURCE: Appendix Table A-1 and Kazushi Ohkawa, Miyohei Shinohara and Mataji Umemura, eds., *Long-term Economic Statistics of Japan since 1868*, Vol. 9 (Tokyo: Toyokeizaishimposha, 1966), pp. 148–165.

Growth in agricultural production by commodity groups

Extremely different patterns in the growth in agricultural production by commodities have emerged, corresponding to differences in the rates of changes in technology and demand (Figure 2–3 and Table 2–3). As a result, both the real and the nominal composition of commodities in total production has changed greatly (Figures 2–4 and 2–5 and Tables 2–4 and 2–5).

Production of rice, by far the most important commodity in agriculture in Japan, grew slowly, compared with other products. However, because of its great value in agricultural production, changes in the rate of growth in rice production have been the

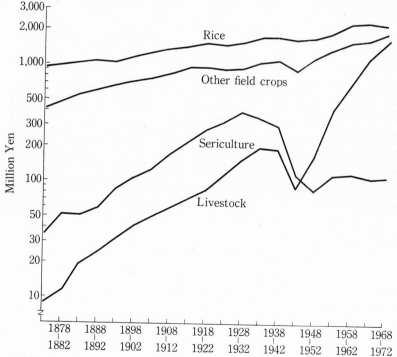

Figure 2–3.   Trends in agricultural production by commodities, 1934–1936 constant prices, five-year averages, semi-log scale.
SOURCE: Same as for Table 2–3.

Table 2-3.   Annual Compound Rates of Growth in Agricultural Production by Major Commodity Groups (%)*

Period	Crops			Sericulture	Livestock
	Rice	Other	Total		
I 1880–1900	0.9	2.1	1.3	3.9	6.8
II 1900–1920	1.7	1.4	1.6	4.7	3.8
III 1920–1935	0.4	0.7	0.5	1.7	5.7
IV 1935–1945	−0.4	−1.6	−0.8	−10.3	−7.6
V 1945–1955	1.4	4.5	2.5	−0.5	16.3
VI 1955–1965	2.2	1.7	2.0	−0.3	11.0
Prewar period :					
1880–1935	1.1	1.5	1.2	3.6	5.4
Postwar period :					
1945–1965	1.8	3.1	2.3	−0.4	13.6
(1945–1970)	(1.4)	(2.7)	(1.9)	(−0.2)	(12.4)
Whole period :					
1880–1965	1.1	1.5	1.2	0.9	5.6
(1880–1970)	(1.0)	(1.5)	(1.2)	(0.9)	(5.7)

* Growth rates between five-year averages centering the years shown.
SOURCE :   Appendix Table A-1.

major determinant of the growth pattern of total agricultural production. Sequences in (*a*) acceleration in output growth rate at the beginning of this century, followed by (*b*) stagnation in the interwar period and (*c*) recovery from the sharp decline during World War II and continued rapid rise are most pronounced in rice production. The trends in rice production set a pace for the growth in total crop production and, also, in total agricultural production.

Rapid growth in the production of sericulture (silk cocoon) until the 1920's, its sharp contraction due to the world depression, and the competition from artificial fibers contribute to the formation of a distinct kink in the rate of agricultural growth from period II to period III. During World War II the share of sericulture was reduced to such a low level that changes in sericultural production no longer affect the aggregate growth rate.

Livestock production started from a negligible level and, in spite of its rapid growth, the share of livestock product in total agricultural production did not rise to a significant level before World War II. However, through a dramatic rise in the two post-

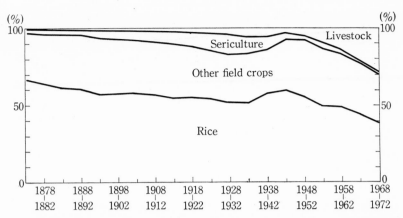

Figure 2–4. Percentage composition of agricultural production by commodities, real composition, 1934–1936 constant prices.
SOURCE: Same as for Table 2–4.

Table 2-4. Percentage Composition of Agricultural Production by Commodities in Terms of 1934-1936 Constant Prices (%)

	Crops			Sericul-ture	Live-stock	Total
	Rice	Other	Total			
1874–1877	67.0	29.8	96.8	2.6	0.6	100.0
1878–1882	64.3	31.6	95.9	3.4	0.7	100.0
1883–1887	62.1	33.7	95.8	3.0	1.2	100.0
1888–1892	60.8	34.6	95.4	3.3	1.3	100.0
1893–1897	57.1	36.4	93.5	4.7	1.8	100.0
1898–1902	57.4	35.2	92.6	5.4	2.0	100.0
1903–1907	57.6	34.4	92.0	5.8	2.2	100.0
1908–1912	56.5	34.2	90.7	6.9	2.4	100.0
1913–1917	54.7	34.8	89.5	7.9	2.6	100.0
1918–1922	55.3	32.5	87.8	9.3	2.9	100.0
1923–1927	53.9	31.1	85.0	11.1	3.9	100.0
1928–1932	52.6	30.1	82.7	12.4	4.9	100.0
1933–1937	51.8	31.8	83.6	10.5	5.9	100.0
1938–1942	52.3	33.0	85.3	9.0	5.7	100.0
1943–1947	59.9	32.6	92.5	4.3	3.2	100.0
1948–1952	55.3	36.8	92.1	2.7	5.2	100.0
1953–1957	49.9	36.7	86.6	2.9	10.5	100.0
1958–1962	48.6	34.4	83.0	2.5	14.5	100.0
1963–1967	45.0	31.3	76.3	2.1	21.6	100.0
1968–1972	40.0	30.2	70.2	1.9	27.9	100.0

SOURCE : Appendix Table A-1.

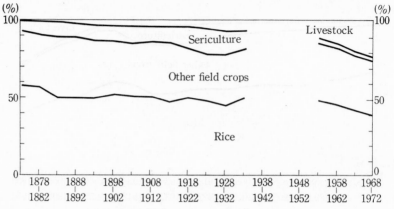

Figure 2–5.   Percentage composition of agricultural production by commodities, nominal composition, current prices.
SOURCE: Same as for Table 2–5.

Table 2–5.   Percentage Composition of Agricultural Production by Commodities in Terms of Current Prices (%)

	Crops			Sericulture	Livestock	Total
	Rice	Other	Total			
1874–1877	58.1	35.2	93.3	5.9	0.8	100.0
1878–1882	57.8	33.0	90.8	8.4	0.8	100.0
1883–1887	50.3	39.4	89.7	8.7	1.6	100.0
1888–1892	51.3	38.5	89.8	8.2	2.0	100.0
1893–1897	50.1	37.1	87.2	10.2	2.6	100.0
1898–1902	52.8	34.5	87.3	10.0	2.7	100.0
1903–1907	51.2	34.6	85.8	10.9	3.3	100.0
1908–1912	51.2	35.6	86.8	10.1	3.1	100.0
1913–1917	47.7	34.9	82.6	14.3	3.1	100.0
1918–1922	50.9	31.9	82.8	13.7	3.5	100.0
1923–1927	48.5	29.8	78.3	16.9	4.8	100.0
1928–1932	45.6	32.6	78.2	15.4	6.4	100.0
1933–1937	50.2	32.0	82.2	11.9	5.9	100.0
1953–1957	48.7	37.8	86.5	3.2	10.3	100.0
1958–1962	48.3	36.8	83.1	2.9	14.0	100.0
1963–1967	44.2	34.2	78.4	2.7	18.9	100.0
1968–1972	39.7	34.9	74.6	2.5	22.9	100.0

SOURCE: Appendix Table A-2.

war decades—exceeding 10 percent per year—livestock has grown to be a critical component in determining the rate of growth in aggregate agricultural output.

2-2 Labor and Land in Agriculture

In this section we will review the trends in the two primary factors of agricultural production, labor and land, and in productivities with respect to these two primary inputs.

Labor

In this study we measure labor in agriculture both in stock and in flow terms. The former is measured by the number of gainful farm workers and the latter by the number of days worked by farm workers. The two series of the number of gainful workers prepared are: (*a*) the simple sum of male and female workers and (*b*) the weighted sum in terms of male equivalents with female workers converted into male equivalents by multiplying the ratio of the male wage rate to the female wage rate (0.72 as the average for the whole period).

The data prepared for the labor input in flow terms are highly provisional. The total number of workdays is calculated by aggregating the days worked in the production of various crops and livestock; the numbers of workdays applied to the different products are estimated by multiplying crop areas and livestock outputs by the number of workdays per hectare or per unit of output. Since it is extremely difficult to estimate the number of workdays per hectare or per unit of output, the estimation of total number of workdays cannot be very far from a rule-of-thumb calculation, especially for the earlier periods. It must also be remembered that our data of workdays count only those directly applied to the production of crops and livestock products and do not include " overhead labor " applied to such farm activities as transportation, marketing, maintenance of irrigation facilities, and cutting of wild grasses for feed and fertilizers. Considering those limitations

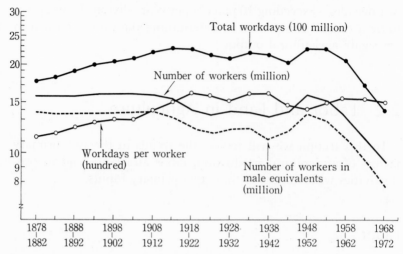

Figure 2–6.   Trends in numbers of gainful workers and workdays in agriculture, five-year averages, semi-log scale.
SOURCE: Same as for Table 2–6.

we must be extremely careful in interpreting the results of an analysis based on flow data.

The trends in the farm labor force and input are shown in Figure 2–6 (growth rates in Table 2–6). The number of farm workers stayed relatively stable before World War II, though it declined by about 10 percent during the boom of World War I. The labor force in agriculture increased immediately after World War II, but it began to decrease sharply with the spurt of economic growth since the mid-1950's. No major difference has been observed between the trends in the simple sum of workers and in man-equivalents.

The trend in flow-labor input in terms of workdays before World War I represents a sharp contrast to the trend in the number of workers, although the two tend to move more or less parallel after 1920. For the period 1880–1920 the number of workdays rose by 30 percent, while the number of farm workers decreased by 10 percent, resulting in an increase in workdays per worker of 40 percent, from about 110 days per year to 160 days. This increase seems to reflect the increase in the rate of labor utilization in agriculture due to (a) progress in double cropping in paddy fields

Table 2-6. Annual Compound Rates of Growth in Numbers of Workers and Workdays in Agriculture (%)*

Period	Number of Workers				Number of Workdays	
			Total			
	Male (1)	Female (2)	Simple Sum (3)	Male Equiva-lents (4)	Total (5)	Per Worker (5)-(3)
I 1880–1900	0.1	0.1	0.1	0.1	0.8	0.7
II 1900–1920	−0.5	−0.7	−0.6	−0.6	0.5	1.1
III 1920–1935	−0.1	−0.1	−0.1	−0.1	−0.2	−0.1
IV 1935–1945	−1.7	2.0	0.1	−0.2	−0.9	−1.0
V 1945–1955	1.5	0.3	0.9	1.0	1.3	0.4
VI 1955–1965	−3.5	−2.5	−3.0	−3.0	−2.7	0.3
(1960–1970)	(−3.7)	(−3.7)	(−3.7)	(−3.7)	(−4.3)	(−0.6)
Prewar period:						
1880–1935	−0.2	−0.2	−0.2	−0.2	0.4	0.6
Postwar period:						
1945–1965	−1.0	−1.1	−1.1	−1.1	−0.7	0.4
(1945–1970)	(−1.5)	(−1.8)	(−1.7)	(−1.6)	(−1.6)	(0.1)
Whole period:						
1880–1965	−0.6	−0.2	−0.4	−0.4	0.0	0.4
(1880–1970)	(−0.7)	(−0.4)	(−0.6)	(−0.6)	(−0.3)	(0.3)

* Growth rates between five-year averages centering the years shown.
SOURCE: Appendix Table A-3.

and (b) expansion in sericultural production as a sideline enterprise to the production of staple cereals within small-scale family farms (see chapter 3, section 2).

Land

Land for agricultural production is also measured both in stock and in flow terms. The former is measured by the area of cultivated land, and the latter by the area planted in crops (abbreviated as " crop area "). Cultivated land areas are aggregated into (a) the simple sum of lowland paddy-field and upland-field areas, and (b) the weighted sum in terms of paddy-field equivalents. Upland-field area is converted to paddy-field equivalents by multiplying the ratio of upland price to paddy-land price (0.43 as

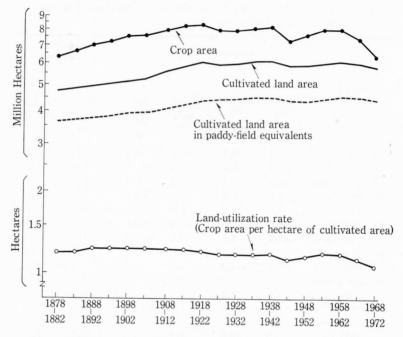

Figure 2–7.   Trends in cultivated land area, crop area, and land-utilization rate, five-year averages, semi-log scale.
SOURCE: Same as for Table 2–7.

the average for the whole period). Those data are plotted in Figure 2–7 (growth rates in Table 2–7).

The amount of cultivated land area increased steadily at the average annual rate of about 0.5 percent until 1920; thereafter it stagnated. One million hectares out of the increase in total cultivated land area of 1.2 million hectares from 1880 to 1920 were of low-valued upland fields in the marginal areas in northern Japan; about 0.8 million hectares were newly brought into cultivation in the northern frontier, Hokkaido. Consequently, the area in paddy-field equivalents grew slower than the simple sum of upland and paddy-field areas during this period.

In general, the crop area moved more or less parallel with the cultivated land area, leaving the rate of land utilization relatively stable. Such trends were the results of two countervailing forces. The expansion of cultivated area in northern frontiers, where

Table 2-7. Annual Compound Rates of Growth in Cultivated Land Area, Crop Area, and Land-utilization Rate (%)*

| Period | Cultivated Land Area | | | | Crop Area | | | Land-Utilization Rate (7)-(3) |
| | Paddy Field (1) | Upland Field (2) | Total | | Rice (5) | Other Crops (6) | Total (7) | |
			Simple Sum (3)	Paddy-field Equivalents (4)				
I 1880-1900	0.2	0.8	0.5	0.4	0.3	1.3	0.9	0.4
II 1900-1920	0.4	1.1	0.7	0.6	0.5	0.5	0.5	-0.2
III 1920-1935	0.3	-0.1	0.1	0.2	0.2	-0.4	-0.2	-0.3
IV 1935-1945	-0.3	-0.6	-0.4	-0.4	-0.8	-1.2	-1.1	-0.7
V 1945-1955	0.3	0.1	0.2	0.2	0.8	1.1	1.0	0.8
VI 1955-1965	0.2	-0.2	0.1	0.2	0.3	-1.4	-0.7	-0.8
(1960-1970)	(0.1)	(-1.2)	(-0.5)	(-0.2)	(-1.0)	(-3.7)	(-2.5)	(-2.0)
Prewar period:								
1880-1935	0.3	0.7	0.5	0.4	0.3	0.5	0.5	0.0
Postwar period:								
1945-1965	0.3	-0.1	0.1	0.2	0.6	-0.1	0.2	0.1
(1945-1970)	(0.2)	(-0.4)	(-0.1)	(0.1)	(0.1)	(-1.1)	(-0.6)	(-0.5)
Whole period:								
1880-1965	0.2	0.3	0.3	0.3	0.2	0.2	0.2	-0.1
(1880-1970)	(0.2)	(0.2)	(0.2)	(0.2)	(0.1)	(-0.1)	(0.0)	(-0.2)

* Growth rates between five-year averages centering the years shown.
SOURCE: Appendix Table A-4.

winter crops cannot be grown, contributed to the reduction in the land-utilization rate as measured by the ratio of crop area to cultivated area. This movement was compensated for by the diffusion of double-cropping practices in other parts of the country (see chapter 3, section 2).

The rate of land utilization has been sensitive to changes in the demand and supply of farm labor. Since typical winter crops, such as wheat and barley, are much less profitable than summer crops, farmers tend to abandon winter crops when the opportunity cost of their labor rises due to the expansion of nonfarm employment. This behavior of farmers is reflected in the decline in the rate of land utilization during the boom of World War I and the acute labor shortage in World War II; it is demonstrated more dramatically by the rapid declines in both total crop area and land-utilization rate, paralleled by the spurt of overall economic growth in the 1960's.

Labor and land productivities

Labor productivity is a major determinant of farm income and wages and has often been used as a measure of economic progress. Land productivity is also a pertinent measure of agricultural productivity or, more broadly, agricultural development in a country like Japan, where land is the limiting factor of agricultural production and farmers are primarily motivated to raise output per unit of cultivated land area.

For expository purposes it is useful to partition labor productivity into two components, the land/labor ratio and land productivity, as in the following identity:

$$\frac{Y}{L} = \frac{A}{L} \frac{Y}{A}$$

where Y is output; L labor; and A land.

Figure 2–8 compares the trends in the indices of labor productivity (Y/L), land productivity (Y/A), and the land/labor ratio (A/L) both in stock terms and in flow terms. Stock variables for labor and land are, respectively, the number of farm workers

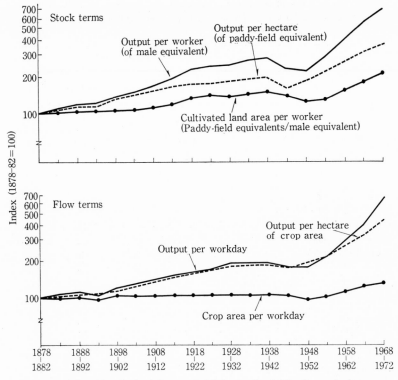

Figure 2–8. Trends in labor and labor productivities in agriculture,
five-year averages, semi-log scale.

Source: Same as for Table 2–8.

aggregated in male equivalents and the area of cultivated land in
paddy-field equivalents.

The major element in explaining the increase in output per
worker in Japanese agriculture was the rise in the yield per
hectare. For the whole period, as well as for the prewar and the
postwar periods, about 70 percent of the growth in output per
worker is accounted for by the increase in output per hectare
(Table 2–8). However, the contribution of improvement in
cultivated land area per worker to the labor-productivity growth
rate has become a major element since the late 1950's when the
absorption of the agricultural labor force by industry and service
sectors has accelerated.

It is likely that the contribution of increased land area per

Table 2-8. Growth Rates of Labor and Land Productivities, and Relative Contributions of Land Productivity Growth to Labor Productivity Growth (%)*

Period	Annual Compound Growth Rates					
	Labor Productivity		Land Productivity		Relative Contribution to Labor Productivity Growth by Land-productivity Growth	
	Per Male Equivalent (1)	Per Work-day (2)	Per Paddy-field Equivalent (3)	Per Hectare of Crop Area (4)	(3)/(1)	(4)/(2)
I 1880–1900	1.6	0.9	1.3	0.7	81	78
II 1900–1920	2.6	1.5	1.4	1.5	54	100
III 1920–1935	1.0	1.2	0.7	1.1	70	92
IV 1935–1945	−1.7	−0.9	−1.5	−0.7	88	78
V 1945–1955	2.2	1.9	2.9	2.1	132	111
VI 1955–1965	6.9	6.5	3.4	4.3	49	66
(1960–1970)	(6.4)	(7.0)	(2.7)	(5.1)	(42)	(73)
Prewar period:						
1880–1935	1.8	1.2	1.2	1.1	66	92
Postwar period:						
1945–1965	4.5	4.1	3.2	3.2	71	78
(1945–1970)	(4.9)	(4.8)	(3.0)	(3.7)	(61)	(77)
Whole period:						
1880–1965	2.0	1.6	1.3	1.4	65	88
(1880–1970)	(2.2)	(1.9)	(1.4)	(1.6)	(64)	(84)

* Growth rates between five-year averages centering the years shown.
SOURCE: Appendix Table A-5

worker during period II, which accounts for almost one-half of the labor-productivity growth rate, is overestimated, for this was the period when less productive land in Hokkaido and Tohoku was brought into cultivation in significant amount.

The contribution of land productivity to the growth in labor productivity is more pronounced in flow terms. The increase in output per workday is almost entirely accounted for by the increase in output per hectare of crop area. It appears, however, that this represents an overestimation of the role of land productivity in the growth of labor productivity. Since the data for the number of workdays do not include the "overhead labor," especially the collection of wild grasses and leaves from the communal pasture and forest lands, which accounted for a large share of the farm-labor input in the earlier days, the trend in the number of work-days overestimates the rates of growth in flow labor input. Consequently, the rates of growth in both labor productivity and the land/man ratio are underestimated by using the number of work-days as the measure of labor input, with the result that the relative contribution of the land/labor ratio to the labor-productivity growth rate is underestimated. Although the rise in land productivity was the dominant factor in explaining the growth in labor productivity in Japanese agriculture, the improvement in the land/labor ratio also played a significant role.

On the whole, the changes in growth trends in labor and land productivities are similar to those in total agricultural output. The rates of growth accelerated from period I to period II and turned into relative stagnation in period III. After the devastation of the war (period IV) they began to rise at faster rates, although there is a sign of deceleration from period V to period VI. It is indicated that the major determinants in the pattern of long-term growth in agricultural output were not the movements in the inputs of the primary factors, land and labor, but rather the productivities with respects to those inputs

2-3 Factor Inputs, Factor Prices, and Factor Shares

We will now compare the trends in the factors of agricultural production that are classified into four major categories: labor, land, fixed capital, and nonfarm current inputs.

In this analysis the measures of labor and land used refer to the number of farm workers in male equivalents and the cultivated land area in paddy-field equivalents, respectively. Fixed capital includes (a) livestock and perennial plants, (b) farm machinery and implements, and (c) farm buildings excluding residential houses, which are aggregated in the 1934–1936 average constant prices. Capital in the form of improvements in land infrastructure, such as irrigation and drainage, are not included. Nonfarm current inputs include (a) fertilizers, (b) agricultural chemicals, (c) feeds

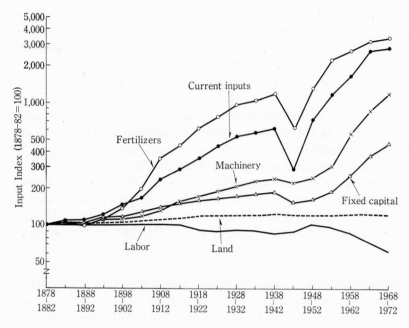

Figure 2–9.   Trends in factor inputs in agricultural production, five-year
averages, semi-log scale.
SOURCE: Same as for Table 2–9.

processed by domestic industry (such as fish meals and oilseed
cakes) and imported from abroad, and (d) other miscellaneous
items, such as fuels.

Trends in those four major categories of agricultural inputs are
compared in Figure 2–9 (growth rates in Table 2–9). In addition
to the four major categories of inputs, the data for " machinery
and implements " and " fertilizers " are also plotted in order to
show the trends in the inputs of factors that typically substitute for
labor and land.

Over the whole period the inputs of the two primary factors,
labor and land, changed slowly relative to other inputs. Capital
grew slowly before World War II, but it began to rise at a rapid
pace in the postwar period, comparable to the progress in farm
mechanization. The rates of growth in current inputs, particularly
fertilizers, far exceeded those of other inputs, especially for the
prewar period.

Table 2-9. Annual Compound Rates of Growth in Factor Inputs in Agriculture (%)*

Period	Labor: Male Equivalents	Land: Paddy-field Equivalents	Capital		Current Inputs	
			Machinery and Implements	Total	Fertilizers	Total
I 1880–1900	0.1	0.4	0.8	0.9	1.6	1.8
II 1900–1920	−0.6	0.6	2.0	1.3	7.7	4.7
III 1920–1935	−0.1	0.2	1.8	0.9	3.4	3.1
IV 1935–1945	−0.2	−0.4	−0.2	−1.4	−5.0	−6.6
V 1945–1955	1.0	0.2	3.1	2.0	13.5	15.0
VI 1955–1965	−3.0	0.2	11.5	7.8	3.6	8.5
(1960–1970)	(−3.7)	(−0.3)	(12.2)	(8.4)	(2.6)	(9.1)
Prewar period:						
1880–1935	−0.2	0.4	1.5	1.0	4.3	3.2
Postwar period:						
1945–1965	−1.1	0.2	7.2	4.9	8.4	11.7
(1945–1970)	(−1.6)	(0.1)	(7.8)	(5.3)	(7.0)	(11.0)
Whole period:						
1880–1965	−0.4	0.3	2.6	1.6	4.1	3.9
(1880–1970)	(−0.6)	(0.2)	(3.0)	(1.9)	(4.0)	(4.2)

* Growth rates between five-year averages centering the years shown.
SOURCE: Appendix Table A-6.

It appears that the differences in the rates of growth in those inputs can, to a large extent, be explained by the differences in the rates of change in factor prices. From a comparison of Figure 2–9 with Figure 2–10 (growth rates in Table 2–10), in which movements in the factor prices relative to the price of farm products are plotted, it should be clear that the rates of change in factor inputs are inversely correlated with those in factor prices. While the relatively stationary levels of labor and land were accompanied by rising trends in their prices, the rapid increases in current inputs were matched by a rapid decline in their prices.

The rapid rise in the price of farmland for the prewar period seems to reflect the fact that land was the most scarce factor limiting agricultural production in this period; whereas the rapid rise in the farm wage rate in the postwar period seems to imply that labor has been becoming increasingly more scarce relative to other factors in recent years. The rapid decline in the price of fertilizers relative to the price of land can be identified as a major

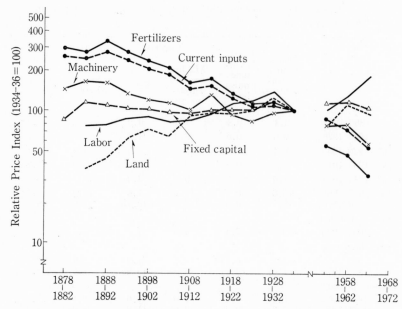

Figure 2–10.   Indices of factor prices of agricultural production relative
to the price of agricultural products, five-year averages, semi-log
scale.

SOURCE: Same as for Table 2–10.

force that induced the substitution of fertilizers for land, thereby
increasing the input of plant nutrients per unit of farmland area.
Likewise, it is clear that the relative decline in the price of machine
capital above the farm wage rate has been a stimulus in the substitution of machinery for labor.

Because factor inputs and prices have moved in opposite directions, the shares of factors in the total cost of agricultural production in current prices have remained fairly stable (Figure 2–11 and
Table 2–11). For the prewar period (until the period of Japan's
military involvement in China beginning in the mid-1930's), the
share of current inputs increased, while the share of land declined.
On the other hand, for the postwar period the share of capital has
increased, which has largely been balanced by a decline in labor's
share.

Assuming a linear homogeneity in the production function and
the competitive equilibrium of a factor market, factor shares in the

Table 2-10. Annual Compound Rates of Change in Factor Prices of Agricultural Production Relative to the Price of Agricultural Products (%)*

Period	Labor Wage Rates	Culti- vated Land Prices	Fixed Capital Prices		Current Input Prices	
			Machin- ery and Imple- ments	Total	Ferti- lizers	Total
I 1890ª–1900	1.5	4.8	−3.2	−0.7	−3.6	−2.8
II 1900–1920	1.3	1.3	−1.1	−0.2	−2.7	−2.5
III 1920–1930	1.9	2.9	0.3	1.3	−1.7	−1.2
Prewar period:						
1890ª–1930ª	1.5	2.6	−1.3	0.1	−2.7	−2.2
Postwar period:						
1955–1965	6.1	4.3	−3.2	−0.9	−5.0	−4.5
(1960–1970)	(7.2)	(−1.1)	(−7.1)	(−1.1)	(−5.4)	(−5.0)
Whole period:						
1890ª–1965	1.2	1.0	−1.4	0.0	−3.0	−2.1
(1890–1970)	(1.5)	(1.1)	(−1.8)	(−0.1)	(−3.1)	(−2.3)

* Growth rates between five-year averages centering the years shown.
ª Because of data limitations, 1890 and 1930, instead of 1880 and 1935, are chosen as the years for the time demarcations into respective periods.
SOURCE: Appendix Table A-8.

total cost of production coincide with both the shares in the functional distribution of factor income and the production elasticities of those inputs. In addition, if we assume the Cobb-Douglas form for the production function, the changes in factor shares become a measure of the direction of factor-saving bias in technical progress.

Although the relevance of those assumptions should wait for empirical testing (see chapter 4), the movements in the factor-share data suggest the hypothesis that the technical progress in Japanese agriculture was of the land-saving and fertilizer-using type for the prewar period and that it began to bias toward the labor-saving and machine-using direction when the labor shortage became serious in the late 1950's and the early 1960's. Further, those factor-saving biases in technical progress were induced by changes in relative factor prices.

In other words, factor substitutions in response to changes in relative factor prices, as indicated in Figures 2–9 and 2–10, were apparently not substitutions along the fixed isoquant of a neoclassical production function but along the envelope of potential

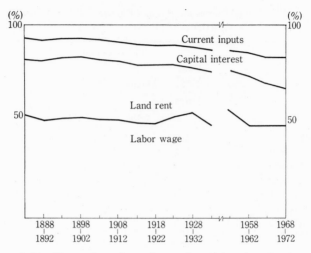

Figure 2–11. Factor shares in total cost of agricultural production.
SOURCE: Same as for Table 2–10.

Table 2–11. Factor Shares in Total Cost of Agricultural Production (%)

	Labor Wage	Land Rent	Capital Interest	Current Input Value	Total
1883–1887	52.7	28.8	10.9	7.6	100.0
1888–1892	50.1	30.7	10.6	8.5	100.0
1893–1897	51.5	31.0	9.7	7.8	100.0
1898–1902	52.0	31.0	9.5	7.5	100.0
1903–1907	50.9	30.7	9.9	8.6	100.0
1908–1912	50.7	30.2	9.8	9.3	100.0
1913–1917	49.0	29.7	10.3	11.0	100.0
1918–1922	49.1	29.6	10.2	11.1	100.0
1923–1927	52.8	26.3	10.0	10.9	100.0
1928–1932	54.5	23.4	10.5	11.6	100.0
1933–1937	48.0	27.6	11.1	13.3	100.0
1953–1957	55.5	20.4	10.3	13.8	100.0
1958–1962	48.3	25.7	11.2	14.8	100.0
1963–1967	48.7	20.3	13.8	17.2	100.0
1968–1972	47.9	19.9	15.2	17.0	100.0

SOURCE: Saburo Yamada and Yujiro Hayami, "Growth Rate of Japanese Agriculture," in *Agricultural Growth in Japan, Taiwan, Korea and the Philippines*, eds. Yujiro Hayami, V. W. Ruttan, and Herman Southworth (Honolulu: University of Hawaii Press, 1975).

isoquants or the isoquant of the metaproduction function in the sense of Hayami and Ruttan.[4]

2-4   Total Input and Total Productivity

Method and data

Indices of labor, land, fixed capital, and nonfarm current inputs are aggregated into a single index of " total input " by factor-share weights. The total input index is sensitive to the choice of factor-share weights. We have, therefore, adopted the chain-linked index:

$$I_t = \left(\sum_i w_{i0} \frac{q_{i1}}{q_{i0}} \right) \cdot \left(\sum_i w_{i1} \frac{q_{i2}}{q_{i1}} \right) \cdots \cdots \left(\sum_i w_{it-1} \frac{q_{it}}{q_{it-1}} \right)$$

where I_t is the total index at period t; q_{it} is the quantity of i-th input at period t; and w_{it} is the share of i-th input in the total cost of production in current prices at period t.[5]

The index of total output divided by the index of total input produces the index of " total productivity." This index is a rough measure of technical efficiency in agricultural production in the sense that it measures the changes in output per unit of input.[6]

The indices of total input and total productivity are constructed both in terms of stock variables for labor and land (the number of farm workers in male equivalents and cultivated land area in paddy-field equivalents) and in terms of flow variables (the number of workdays and crop area). As a measure of technical efficiency in production it may appear theoretically more appropriate to use input data in flow terms for the construction of a total productivity index. However, in the case of agriculture characterized by sharp seasonal fluctuations in labor requirements, it is the labor input available for the peak seasons, such as planting and harvesting, that really matters for agricultural production. The marginal product of farm labor in the slack seasons should have been very low, especially in earlier days when off-farm employment was not readily available. Since it is reasonable to assume that the labor input that can be mobilized in the peak seasons is more or less proportional to the labor population in agriculture, the number of farm workers adjusted for male-female quality difference seems a more appropriate variable for the input of labor within the context of the production function for agriculture.[7]

Also, it is likely that the aggregation of land in terms of area planted in crops involves bias because winter crop areas are less productive than summer crop areas. Again, the cultivated land area in paddy-field equivalents, which adjusts for the quality differences among paddy- and upland-field areas, seems a more accurate measure for the input of land within the context of the agricultural production function.

Further, we should remember that our data of labor and land flows are statistically very weak and are likely to involve much larger measurement errors than the stock data. For those limitations it is more appropriate to consider the total productivity index based on flow data as providing supplementary information to the analysis based on stock data.

Trends in total input and productivity

Figure 2–12 shows trends in total productivity in both flow and stock terms, in relation to the trends in total output and total input (growth rates in Table 2–12).

Over the whole period the indices of total input in stock and flow terms increased at the annual rates of 0.7 and 0.8 percent, respectively, while total output grew at 1.6 percent. Consequently, total productivity rose at 0.9 percent per year in stock terms and 0.8 percent in flow terms. This implies that roughly one-half of the growth in total output is explained by the growth in inputs, whereas the other one-half is explained by " technical progress "; or, stated more correctly, one-half of the output growth in agriculture is left unexplained by increases in conventionally measured inputs.

There were large variations among periods in the rate of growth in total productivity as well as in its relative contribution to the output growth rate. In stock terms the increase in the rate of output growth from period I to period II was associated with both a rise in the input growth rate and an acceleration in productivity growth. Throughout periods I and II, productivity growth was the dominant factor in determining the growth rate of total output. More conspicuous is the fact that the interwar stagnation in the growth rate of total output is almost entirely explained by the deceleration in the rate of growth in productivity from period II to period III.

The rate of increase in total input in flow terms for the period before 1920 was much faster than in stock terms, resulting in the lower estimate for the growth rate in total productivity. This difference was caused primarily by an increase in the rate of labor utilization measured by the average number of workdays per worker. If we bar the possibility of statistical measurement errors, it seems to reflect the fact that technical change in this period was of such a nature as to reduce the seasonal slack in the utilization of farm labor by facilitating the diffusion of double cropping and of

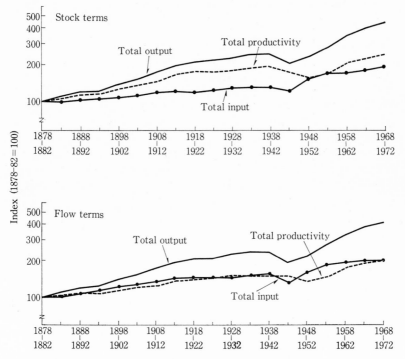

Figure 2–12. Trends in total output, total input, and total productivity in agriculture, five-year averages, semi-log scale.

Source: Same as for Table 2–12.

Table 2-12. Contributions of Growth Rates of Total Input and Total Productivity to Growth Rates of Total Output in Agriculture (%)*

		Annual Compound Rates of Growth					Relative Contribution of Total Productivity Growth to Output Growth	
	Total Output (1)	Total Input		Total Productivity				
		Stock Terms (2)	Flow Terms (3)	Stock Terms (4)	Flow Terms (5)		(4)/(1)	(5)/(1)
I 1880–1900 (1880–1895)	1.6 (1.4)	0.4	0.9 (1.0)	1.2	0.7 (0.4)		75	44 (29)
II 1900–1920 (1905–1920)	2.0 (2.0)	0.5	1.0 (1.0)	1.5	1.0 (1.0)		75	50 (50)
III 1920–1935	0.9	0.4	0.3	0.5	0.6		56	67
IV 1935–1945	−1.9	−1.1	−1.7	−0.8	−0.2		−42	11
V 1945–1955	3.2	3.6	3.6	−0.4	−0.4		−13	−13
VI 1955–1965 (1960–1970)	3.6 (2.4)	1.0 (1.1)	0.9 (0.4)	2.6 (1.5)	2.8 (2.3)		72 (60)	78 (96)
Prewar period: 1880–1935	1.6	0.4	0.8	1.2	0.8		75	50
Postwar period: 1945–1965 (1945–1970)	3.4 (3.1)	2.2 (1.9)	2.3 (1.8)	1.2 (1.3)	1.1 (1.4)		35 (42)	32 (45)
Whole period: 1880–1965 (1880–1970)	1.6 (1.6)	0.7 (0.7)	0.9 (0.8)	0.9 (0.9)	0.7 (0.8)		56 (56)	44 (50)

* Growth rates between five-year averages centering the years shown.
SOURCE: Appendix Table A-9.

sericultural production as sideline enterprises (see chapter 3, section 2).

Both in stock and in flow terms the contribution of productivity to the growth in total output continued to be relatively small from period III to period IV, the latter being subject to war devastation. Remarkable is the change from period V (recovery from the war) to period VI (post-recovery spurt) in the relative contributions in inputs and productivity. Both periods marked rapid rates of growth in total output in agriculture. However, while the output growth in the recovery process was largely explained by the increase in inputs, the growth in the post-recovery process can be largely explained by a rise in productivity. This seems to imply that the sharp decline in agricultural production during the war was caused primarily by the shortage in inputs and that the decline was recovered according to the recovery in the supply of the inputs.

Although the patterns of growth in total input and total output are substantially different between stock and flow terms, especially for the earlier period, the ways in which total productivity grew and contributed to the emergence of distinctive growth phases in agricultural output are more or less the same in both cases.

2-5 Summary of Major Growth Trends

From the beginning of industrialization in the early Meiji period until today (approximately from 1880 to 1965) agriculture in Japan attained real rates of growth in output at the annual compound rate of about 1.5 percent. Total output almost quadrupled during the period covered in this study. Japanese agriculture continued to be dominated by the production of field crops, particularly rice, although the rise and fall in sericulture and the rapid increase in livestock production in recent years were more dramatic.

In contrast to output growth, the two primary inputs in agriculture, labor and land, remained fairly stable. As a result, productivities of labor and land increased at a rate comparable to the growth rate of output. Since the land/labor ratio improved only slightly, the growth in labor productivity was primarily brought about by the rise in the yield per hectare of farmland. However, since the beginning of the postwar spurt of economic development in the mid-1950's, which accelerated the rapid outmigration of the agricultural labor force, the improvement in the land/man ratio has become the major component in the growth in labor productivity.

The growth in land productivity was associated with the rapid increase in fertilizer and other current inputs, which are primarily substitutes for land. The improvement in the land/labor ratio was associated with an increase in capital stock, particularly in the form of farm machinery and implements per worker, which are primarily substitutes for labor. As the data suggest, those input substitutions among production factors represent the rational response of farmers to changes in relative factor prices, while they are facilitated by changes in production isoquants induced by the relative price changes.

Overall, the index of total input, which aggregates the four major categories of inputs, labor, land, fixed capital, and nonfarm current inputs, increased at a rate of only about one-half the growth rate in total output. Consequently, another one-half was accounted for by the growth in total productivity.

It was primarily the changes in the growth rate in total productivity rather than total input that determined the changes in the rate of growth in agricultural output over time. The same pattern of changes in growth rates can be observed in the partial productivities of labor and land.

In terms of aggregate output and productivities the following chronology in Japanese agriculture can be ascertained: period I, approximately 1880–1900, a steady rise to the point in acceleration; period II, 1900–1920, accelerated growth; period III, 1920–1935, relative stagnation; period IV, 1935–1945, devastation by World War II; period V, 1945–1955, postwar recovery; period VI, 1955–1965, sustained growth following the recovery.

As a more broad phaseology it is convenient to combine periods I and II, which we may call the "Initial Growth Phase." In contrast, period III may be called "Interwar Stagnation Phase," and period V and period VI combined may be called the "Postwar Growth Phase."

It should be remembered that those time demarcations are not very strict and are adopted primarily for the convenience of historical description.

Notes to Chapter 2

[1] This chapter draws heavily on Saburo Yamada and Yujiro Hayami, "Growth Rates of Japanese Agriculture, 1880–1970," paper prepared for the conference, *Agricultural Growth in Japan, Korea, Taiwan, and the Philippines,* held at the East-West Center, Honolulu, February 6–9, 1973; and Masahiko Shintani, "Nogyo Bumon ni okeru Toka Rodo Nissu no Suikei" (Estimation of Labor Input in Agriculture since 1874), *Keizai Kenkyu* 25 (July 1974): 264–271.

[2] Reliability of agricultural production statistics in Meiji Japan has been strongly questioned by Nakamura. See James I. Nakamura, *Agricultural Production and the Economic Development of Japan: 1873–1922* (Princeton: Princeton University Press, 1966). The questions regarding the official statistics of Japan raised by Nakamura have been widely discussed: Yujiro Hayami, "On the Japanese Experience of Agricultural Growth," *Rural Economic Problems* 4 (May 1968): 79–88; Yujiro Hayami and Saburo Yamada, "Agricultural Productivity at the Beginning of Industrialization," *Agriculture and Economic Development: Japan's Experience,* eds. Jazushi Ohkawa, Bruce F. Johnston, and Hiromitsu Kaneda (Tokyo: University of Tokyo Press, 1969), pp. 105–135; J. I. Nakamura, "The Nakamura versus the LTES Estimates of Growth Rate of Agricultural Production," *Keizai Kenkyu* 19 (October 1968): 358–362. Appraisals by other scholars include: Henry Rosovsky, "Rumbles in the Ricefields: Professor Nakamura vs. the Official Statistics," *Journal of Asian Studies* 27 (February 1968): 347–360, and Colin Clark's review of Nakamura's book in *Journal of Agricultural Economics* (September 1967): 428–430. The data used in this study are those that have been revised by taking into consideration the previous controversies.

[3] For the rates of industrial growth, see volume 10 of Kazushi Ohkawa, Miyohei Shinohara, and Mataji Umemura, eds., *Estimates of Long-term Economics of Japan since 1868* (Tokyo: Toyokeizaishimposha, 1972).

[4] Yujiro Hayami and Vernon W. Ruttan, *Agricultural Development: An International Perspective* (Baltimore and London: John Hopkins University Press, 1971), pp. 82–85.

[5] This index is equivalent to the Divisia Index recommended by Dale W. Jorgenson and Zvi Griliches, "The Explanation of Productivity Change," *Review of Economic Studies* 34 (July 1967): 249–283. For the calculation of the index, it is assumed that the factor shares for 1878–1882 were the same as for 1883–1887; and the averages of factor shares for 1938–1942 and 1948–1952 are used as weights for linking the index between those two periods.

[6] For detailed discussions on the theoretical aspects of the total productivity index, see Willis L. Peterson and Yujiro Hayami, "Technical Change in Agriculture," paper prepared for the American Agricultural Economics Association Literature Review Committee, University of Minnesota, Department of Agricultural and Applied Economics, 1973.

[7] This assumption was supported by a study of the agricultural production function based on interfarm cross-section data by Keizo Tsuchiya, *Nogyo Keizai no Keiryo Bunseki* (Econometric Analysis of Agricultural Economy), (Tokyo: Keiso Shobo, 1962), pp. 88–96.

Chapter 3 Institutional Aspects of
Agricultural Development[1]

3-1 Transition to Modern Agricultural Growth

Evolution during the Tokugawa period[2]

During the Tokugawa period, which lasted for some three hundred years preceeding the Meiji Restoration in 1868, Japan was divided into more than two hundred fifty fiefs (*han*) ruled by feudal lords (*daimyo*) and their armed retainers (*samurai*) under the hegemony of the Tokugawa Shogunate.[3] The rule of the Shogunate in Edo (Tokyo) was authorized by the emperor in Kyoto, who had nothing but spiritual significance.

Society under the Tokugawa regime was characterized by a rigid hierarchial class structure. Social mobility was low, and occupations were determined by birth. Feudal restrictions on farm people were especially stringent, because this class represented the basic source of income to feudal lords and the *samurai* class in the form of land tax in kind (usually in rice). In principle, peasants were bound to their land and were not allowed to leave their villages except for such occasions as religious pilgrimages. Their title to land was restrictive, and they could not sell or mortgage their land. Nor were they free to choose which crops to plant. In order to secure tax revenue in the form of staple food grains, planting such nonfood crops as mulberry and tobacco on the regular taxable farmland was generally prohibited, especially in the paddy fields.

However, these strong restrictions on the farmers' social and economic behavior were gradually undermined as the market economy developed. Throughout the Tokugawa period we see slow but steady development in both local and interregional trade as the population expanded in such major cities as Edo, Kyoto, and Osaka, and in numerous castle towns.[4] Increasingly, peasants were involved in market transactions, and they developed devices for evading the feudal regulations that were inconsistent with the market economy.

Market demand gave peasants a strong incentive to raise productivities in order to increase surpluses of their produce for sale.[5] Through the trials and errors of farmers better farming practices and seed varieties were developed, and such commercial fertilizers as dried sardines and oilseed cakes were applied in the most advanced regions in Kinki (around Osaka) on cotton and other high-valued commercial crops. Improvements in land infrastructure, including flood control and irrigation, which were promoted both by local initiative and by the leadership of feudal lords, provided the basis for the development of a technology that increased the productivity of the land.[6]

This development in agricultural technology had a significant impact on the agrarian structure. It appears that technical progress in Tokugawa agriculture, especially since the middle of the eighteenth century, was of a nature that promoted the relative efficiency of the small-scale farms that were dependent on family labor. In the earlier period the more dominant mode of farming had been large holdings, ranging from a few hectares to a few dozen hectares, which were cultivated by the labor of extended family and/or hereditary or indentured servants. These large farms were gradually reduced through the dissolution of the extended family or by renting land to the ex-servant class. Thus, the small-scale family farm of around one hectare of cultivated land became the dominant mode of agricultural production, even though traditional large-scale operations persisted in the backward regions, such as Tohoku (Northeast), until the Meiji period.[7] Through this process and also through the illegal practices of mortgage and foreclosure among peasants, the landlord-tenant system was developed, despite feudal regulations against it.[8]

Reforms at the Meiji Restoration

The development of the market economy was accelerated in the nineteenth century, especially after the Shogunate conceded rights to Commodore Perry and his fleet, opening the doors of Japan to foreign countries (1854); the effect was a serious undermining of the economic basis of feudal rule. The threat of colonialization by Western powers gave rise to a strong nationalism among the Japanese people. The authority of the Tokugawa Shogunate, which could not adequately countervail the demand of the Western powers, was challenged. After political and military struggles the Shogunate was finally overthrown in 1868, and the rule of the emperor was restored.[9]

Under the absolutistic government of Emperor Meiji, Japan moved toward the creation of a modern nation-state.[10] Feudal fiefs were abolished and were replaced by prefectures with governors appointed by the central government (1871). Feudal barriers among regions and social classes were removed. Conditions were thus prepared to unite the nation into a single economy.

The major goal of the newly established Meiji government was to have Japan catch up with the economic and military strength of the Western powers. The national slogan was to " build a wealthy nation and a strong army " (*fukoku kyohei*). To attain this goal it was considered necessary to " develop industries and promote enterprises " (*shokusan kogyo*) within the framework of capitalism.[11] As a prerequisite the modern system of market economy, based on private property rights and free contracts, had to be established.

Feudal constraints on economic activities were removed one by one. In agriculture it was announced that land utilization and the choice of crops were to be left free to the decision of farmers (1871). The prohibition on the sale and the mortgage of farmland was removed (1872). Title to land in fee simple was granted to farmers in the Land Tax Revision, which was sanctioned by the Civil Code of 1895. Through these reforms farmers became free economic agents in allocating resources in response to market incentives.[12] Furthermore, their ability to allocate resources was increased by the spread of general education, facilitated by the establishment of compulsory education system.

Land Tax Revision

Perhaps the single most important reform of the Meiji Restoration was the Land Tax Revision.[13] The Revision changed the feudal tax in kind, levied in proportion to quantities harvested, into a modern land tax in cash based on the value of land.

In the new land-tax system the annual tax rate was fixed at 3 percent of the land value. The price of land was evaluated by discounting the estimated annual net income from land by the interest rate. The Revision involved the nation-wide cadastral survey for ascertaining the area, price, and ownership of land. Certificates to titles of land were issued to the owners on ascertained private land. It took nine years (1873–1881) to complete and cost the government almost one full year's revenue.[14]

The primary purpose of the Land Tax Revision was, of course, to secure a stable source of government revenue for carrying out various modernization measures, including industrialization. Undoubtedly the new land-tax system worked as a means of resource transfer from the agricultural to the nonagricultural sector.[15] At the same time it had far-reaching effects on agrarian structure and economy.

The land-tenure system established by the Revision (and the Civil Code) was largely an acknowledgment of the status quo that had developed during the Tokugawa period, although the dual ownership of land, including perpetual tenancy (*eitai kosaku*), was negated. Formal titles were given to landlords who had accumulated farmland through mortgage and other means that had been against feudal regulations, thus laying the foundation for the development of landlordism in the Meiji period. Another important aspect was that in the process of establishing the land titles during the Land Tax Revision the major part of the communal pasture and forest land was shifted to the ownership of wealthy landlords or to the ownership of the government.[16]

The new tax and tenure system had the effect of forcing farmers to be more involved in the market economy and contributed to the concentration of land titles in the hands of landlords. To pay the land tax in cash, farm producers needed to market nearly one-quarter of their produce. In many cases small producers had to increase their cash outlay for their production and consumption because the communal pasture and forest land, which previously had been an important source of fertilizers, feeds, and fuel, became unavailable to them. Because the new land tax was fixed in cash, small peasants were often unable to pay the tax in years of poor harvest or low farm prices. They were compelled to borrow money from landlords, and many of them lost their land through foreclosure.

This process accelerated during the Matsukata deflation in the 1880's resulting in a drastic decline in farm prices.[17] The land cultivated under tenancy was less than 30 percent of the total arable land area at the time of the Land Tax Revision. It rose to 40 percent by 1892 and to nearly 50 percent by 1930.[18]

In those days land rent, particularly for paddy fields, was paid in kind, roughly 50 percent of harvest; and the landlords, who had a much lower marginal propensity to consume rice, received an increasing share of the output. In turn, there was an increase in the marketable surplus of rice, the critical wage good for urban workers. Also, the landlords invested a significant amount of their increased rent income in nonfarm business, either directly or through financial intermediaries. Thus, landlordism developed under a new system and provided a condition for the transfer of resources from agriculture to industry.

It must be emphasized, however, that the concentration of land titles to landlords did not promote polarization into large commercial farms and landless laborers. Instead, the concentration of farm sizes in the 0.5- to 2-hectare range increased up to the 1930's, as shown in Table 1–3 (chapter 1), although data for the early Meiji period are not available. This observation seems to suggest that technical progress in agricultural production in modern Japan from the Meiji Restoration until World War II was along the extension of technical progress during the Tokugawa period, which was biased toward increasing the relative efficiency of small-scale family farms.

Early efforts at agricultural improvement

Although the major preoccupation of the leaders of the Meiji government was to build modern industry and military strength that could rival those of the Western powers, they did not neglect the need for improving the productivity of agriculture, by far the dominant sector of the economy. Initially, as in industrialization and other modernization measures, they looked to Europe and the United States as models for agricultural development.

It appears that the basic agricultural-development strategy of the government leaders was formulated from observations of European and U.S. agriculture by the 1871–1873 mission of Lord Iwakata. This large-scale mission, which included almost half of the cabinet members, aimed at negotiating with the Western powers on the termination of exterritoriality, and, at the same time, at collecting all the data in the advanced countries that might be useful in the modernization of Japan.[19]

The report of the Iwakata mission recognized the superiority of Western agriculture in the form of the organic combination of crops and livestock and in the high level of application of modern inputs, such as fertilizers and machinery. It identified the source of high productivity as the application of science and technology developed and diffused by agricultural associations, fairs, schools, and experiment stations. Those organizations were considered necessary for agricultural improvements in Japan.[20]

Subsequently, the ideas of the mission report were carried out by Toshimichi Okubo and his followers.[21] The Naito Shinjuku Agricultural Experiment Station was set up in 1873, where the operations of farm machineries imported from the United States and England were demonstrated. In 1879 the Mita Farm Machinery Manufacturing Plant was established to produce farm machinery modeled after the imported machines. The government established agricultural colleges—the Komaba Agricultural School (founded in 1877 and redesignated as the University of Tokyo College of Agriculture in 1890) as an education and training center for agriculture on mainland Japan, and the Sapporo Agricultural School (founded in 1875 and redesignated as the Hokkaido University College of Agriculture in 1918), designed to develop the last frontier, Hokkaido. Instructors were invited from Britain to the Komaba School and from the U.S. to the Sapporo School. The curriculum at the new agricultural colleges was based on the science and technology developed for Anglo-American large-scale farming. The government also tried to transplant foreign plants and livestock to Japan. The Mita Botanical Experiment Yard (1874), the Shimofusa Sheep Farm (1875), the Kobe Olive Farm (1879), and the Harima Grape Farm (1880) represented such trials.[22]

These trials were based on the broad strategy of attaining rapid modernization and economic development by borrowing advanced technology from the Western world, and the strategy was highly successful in the case of industry. However, direct importation of Western technology was largely unsuccessful in agriculture, except in Hokkaido. A farmer, observing the imported machinery, remarked, " These machines may be applicable in a vast area like Hokkaido, but it would be as if a camel were to dress in the hide of an elephant to use them in the small patches of land as in our region."[23] The factor endowments in Japanese agriculture were simply incompatible with the foreign machineries. Nor were the efforts of transplanting exotic plants and animals successful, because they did not adapt to the Japanese climate, at least in a short time.

3-2   Initial Growth Phase

Reorientation of agricultural-development strategy

The government perceived the failure of a hasty attempt to develop agriculture by the direct importation of foreign technology. The newly founded Ministry of Agriculture and Commerce (1881; redesignated the Ministry of Agriculture and Forestry in 1925) began to search for a way to develop technology consistent with the resource endowments and the ecological conditions of Japanese agriculture.

The facilities for the demonstration of Western machinery, plants, and livestock were largely discontinued. In turn, the government tried to develop institutions for improving indigenous farming techniques in Japan. The Itinerant Instructor System and the Experiment Farm for Staple Cereals and Vegetables were established in 1885. In contrast with earlier emphasis on the direct transplanting of Western technology, the Itinerant Instructor

System, in which the instructors traveled around the country holding agricultural-extension meetings, was designed to diffuse better seed varieties and more productive cultural practices already in use by Japanese farmers. The Experiment Farm was designed to test which varieties or practices were, in fact, superior. Not only the graduates of agricultural colleges but also veteran farmers (rōnō) were employed as itinerant instructors, in order to combine practical experience with the scientific knowledge of inexperienced college graduates.[24]

The curriculum at the agricultural colleges was also reoriented. The British agricultural instructors were replaced by German scientists. Thereafter, the primary emphasis of agricultural education and research in colleges and universities was placed on German agricultural chemistry and soil science of the von Liebig tradition.[25]

The Experiment Farm for Staple Cereals and Vegetables was further strengthened and designated in 1893 as the National Agricultural Experiment Station, with six branch stations throughout the nation. The Itinerant Instructor System was subsequently absorbed into the program of the National Agricultural Experiment Station. Meanwhile, the national government encouraged the prefectural governments to set up local experiment stations. However, only a few prefectures had established their experiment stations before the Law of State Subsidy for Prefectural Agricultural Experiment Stations was enacted (1899).

These measures of developing agricultural technology were partly aimed at counteracting the appeal for a reduction of the newly established land tax.[26] The Konoronsaku (A Treatise on the Strategy of Agricultural Development), which was drafted in 1891 by the Agricultural Science Association (Nogakukai) and which had immediate impact on the establishment of the National Agricultural Experiment Station, denied the argument for a land-tax reduction on the basis that it would only contribute to the welfare of landlords and give no benefit to a large number of tenant farmers. It advocated " more positive measures to develop agriculture, such as agricultural schools, experiment stations, itinerant lectures, and agricultural societies " to reduce the burden of farmers.[27]

The establishment of the system of the National Agricultural Experiment Station in 1893 represented a partial realization of the proposal by the Agricultural Science Association. However, the resources allocated to activities for agricultural research and development were very meager. The initial staff size of the National Agricultural Experiment Station, including branch stations, was only twenty research staff and seven technicians, and was only increased to thirty and fifteen respectively, in 1899. Experiments were always handicapped by insufficient facilities and logistical support.[28] Under such conditions it was only possible to conduct simple field experiments comparing certain varieties of seeds or husbandry techniques. Facilities, personnel, and, above all, the state of knowledge did not permit conducting research beyond simple tests and demonstrations.

Famers' initiative and organizations

In spite of the weak basis for agricultural research and experimentation the growth in agricultural output and productivity began to accelerate at the beginning of this century (chapter 2). The reason should be sought in the existence of indigenous technological potential that could be further tested, developed, and refined at the new experiment stations, combined with a strong aspiration among farmers to innovate, especially among those who belonged to the *gōnō* class (landlords who personally farmed part of their holdings).

As discussed previously, landlords played a role in channeling resources from agriculture to nonagriculture. At the same time, they played a key role in raising agricultural productivity by acting as village leaders, both in the introduction of new technology and in improvements in the infrastructure, such as irrigation.[29] The reforms of the Meiji Restoration removed feudal constraints on their economic activities. In particular, the Land Tax Revision that transformed the feudal share-crop tax to the fixed-rate cash tax increased their incentive to raise farm productivity.

The *gōnō* farmers and landlords took the initiative of organizing agricultural societies called *nodankai* (agricultural discussion society) and *hinshukokankai* (seed-exchange society) as the medium for introducing new agricultural technology.[30] Those among the *gōnō* who were especially experienced and skillful in farming were called *rōnō* (veteran farmers).

Such improved techniques in rice production as use of salt water in seed selection, oblong-shaped nursery bed preparation, and checkrow planting were developed and diffused through the initiative of the veteran farmers, while encouraged by the itinerant instructors and sometimes enforced by the sabers of police. The major improved varieties of seeds during the Meiji period were also the result of selections by veteran farmers. For example, the *Shinriki* variety, which was more widely diffused in the western half of Japan than any other single variety that has since been propagated, was selected in 1877 by Jujiro Maruo, a farmer in Hyogo prefecture. (The variety was called *Shinriki*, meaning the " Power of God," by the farmers who were surprised by its high yield.) Also, the *Kameno-o* variety, which was propagated widely and contributed greatly to stabilizing the rice yield in northern Japan, was selected in 1893 by Kameji Abe, a farmer in Yamagata prefecture.

The government tried to encourage and organize such movements at the grass roots. Taking the opportunity of the Second National Exposition of Industrial Development in 1881, the government invited veteran farmers to Tokyo and held the National Agricultural Discussion Meeting. Under the strong leadership of Yajiro Shinagawa, the vice minister of agriculture and commerce, these farmers organized the Agricultural Society of Japan (*Dai Nippon Nokai*), modeled after the Royal Agricultural Society of England.[31]

The Agricultural Society of Japan was engaged primarily in the dissemination of technical information by publishing bulletins and holding agricultural fairs and extension meetings. Some of the members of the society considered that a larger and more systematic organization was required for promoting agricultural interests that could exercise political influence. In 1894 the National Agricultural Association (*Zenkoku Nojikai*) was established for this purpose, and this organization developed into the Imperial Agricultural Association (1910). It was organized in a pyramidal structure, with the Imperial Association on the top, down to the prefectural associations and the village associations on the bottom. By law the participation of farmers in the association and the payment of membership fees were compulsory.[32] The Association encompassed activities ranging from agricultural-extension services to political lobbying for agricultural protection.[33]

Another important organizational development was agricultural cooperative associations.[34] The idea of protecting farmers against exploitation by middlemen and money-lenders through credit and marketing cooperatives gained momentum during the Matsukata deflation in the 1880's. However, the Credit Cooperative Association Bill, drafted in 1891 according to the German model, failed to pass the Diet because it was considered too radical. A modified bill was approved, finally, in 1900. The law provided for four kinds of cooperative associations—credit, purchasing, marketing, and production. The government adopted several measures of fostering agricultural cooperatives, including tax exemptions and subsidies.

The cooperatives were organized into national federations, such as the Central Union of Cooperative Associations (1909) and the Central Bank of Cooperative Associations (1923). No doubt, the development of agricultural cooperative associations contributed to preserving unimodal distribution in the agrarian structure by increasing the availability of credit and marketing services to smaller farmers and by protecting them against damages from business fluctuations. The role of the cooperatives became more important during the recession in the interwar period.

Basis for agricultural productivity growth

One critical element stands out in the acceleration in the growth of agricultural productivity since the last decade of the nineteenth century: the success in developing technology consistent with the resource endowments of Japan by improving indigenous *rōnō* techniques through the application of modern science. Simple tests and demonstrations in the experiment stations were effective in screening and refining the results of farmer innovations.

The *rōnō* techniques were based on experiences in the specific localities where they originated. They tended to be location-specific and to require modification when transferred to other localities. Simple comparative tests effectively screened the *rōnō* techniques and varieties, thereby reducing the risk to farmers adopting the new technology. Slight modifications or adaptations of indigenous techniques on the basis of experimental tests often gave them universal applicability. A good example is the technique of rice-seed sorting in salt water. Jikei Yokoi, who later became the foremost leader of agriculture and agricultural science in Japan, found this technique practiced by farmers when he was a young instructor at a vocational agricultural school in Fukuoka prefecture. After he perfected the technique and it was subjected to repeated tests at the National Agricultural Experiment Station, it was propagated throughout Japan.

The technology developed in this process was, by necessity, motivated to increase land productivity or was biased toward saving land, which represented the major constraint on agricultural production in Japan. However, it required an increase in the application of the input that substitutes for land, that is, fertilizer. Agricultural growth based on the development of the *rōnō* techniques was supported by an improvement in the supply of fertilizers, which depended on active entrepreneurship in farm supply industries.

Traditionally, the major sources of plant nutrients in Japanese agriculture were wild grasses and leaves collected from the communal pasture and forest land, supplemented by stable manure and night soil. In fact, the night soil from cities was sold to farmers as a " commercial fertilizer " during the Tokugawa period and even in the early Meiji period. Commercial fertilizers in the form of dried sardines and oilseed cakes were applied on a very limited scale to the cash crops, such as cotton.[35] Even though farmers knew the effect of applying the fertilizers, the prices were too high to apply them to staple food crops.

Fertilizer traders and manufacturers responded to the pressing demand by farmers for land substitutes and exploited the opportunity opened by the Meiji Restoration. First, increased efficiency in transportation, especially the introduction of the steamship, greatly reduced the cost of herring meals from Hokkaido. Application of herring meals to rice production began in the Kinki region, where farmers were accustomed to using commercial fertilizers for cotton, and in other coastal areas from Hokkaido to Kinki. Search for a cheap source of nitrogen brought about the enormous inflow of Manchurian soybean cake in the 1900's and 1910's. The application of phosphate fertilizers began on an experimental scale with the importation of guano and the manufacture of bonemeal. The production of superphosphate of lime on a commercial scale began in 1888 with the establishment of the Tokyo Artificial Fertilizer Company, which grew to become the major source of the supply of phosphate by the 1910's.

These innovations in the supply of fertilizers reduced the cost of artificial plant nutrients and induced innovations of the fertilizer-using and land-saving types in crop production. Seed varieties developed by *rōnō* in response to the inflow of cheap Manchurian soybean cakes (such as *Shinriki* and *Kameno-o*) were characterized by high fertilizer-responsiveness—varieties that did not lodge easily and that were less susceptible to disease at high levels of nitrogen application. Both the economic logic and the demand from farmers pressed agricultural scientists to develop a technology geared to high levels of fertilizer application and yield, the so-called " fertilizer-consuming rice culture."[36] In this respect the discipline of agricultural chemistry and soil science of the German tradition was extremely effective.

The increased application of fertilizers was greatly facilitated by the Fertilizer Control Law (1899), which protected farmers from fraud in the quality of fertilizers. The manufacture and trade of fertilizers were made subject to license by the government. By law the government was authorized to inspect the ingredients of fertilizers. The risk involved in the purchase of commercial fertilizers was reduced, thereby facilitating the adoption of new forms of fertilizers by farmers.

A prerequisite for such development in the seed-fertilizer technology was an irrigation and drainage system that adequately controlled the supply of water. In this respect Meiji Japan was favored by the inheritance of a relatively well developed land infrastructure from the Tokugawa period.

Improvement in the irrigation system was the major source of productivity growth during the feudal period. It was the prime

responsibility of feudal rulers to control rivers and major irrigation systems, and villages were experienced in mobilizing communal labor to maintain and improve irrigation infrastructure.[37]
Even at the beginning of the Meiji period almost all paddy fields
in Japan were irrigated in some way or other, although water
supply was not necessarily sufficient, and appropriate drainage was
lacking in many cases. The development and diffusion of seed-
fertilizer technology were facilitated by this Tokugawa heritage.

After the Meiji Restoration the government tried to improve the
major rivers which had deteriorated during the internal strife
preceding the Restoration. The riparian works of the major rivers
were placed under the auspices of the Ministry of Interior, and
Dutch engineers were invited for consultations on the reconstruc-
tion and improvements of river control.[38]

At the same time the government encouraged land-improvement projects undertaken by the *gōnō* class, including the construction of irrigation and drainage facilities and the replotment
of irregular small-sized paddy fields into more efficient units. The
major limitations on such projects were the difficulties in getting
the consent of farmers and landlords concerned and in securing
sufficient amounts of long-term credit.

In order to facilitate the land-improvement projects, the government enacted the Arable Land Replotment Law in 1899 (revised
in 1905 and 1909). By the law, (*a*) participation in the project was
made compulsory upon the consent of more than two-thirds of the
landowners owning more than two-thirds of the arable land area
in the district concerned, and (*b*) a legal-person status was given
to the associations of land-improvement projects, so that they
could receive credit.[39] Also, the government established the
Japan Hypothec Bank in 1897, which aimed to advance long-term
credit for land-infrastructure investments. As a supplement to the
Hypothec Bank, the Banks of Agriculture and Industry were
established, one for each prefecture (1880–1900). Later, the
government advanced low-interest credit from funds mobilized
from the postal savings for land-improvement projects through
the Hypothec Bank and the prefectural Banks of Agriculture and
Industry.[40] Also, both central and local governments promoted
the land-improvement project by giving subsidies through agricultural associations.

The nation-wide diffusion of the seed-fertilizer technology progressed on the basis of improvement in land infrastructure. It originated in such advanced regions as Kinki, where the population density was higher and the irrigation infrastructure better established. Later, beginning in the first decade of this century, this process was transmitted to the relatively backward eastern part of Japan (see detailed quantitative analysis in chapter 5).

It must be emphasized that this diffusion was not a simple one of seeds or practices but rather a diffusion of the concepts and methods of improving seed varieties and cultural practices suited for local environmental conditions. At the same time, it involved the process of assimilating environmental conditions for agricultural production in the east of Japan to those in the west by improving the irrigation and drainage systems. Improvement in drainage facilities was an especially critical condition for eastward diffusion of the seed-fertilizer technology, and it enabled the full exploitation of fertilizer-response capacity of the high-yielding varieties. It also facilitated the introduction of horse-ploughing. Deep ploughing by animal power and improved ploughs contributed to the increase in the application of fertilizers and in the productivity of land.

Improvements in land infrastructure also facilitated a more intensive utilization of farm land by promoting multi-cropping. The construction of drainage facilities was the key for the introduction of winter crops (such as wheat, barley, and vegetables) into paddy fields. Needless to say, progress in multi-cropping enabled the more intensive utilization of farm labor by eliminating idle seasons.

The development of sericulture was another major factor that contributed to the intensification of labor utilization. In most cases sericultural production developed as a sideline enterprise to staple cereal production in peasant farms. The rapid growth of the sericulture industry was stimulated by the expanding world demand for silk. At the same time it was supported by a number of technical and institutional innovations.

The technical innovations were the artificial incubation of silkworms and the breeding of the F-1 hybrid varieties that allowed for the practice of summer-fall rearing of silk worms. Traditionally, spring—April to June—was the period of cocoon production.

However, this season coincided with the peak labor requirements for rice and other crop production, during which the allocation of family labor for sideline enterprises was limited.

Summer-fall culture, using the nonhibernating bivoltine varieties, had been practiced on a very small scale before the Meiji period, but it was a high-risk business because of the high death rate of silkworms. Shortly after the Meiji Restoration a method was devised that postponed the hatching of hibernating varieties by storing the silkworm eggs in cool caves. Later a method of artificial hatching by a chemical process was developed. The risk of the summer-fall culture was reduced by the introduction of the hybrid varieties, which resulted in the dramatic improvement in the survival rate of summer-fall reared silkworms.[41]

Summer-fall rearing had a number of advantages in the use of resources. It increased the efficiency of capital use for farmers because it enabled the use of rearing equipment and utensils more than once in a year. Also, reelers could economize on the use of circulating capital because they were able to divide payments for cocoons between the spring and summer-fall seasons. It reduced the risk of frost on mulberry leaves, which often damaged early spring culture. The most critical contribution, however, was the increase in the efficiency of labor utilization by providing employment for seasonally idle labor.

Cocoon production from summer-fall culture rose from a negligible level at the beginning of the Meiji period to 12,000 tons in 1890, about 25 percent of the total production, and to 119,000 tons in 1920, about half of the total production. This development was the key that enabled the Japanese sericulture industry to surpass France, Italy, and China.

Such technical innovations were supported by a number of institutional innovations, among them the establishment of silk inspection stations (1895), national and prefectural silkworm egg-multiplication stations (1910–1911), and sericultural colleges in Tokyo (1896), Kyoto (1899), and Ueda (1920). In addition to these government institutions, the development of sericulture cooperatives was crucial. The activities of these cooperatives ranged from transmitting technical information and the cooperative rearing of young worms to managing cooperative silk-reeling mills and training centers.[42]

3-3   Interwar Stagnation

Changing role of landlords and the exhaustion of indigenous potential

Rapid agricultural growth in the latter half of the Meiji era was based on a backlog of indigenous technological potential, previously dammed by feudal constraints, which was released by the reforms of the Restoration (see chapter 5 for quantitative evidence). The interaction among farmers, agricultural scientists, and agricultural-supply firms was effective in exploiting the potential. The initiative of innovative farmers and landlords, together with the proper guidance of the government, was the key to the effective interaction.

Such favorable environments for agricultural progress were gradually undermined. As industry rapidly developed, opportunities for nonfarm investments increased. Landlords found it more profitable to invest their rent revenue in nonfarm businesses rather than to reinvest in agriculture, and they began to lose interest in agricultural improvements. Thus, the shift from "innovative landlords" to "parasitic landlords" progressed in the late Meiji era and the Taisho era (1912–1925).[43]

The major target of the landlords in exercising their political influence through the agricultural associations shifted from measures of increasing agricultural productivity to agricultural protectionism, including tariffs and price supports on farm products. Voices for tariff protection, in terms of foreign exchange and national security considerations, began to be raised when Japan became a net importer of rice during the mid-1890's. It was in the first year of the Russo-Japanese War (1904–1905) that the 15 percent *ad valorem* tariff was first imposed on rice imports. This tariff was aimed at increasing government revenue for financing the war, and it was to be terminated at the war's end. However, the landed interests lobbied to preserve this tariff and succeeded in making it permanent in the form of a specific duty.

Subsequently, the rice tariff became a major issue of public controversy, similar to those over the British Corn Laws and the

German grain tariffs. The Imperial Agricultural Association, representing the landed interests, and the Tokyo Chamber of Commerce, representing the manufacturers and the traders of export commodities, lobbied strongly for opposite ends. In 1912 the tariff controversy in the Diet came to a conclusion with the specific duty of one *yen* per 60 kolograms.[44]

The process of transformation from innovative landlords to parasitic landlords was accompanied by the exhaustion of indigenous technological potential. As stated previously, in the Meiji period simple applied research at the agricultural experiment stations was effective in exploiting the backlog of the potential, but the experiment stations were not yet developed to where they could conduct the more sophisticated and basic research necessary to increase the potential. Scholars at agricultural colleges were engaged primarily in the study of principles and theories developed abroad. Although a few research results of empirical significance were produced, they were grossly insufficient in recharging the declining indigenous potential.

Rice Riot to agricultural depression

The exhaustion of technological potential in Japanese agriculture became evident in the 1910's, when the rate of growth in agricultural output and productivities began to decelerate. Unfortunately this decline coincided with an increase in demand due to the boom of World War I, forcing farm prices to rise to an unprecedented high level. The rising price of food, which exceeded increases in wage rates, caused serious social unrest and culminated in the Rice Riot (*Kome Sodo*) of 1918. The riot, triggered by fishermen's wives in Toyama prefecture, swept over major cities in Japan.

The reaction of the government to the Rice Riot was to organize programs for importing rice from the overseas territories of Korea and Taiwan. In order to create a rice surplus to export to Japan, short-run exploitation policies involved importing sorghum from Manchuria to Korea, forcing Korean farmers to substitute this lower-quality grain for rice in domestic consumption. A similar squeeze was practiced in Taiwan, which forced Taiwanese farmers to substitute sweet potatoes for rice in their diet. This policy was enforced by a squeeze on real income through taxation and government monopoly sales of such commodities as liquor, tobacco, and salt. The longer-run program was to introduce development programs designed to increase the yield and output of rice in these colonial territories. Under this program, titled *Sanmai Zoshoku Keikaku* (Rice Production Development Program), the Japanese colonial governments invested in irrigation and water control and in research and extension, in order to develop and diffuse high-yielding Japanese rice varieties adapted to the local ecology of Korea and Taiwan.[45] The success of this effort created the tremendous rice surplus that flooded the Japanese market. In the twenty years from 1915 to 1935 net imports of rice from Korea to Japan rose from 170 to 1,212 thousand metric tons per year, and net imports from Taiwan rose from 113 to 705 thousand metric tons. As a result of the inflow of colonial rice, the net import of rice rose from 5 to 20 percent of the domestic production.

The increase in the inflow of colonial rice coincided with the postwar recession, which was aggravated by the deflationary policy of the government aiming to return to the gold standard at prewar parity. During the 1920's the contraction of demand in the face of competition from the colonies depressed agricultural prices and income.[46] Finally, the world depression hit Japan, resulting in a serious agricultural crisis, and the government was compelled to rescue this situation by supporting farm prices.

When the price of rice began to fall in the 1920's, the Imperial Agricultural Association pressed the government to adopt a rice-control program, the so-called Ever-Normal Granary Plan. This demand brought about the Rice Law of 1921, which empowered the government to adjust the rice supply in the market by (*a*) operating the purchase, sale, storage, and processing of rice within the financial limit of 2,000 million *yen*, and (*b*) reducing or increasing the import duty and restricting imports from foreign countries.

In response to the rapid decline in rice prices in the late 1920's and 1930's, the Rice Law was amended in 1925, 1931, and 1932, raising the financial limit finally to 4,800 million *yen*. In 1933, when a bumper crop caused a phenomenal surplus of rice, the

Rice Law was replaced by the Rice Control Law, which authorized the government to buy and sell unlimited quantities of rice
at the floor and ceiling prices. The government rice-control operation was extended to colonial rice.[47]

In addition to the farm price support the government developed various programs to mitigate the agricultural crisis. These
included: (a) government spending on construction of physical
infrastructure in rural areas in order to provide wage-earning
opportunities; (b) liquidation of farm debts from usury by re-
leasing credits from the postal savings fund; and (c) organization
of economic recovery movements for villages that promoted self-
sufficiency both in production inputs and in consumption goods,
thereby reducing the cash expenditures of farm households.[48]
Further, the government encouraged the organization of agricultural cooperatives to ensure the protection of farmers from the
exploitation of middlemen and usuries.

In spite of all those efforts the level of income and the living
standard of farm people did not improve appreciably. The tenant
farmers, who were especially immiserized, demanded a reduction
in rent. By this period the paternalistic relations between landlords and tenants, which characterized the agrarian society of
Meiji Japan, had already been fading away as landlords were
transformed into a parasitic class. The tenant-union movements
for rent reduction and the establishment of stronger tenancy
rights gained momentum, and landlords often retaliated by
deprivation of tenanted land. Subsequently, tenancy disputes
became a common feature in rural areas in Japan.[49]

In 1920 the Ministry of Agriculture and Commerce set up the
Tenancy System Research Committee. The committee prepared
a plan for drafting a tenancy law that was designed to give
tenants more stable tenure in that the landlords could not refuse
them the renewal of their tenancy contract. The plan did not
materialize, however, because of the opposition of the landlords.
Instead, the Tenancy Arbitration Law was enacted in 1924,
authorizing local courts and tenancy-arbitration committees to
mediate tenancy disputes. The interests of the tenants were unfortunately not sufficiently protected by this law, because the
majority of the members of the arbitration committee were
landlords and owner-farmers.[50]

The government also tried to transform tenants into owner-farmers. Since 1920 low-interest loans were advanced through credit cooperatives to tenant farmers for the purchase of farm land. Further, with the ordinance of the Ministry of Agriculture and Forestry in 1926 a part of the interest payment was subsidized. The Ministry planned to convert 113,000 hectares of farm land under tenancy into owner-cultivated area within twenty-five years. In fact, within twelve years, from 1926 to 1937, 115,000 hectares of land were converted into the owner-cultivated area. This amount, however, represented only about 4 percent of the farmland under tenancy and did little to change the agrarian structure of Japan.

Emergence of new technological potential

Thus, the interwar period was characterized by stagnation in the rates of growth in real output and productivity in agriculture as well as by depressed income and welfare of the rural population. However, this period also saw a gradual accumulation of new potential in agricultural technology.

The movement for building up new technological potential by more sophisticated and basic research had already begun before World War I. While the capacity of the National Agricultural Experiment Station for conducting more basic research was gradually strengthened, the prefectural experiment stations began to accept the responsibility for carrying out more applied research tests and demonstrations. The extension services of the agricultural associations were greatly expanded.[51] Relieved of those activities, the National Agricultural Experiment Station could now direct its resources toward more basic research.

In response to the development of a network of prefectural experiment stations the national experiment station reduced its branch stations from nine to three in 1903. This reduction was aimed at exploiting scale economies in more basic research by concentrating research resources in fewer stations. In the next year, for the first time, the National Agricultural Experiment Station launched an original crop-breeding program at the Kinai branch. The object of this project was to develop new rice varieties by artificial crossbreeding, based on the Mendelian principles rediscovered in 1900. It took almost two decades before new varieties of major practical significance were developed, though the project contributed greatly to the accumulation of experience and knowledge. Another project was started in 1905 at the Rikuu branch to improve rice varieties by pure line selection. This approach brought about quicker practical results. Thereafter the main efforts of crop breeding in the Taisho era were directed to pure line selection.[52]

Rice breeding by the method of pure line selection represented the final stage in exploiting the indigenous technological potential embodied in the *rōnō* varieties. As the purity of those varieties was raised the potential was exhausted.[53]

Meanwhile, not only the National Agricultural Experiment Station but also the prefectural stations began crossbreeding projects. However, those projects were handicapped by the lack of coordination under the constraint of research resources. Under such circumstances, the nation-wide coordinated crop-breeding program called the "Assigned Experiment System" (the system of experiment assigned by the Ministry of Agriculture and Forestry), was established, first for wheat (1926), then for rice (1927), and for other crops and livestock in subsequent years.

Under the Assigned Experiment System the national experiment stations were given the responsibility for conducting crossbreeding up to the selection of the first several filial generations. The regional stations, in each of eight regions, conducted further selections in order to achieve adaptation to the regional ecological conditions. The varieties selected at the regional stations were then sent to prefectural stations to be tested for their acceptability in specific localities. The varieties developed by this system were called *Norin* (abbreviation for the Ministry of Agriculture and Forestry) varieties.

This system was outstandingly successful, as demonstrated by the fact that the Mexican dwarf wheat, which is revolutionizing Mexican and Indo-Pakistan agriculture, was based on the *Norin No. 10* wheat variety. The *Norin* numbered varieties were developed and successively replaced older varieties in the latter half of the 1930's. If the supply of fertilizer and other agricultural inputs had not been restricted due to the diversion of resources for military purposes during World War II, the second epoch of agricultural productivity growth in Japan, which was experienced after the war, would probably have begun in the late 1930's.

3-4 Agricultural Development Since World War II

Reorganization of agricultural institutions

After the devastation of World War II Japan was left with a territory reduced by almost one-half and a population increased by repatriation from overseas territories. The productive capacity of manufacturing plants was devastated, and the industrial production declined to one-fourth of its prewar level. It was of the utmost urgency to secure food supplies from domestic agriculture.

Emergency measures involved the compulsory delivery of food products as well as the use of several incentive schemes, such as giving bonuses to producers who completed their delivery quota. The government also developed emergency land-settlement programs for the purposes of increasing food output and for providing employment opportunities for the repatriates and the demobilized soldiers.

The critical impediment to the recovery of agricultural production was the shortage of fertilizers. In the program for the rehabilitation of industry, called *Keisha Seisan Hoshiki* (Differential Production Scheme), which began in 1946, the fertilizer industry was given high priority together with the coal-mining and iron-steel industries. In this scheme the government fund was first allocated to coal mining; the increased outputs of coal were delivered to fertilizer, iron, and steel industries; and the increased output in food from fertilizers and in iron and steel were returned to coal mining to expand the cycle of reproduction.

Meanwhile, the policies of "democratizing" agrarian society and institutions were promoted under the direction of the U.S. occupation forces. Of special significance were land reform and the reorganization of the agricultural cooperative associations.

The land reform, which became effective in postwar Japan, was carried out for the 1946–1950 period in accordance with the strong recommendations of the occupation authorities.[54] The position of landlords had already been seriously undermined, during the war. The urgent need to increase agricultural production by increasing production incentives to the tillers had overcome the opposition of the landlord class in strengthening the tenancy right (the Farmland Adjustment Law in 1938), in fixing the rent (the Rent Control Order in 1939), and in controlling land prices (the Farmland Price Control Order in 1941). Immediately after the war (December 1945), in response to the occupation policy and, in part, for the purpose of mitigating the food crisis, the government submitted to the Diet an amendment to the Farmland Adjustment Law, which included a clause that farmlands exceeding five hectares leased by a resident landlord and all the farmland leased by an absentee ladlord should be surrendered to the tenants within five years.

The occupation authorities were not satisfied with this reform program and issued a memorandum requesting a more radical one. In the next year the government drafted a land-reform program along the direction of the GHQ (the General Headquarters of Supreme Commander of Allied Powers). It took the form of the Revision of the Farmland Adjustment Law and the Owner-Farmer Establishment Special Measures Law, which were approved by the Diet in October 1946.

The government was authorized to enforce the purchase of all farmlands owned by absentee landlords as well as the land holdings of resident landlords exceeding one hectare (4 hectares in Hokkaido), which should be sold to tenants within two years after the proclamation of the law. To execute the land transfers, an Agricultural Land Commission was established in each village, consisting of three representatives from the landlords, two from the owner-farmers, and five from the tenant farmers.

The land prices paid to the landlords were determined as forty times the annual rent in the case of paddy fields and forty-eight times in the case of upland fields. In this formula the rents in kind were evaluated by the commodity prices of November 1945. Consequently, in the process of rapid inflation from 1945 to 1949, the real burden of tenant farmers in procuring land was reduced to a negligible level.[55]

For the four years from 1947 to 1950 the government purchased 1.7 million hectares of farmland from landlords and transferred 1.9 million hectares, including state-owned land, to tenant farmers, which amounted to about 80 percent of the ex-tenanted land area. As a result, the ratio of farmland under tenacy declined from 45 percent in 1945 to 9 percent in 1955. Further, for the remaining land under tenancy, the right of tenants was strengthened and the rent was controlled at a very low level by the Agricultural Land Law (1952). This law also imposed a limit on land-holding to three hectares (12 hectares in Hokkaido) in order to prevent the revival of landlordism.

The success of the drastic land reform in Japan was, to a large extent, based on the power of the occupation forces. Equally critical was the backlog of knowledge and experience of the land-tenure system, accumulated by the reform-minded officials in the Ministry of Agriculture and Forestry since the establishment of the Tenancy System Research Committee in 1920. Also important were the various measures of controlling the tenure relations that had developed during the war and that had weakened the position of the landlords.

There is no doubt that the land reform promoted more equal assets and income distributions among farmers, thereby contributing critically to the social stability of the rural sector. However, the farm-size distribution did not change, and the small-scale family farms remained the basic unit of agricultural production. Although land reform contributed to an increase in the level of living and consumption, its contributions to capital formation and productivity growth in agriculture have not been clearly visible or are not significant in terms of quantitative analysis.[56]

Another reform, which had a major impact on agricultural economy and rural society, was the reorganization of agricultural cooperative associations. During the war the agricultural associations and the agricultural cooperatives were integrated into a semi-governmental organization called *Nogyokai* (Agricultural Society) that was designed to share the responsibility of controlling and mobilizing village economies for war purposes. This organization was dissolved by the direction of the GHQ. All the economic functions of the *Nogyokai*, including marketing and credit, were transferred to the agricultural cooperative associations reestablished by the Agricultural Cooperative Law in 1947.

The agricultural cooperative associations inherited the nationwide organizations from the *Nogyokai*. The village associations, numbering more than 30,000, were organized into prefectural and national federations. The national federations at the top of the pyramid include the National Federation of Agricultural Cooperatives for marketing; the Central Bank of Agriculture and Forestry for credit; the National Federation of Mutual Insurance for life and casualty insurance; and the Central Union of Agricultural Cooperatives for political lobbying.

The development of the cooperative associations was facilitated by pervasive government control on agricultural products and inputs during the early postwar period. The cooperatives almost monopolized the delivery of food products, above all rice, to the Food Agency of the Ministry of Agriculture and Forestry and the distribution of government rations of fertilizers and other inputs. Even today, as much as 75 percent of the rice and fertilizers is marketed through the agricultural cooperatives.

Such an organization gave farmers highly effective countervailing power over large private business. On the other hand, since it became so dominant in the rural economy, it has been criticized for inefficient bureaucracy and for exercising monopolistic power.[57] However, there is no denying that the strong cooperative organization, with some 5 million members and 400,000 employees, added to the social stability of the rural sector, on which agricultural development and economic growth in postwar Japan have been ultimately dependent.

When the *Nogyokai* was dissolved at the birth of the new agricultural cooperative associations, the extension-service activities that had been carried out by the *Nogyokai* were assumed by the prefectural governments. Again, according to the instruction of the GHQ, the new system was modeled after the U.S. system of agricultural-extension services. Unlike the trinity of education, research, and extension in the U.S. land-grant college system, the new extension service was established separately from experiment stations and agricultural colleges. However, because both the prefectural experiment station and the extension services

were placed under the auspices of the same agricultural depart-
ments of the prefectural governments, they have been operating
in close cooperation. In many cases senior extension specialists are
stationed in the experiment stations as contact points. Activities
in the prefectural extension services have been reinforced by subsidies from the central government amounting about 40 percent
of the total extension budget.

Basis for postwar agricultural growth

Agricultural production in Japan recovered rapidly from the
1945–1947 bottom. By 1952 direct goverment controls on food
commodities, except for rice, had been lifted, The food shortage
was completely dissolved by the bumper crop of rice in 1955.
The growth rates of agricultural output and productivity have
decelerated since the mid-1950's, when the recovery was completed, but they have been maintained at much higher levels
than the prewar growth rates (Chapter 2).

The major factor underlying rapid agricultural growth in the
post-World War II period may be identified as the backlog of
technological potential accumulated since the 1930's under the
Assigned Experiment System, a potential which had been
dammed by critical shortage of fertilizers and other complementary inputs during the war. The new potential of agricultural
technology was quickly realized along with the recovery in the
supply of those technical inputs. This process was also assisted
by the rehabilitation and improvement of flood-control and irrigation facilities. The land-infrastructure improvement projects promoted by government investment and credit covered 1.6 million
hectares of paddy fields, as much as 60 percent of the total area,
for 1946–1957.[58]

The postwar agricultural growth was further enhanced by the
supply of new industrial inputs, such as chemical pesticides, insecticides, and garden-type tractors and tillers. Such inputs were
based on the progress of industrial technology and scientific
knowledge accumulated during the war. Agricultural scientists
developed techniques that pushed forward the "fertilizer-consuming rice culture" to an extreme. Basic to this move forward

was a dynamic interaction among various scientific and engineering disciplines. Increased fertilizer application made rice plants susceptible to pests and insects, inducing research on agricultural chemicals, in plant physiology and in entomology. Success in these areas reinforced the development of varieties that were even more responsive to high levels of fertilizer application.

A distinct aspect of postwar agricultural development was the progress in farm mechanization. Before World War II, mechanization in Japanese agriculture was limited to irrigation, drainage, and postharvesting operations, such as threshing, The introduction of tractors was attempted only on an experimental scale. The postwar spurt of "mini-tractorization," a rapid introduction of small-scale tractors of less than 10 horsepower, was paralleled by the spurt of industrial and economic development since the mid-1950's that resulted in the rapid absorption of the agricultural labor force by the nonagriculture sector.[59] The number of hand tractors on farms rose sharply, from virtual nonexistence in the 1940's, to 89,000 in 1955, 517,000 in 1960, and 2,500,000 in 1965.

Such rapid progress in tractorization was induced by the relative rise in farm wage rates due to labor outmigration from agriculture. At the same time it was supported by the capacity of the machinery industry to supply the farm machineries and implements suitable for the farming conditions of Japan.[60] The hand tractors were first manufactured according to designs from the United States. They were subject to several defects: heavy body weights relative to the power that they could generate and engines without waterproof devices, which made operations in wet fields difficult. The replacement of draft animals by tractors was made possible by the development of new designs that overcame those critical defects. The engineering capacity in Japanese industry, increased during the war, served as a backlog for the local adaptation and diffusion of mechanical technology in agriculture for the postwar period.

Until the late 1960's the use of tractors had largely been limited to land preparations, such as ploughing and harrowing. Transplanting and harvesting were still performed manually, creating sharp seasonal peaks in labor requirements. Substantial efforts have been made in developing rice-transplanting machines and harvesting machines, such as the cutter, binder, and small-scale combine. Small-scale mechanization for the whole process of rice production in Japan has now been nearly completed.

Introduction of large-scale riding tractors for farm operations began in Hokkaido in the late-1950's, and usage has been progressing rapidly on a nation-wide scale since the acceleration in labor outmigration from agriculture during the 1960's.

The major constraint on the efficient use of large-scale machineries in Japan is, of course, the small-scale farm unit. The land-reform laws have served as a restriction on the growth of farm size. Organizational innovations, such as the cooperative tractor station and contract farming, as well as revision of the land-reform laws, will be required for further development of mechanical technology consistent with the increasing need for labor-saving in agriculture.

Agricultural adjustment problems

When Japan recovered from the devastation of the war and set off on its "miraculous" economic growth since the mid-1950's, agriculture began to face serious adjustment problems.

The rate of growth in agricultural productivity, which was rapid by international standards, was not rapid enough to keep up with the growth in the industrial sector. The growth rate of real per-worker output in manufacturing was almost twice that of agriculture. Intersectoral terms of trade did not improve for agriculture during the 1950's, since the end of the Korean War, partly because of the pressure of surplus agricultural commodities in the United States and other exporting countries and partly because the domestic demand for major staple cereals, especially rice, approached the saturation point after the bumper crop of 1955. In consequence, the levels of income and living for farm households lagged behind urban households.

In such a situation the major goal of agricultural policy shifted from an increase in the production of food staples to a reduction in the rural-urban income gap. To attain this goal the New Village Construction Program was initiated in 1956. This program was aimed at improving the rural economy by providing a package of economic and social infrastructure for the villages that prepared village-development plans. Each village was encouraged to promote the cooperative agricultural-development plan in order to increase the production of commodities having high-income elasticities, such as livestock, fruits, and vegetables. Long-term credits were advanced from the Agriculture, Forestry and Fishery Credit Cooporation, funded by the government, for the purchase of livestock, pasture improvement, and so on.

The need for assisting agricultural adjustments increased from the 1950's to the 1960's as the rural-urban income gap progressively widened and the outmigration of agricultural labor accelerated. These difficulties led to the enactment of the Agricultural Basic Law, a national charter for agriculture, in 1961.[61] The law declared that it was the government's responsibility to raise agricultural productivity and thereby close the gap in income and welfare among farm and nonfarm people. Among the measures identified as necessary for this purpose were encouragements to selectively expand the production of agricultural commodities in response to a changing demand structure and to enlarge the scale of the production unit. An important direction of agricultural development policy suggested by the law was to foster family farms selectively into "viable units" that can earn income from agricultural production comparable to the level of nonfarm household income. In order to improve farming efficiency it was considered essential to increase the scale of the farm operation by promoting both the exodus of inefficient farm units and cooperative operations among the remaining farms.

In spite of all these efforts the rate of agricultural productivity growth was not raised sufficiently to prevent the rural-urban income gap from widening. The major constraint on the increase in agricultural productivity was the small size of the farm unit. Although the outmigration of the agricultural labor population was accelerated from the annual rate of 3 percent in the 1950's to nearly 5 percent in the 1960's, the rate of decline in the number of farms remained relatively slow, at a 2 to 3 percent range. At this rate it would take more than twenty years to double the average farm size, which is grossly insufficient to keep the farm income in balance with the urban wage rate that has been doubling every five years.

The reaction of farmers against the deterioration in their economic position involved group action requesting government support for farm-product prices, and allocation of farmer's labor to nonfarm employment in order to supplement the income from farming.

The demand for price support took the form of pressuring the government to raise the price of rice, which had been kept under the direct control of the Food Agency. Immediately after the war, according to instructions of the GHQ, the parity price formula was introduced for determining the government procurement price from rice producers. This formula was modified in 1952 to account for (a) the lag in the level of consumption and living of rural households compared to urban households and (b) changes in the levels of material inputs to rice production. It was later decided that the government should consult not only the parity index but also the cost of rice production in determing the producer price of rice.

Despite these changes in the price-determination formula, the price of rice was remarkably stable before 1960, and the deficit of the Food Control Special Account did not rise.[62] During the 1950's Japanese exports were still dominated by the products of labor-intensive light industries, such as textiles and toys. The balance of payments was the ceiling of the rate of industrial expansion and economic growth. In such situations it appears the rice policy was successful during the 1950's in contributing to industrial development by keeping the price of a critical wage good from rising, without causing a drain on foreign exchange and undue pressure on the national budget.

Meanwhile, the discontent of farmers had mounted. In 1960 strong political pressure from farm organizations finally resulted in a rice price-determination formula called the "Production Cost and Income Compensation Formula."

By this formula the price of rice is determined by the cost of production at the paddy field, where yield per hectare is lower than the national average by one sigma (one standard deviation). Since the rice yield per hectare is, in general, inversely correlated with the cost of production per unit of output, this formula implies that the price thus determined covers the cost of production of marginal producers ("marginal" in the sense of a cost higher than average by about one standard deviation). A critical point in this formula is that wages for family labor are valued by nonfarm wage rates in order to guarantee "fair returns" for the labor of rice producers.

With this formula the producer price of rice rose rapidly, corresponding to the rise in industrial wages. It doubled from 10,400 *yen* per 150 kilograms of brown rice (193 U.S. dollars per metric ton) in 1960 to 20,600 *yen* (382 U.S. dollars) in 1968.[63] The difference between producer price and import price increased from less than 20 percent to more than 100 percent.

The rice price support contributed to the reduction in the gap between farm and nonfarm income and wages. Income per agricultural worker relative to the income of manufacturing workers, which had declined in the 1950's, began to improve after 1960 when the new price formula was introduced. The remarkable improvement in terms of trade for agriculture more than compensated for the relative decline in the net product per farm worker in real terms (Table 3–1).

However, the price support has not been sufficient to attain the goal of farm-nonfarm income parity. Farmers have been compelled to supplement their income by earnings from nonfarm employments. The rapidly growing nonfarm sector has provided abundant opportunities for off-farm employment. Since 1963 the off-farm income of farm households has exceeded the income from farming (Table 3–2). Thus, part-time farming became a secular feature of rural Japan. According to the 1965 Census of Agriculture, almost 80 percent of the farms were classified as part-time farms, of which about half were classified as "part-time farm of the second type" (farms with more than half of their total incomes earned from nonfarm sources). The 1970 Census indicated that the percentages of the part-time farms and of the "part-time farms of the second type" increased to 85 and 50 percent, respectively.

Price support, together with an increase in off-farm income, resulted in a marked reduction in the gap between agriculture and nonagriculture in income per person and per household (Table 3–2). Satisfaction of the income-parity objective, however, involved a substantial loss in economic efficiency. High rice prices have reduced consumers' welfare by contracting the de-

Table 3-1. Changes in Relative Productivity and Relative Prices between Agriculture and Manufacturing, 1953–1970

| Fiscal Year | Net Product per Worker[a] (current prices) | | Relative Productivity (current prices) C=A/B | Index of Products Prices (1960=100) | | Relative Price Index F=D/E | Relative Productivity (constant prices) G=C/F |
	Agriculture A	Manufacturing B		Agriculture[b] D	Manufacturing[c] E		
	1,000 yen		%				%
1953–1955 av.	68	227	30	101	102	100	30
1960	99	438	23	100	100	100	23
1961	113	499	23	109	100	109	21
1962	126	508	25	120	98	122	20
1963	138	616	22	128	99	129	17
1964	155	654	24	134	99	135	18
1965	182	666	27	149	99	150	18
1966	213	791	27	160	101	158	17
1967	293	936	31	174	102	171	18
1968	317	1,048	30	177	102	173	18
1969	338	1,274	27	190	104	182	15
1970	361	1,426	25	195	109	179	14

[a] Net domestic product at factor cost per gainful worker. Agricultural workers include forestry workers.

[b] Ministry of Agriculture and Forestry index of agricultural product prices at farm gate.

[c] Bank of Japan index of wholesale prices of manufacturing products.

SOURCE: Economic Planning Agency, *Kokumin Shotoku Tokei Nenpo* (Annual Report on National Account Statistics), 1970 and 1973 issues; Bank of Japan, *Bukka Shisu Nenpo* (Annual Report on Price Indices), 1970–1972 issues; Ministry of Agriculture and Forestry, *Noson Bukka Chingin Chosa Hokoku* (Report on Prices and Wages in Rural Villages), 1965 and 1972 issues. Prime Minister's Office, Bureau of Statistics, *Nihon Tokei Nenkan* (Japan Statistical Yearbook), 1962 and 1972 issues.

Table 3-2. Changes in Relative Income between Farm and Urban Worker Households, 1953-1970

Fiscal Year	Farm Household				Urban Worker Household Income per		Relative Income per	
	Income per Household		Total A	Total Income per Person B	Household[a] C	Person D	Household A/C	Person B/D
	Farm Income	Off-farm Income						
	‥‥‥‥‥‥‥‥‥‥‥‥‥‥‥1,000 yen‥‥‥‥‥‥‥‥‥						‥‥‥%‥‥‥	
1953-1955 av.	223	127	350	55	334	70	105	79
1960	225	224	449	78	491	112	91	70
1961	237	264	501	89	542	128	92	70
1962	270	302	571	103	610	146	94	71
1963	289	353	642	118	681	163	94	72
1964	319	413	732	136	761	184	96	74
1965	365	470	835	157	821	200	102	79
1966	413	535	948	182	904	223	105	82
1967	510	625	1,135	221	992	247	114	89
1968	527	721	1,248	247	1,082	275	115	90
1969	529	870	1,399	283	1,206	312	116	91
1970	508	1,084	1,592	326	1,385	358	115	91

[a] Includes transfer income.

SOURCE: Ministry of Agriculture and Forestry, Statistical Research Division, *Noka Keizai Chosa Hokoku* (Report on Farm-household Economy Survey), various issues; Prime Minister's Office, Bureau of Statistics, *Toshi Kakei Chosa Nenpo* (Annual Report on Urban Household Expenditures), various issues.

mand for rice itself, but also by obstructing the shift of resources from rice to other high-demand agricultural products, such as livestock and vegetables.

More conspicuous wastes were the rapidly accumulating surplus rice in government storage and the multiplying deficit from the food-control program. Rice production continued to rise until it reached a record 14.4 million tons in 1967. Meanwhile, consumption remained stable until 1965, when it rapidly declined, resulting in an annual addition of 2 million tons to the government rice storage. In 1968 the deficit from the rice-control program reached 463 billion *yen* (1.3 billion U.S. dollars), which amounted to 40 percent of the budget of the central government for agriculture and forestry, nearly 5 percent of the total national budget.

The ever-increasing rice surplus and the rice-control program deficit finally worked as brakes on further price increases in 1968. A program for retirement and diversion of paddy fields was launched in 1969, partly to stop the increasing deficit and partly to counteract the drain of resources to rice. Subsequently, rice prices were fixed for three years.

The progress of part-time farming also involved inefficiencies in the use of land and capital for agriculture. Increasingly farmers have abandoned winter crops, such as wheat and barley, in order to engage in off-farm economic activities. This has resulted in a decline in the rate of utilization of farmland and capital, such as machinery. Also, the increasing dependence of farm households on off-farm income has been accompanied by serious social problems. Farmers located in remote areas, where off-farm employment opportunities are unavailable within a commuting distance, migrate to metropolitan areas during the winter months, and family tragedies often result. In spite of these economic and social problems, however, it seems reasonable to assume that the progress of part-time farming has made a positive contribution to the welfare of society by increasing the capacity of holding the population in the rural sector, thereby preventing rural depopulation and urban congestion.

For the past decade Japanese agriculture has been progressively interlocked in the international division of labor. Corresponding to the shift to manufacturing's comparative advantage,

Table 3-3. Changes in Self-Sufficiency in Food and Feed (%)

	1960	1965	1970
Total Food[a]	90	81	76
Rice	102	95	106
Wheat	39	28	9
Barley	107	73	34
Soybean	28	11	4
Fruits	100	90	84
Meat	91	89	88
Dairy products	89	86	89
Eggs	101	100	97
Sugar	18	30	23
Concentrate feed[b]	67	36	33

[a] Domestic production divided by domestic consumption; both deducted for feed use.
[b] In terms of digestible nutrient.
SOURCE: Ministry of Agriculture and Forestry, *Showa 47 Nendo Nogyo no Doko ni kansuru Nenji Hokoku* (Annual Report on the State of Agriculture, 1972), (Tokyo, 1973), p. 16.

the rates of self-sufficiency in food and agricultural products have declined (Table 3–3). Especially dramatic was the decline in self-sufficiency for winter cereal crops (wheat and barley) and soybeans. The efforts to increase domestic agricultural production was weakened in the late 1960's under the pressure of surplus rice as well as by the optimistic prospect for world food supplies due to the spread of the "green revolution" in Asia.

Voices for the international division of labor have been reversed by the world food shortage and high prices caused by the worldwide poor crop of 1972. Once again, food self-sufficiency has become a popular political slogan. This mood was reinforced by the energy crisis emerging from oil-supply cuts by the Arabs. The farm block took advantage of this situation and succeeded in increasing the government procurement price of rice. Demand for government policy to increase agricultural production, such as land-infrastructure investment, has been strengthened.

Aside from the emotional appeal for food self-sufficiency, it is important for national welfare, as well as for security, to maintain and increase the capacity of agricultural production while improving the efficiency of production. An important consideration must be to promote economic efficiency without causing undue strain on social stability by rural depopulation and urban congestion.

In an economy in which labor is becoming relatively more scarce and the wage rate is rising relatively faster, it is necessary to develop technology that facilitates the substitution of labor by capital in order to improve efficiency in agricultural production. The efficient use of capital generally requires a large-scale operation. A condition for exploiting labor-saving technology in the face of the irreversible trend in the progress of part-time farming could be an institutional innovation, such as contract farming, which would enlarge the scale of operation within the framework of small-scale farm units. The problem of attaining the goal of economic efficiency in agricultural production, while maintaining sufficient equity in welfare among the rural population and between rural and urban sectors, will require extreme skill. The achievement of this goal will depend ultimately on the flexibility of the Japanese society to transform itself in response to changes in technology and relative resource endowments in the course of economic development.

Notes to Chapter 3

[1] This chapter draws extensively on Yujiro Hayami and Vernon Ruttan, *Agricultural Development: An International Perspective* (Baltimore: Johns Hopkins University Press, 1971), pp. 153–164. It also depends heavily on Nogyo Hattatsushi Chosakai (Research Committee on Japanese Agricultural Development), *Nihon Nogyo Hattatsushi* (History of Japanese Agricultural Development), 10 vols. (Tokyo: Chuo-koronsha, 1953–1958), henceforth abbreviated as *NNHS*. For an English summary of the history of agricultural policy and institutions in modern Japan, see Takekazu Ogura, ed., *Agricultural Development in Modern Japan* (Tokyo: Fuji Publishing Co., 1963).

[2] Literature on agriculture in the Tokugawa period is prolific, including the classical studies by Toshio Furushima: *Nihon Hoken Nogyo Shi* (Agricultural History of Feudal Japan), (Tokyo: Shikai Shobo, 1941); *Kinsei Nihon Nogyo no Kozo* (Structure of Japanese Agriculture in the Late Middle Age), (Tokyo: Nihon Hyoronsha, 1943); *Nihon Nogyo Gijutsu Shi* (History of Agricultural Technology in Japan), 2 vols. (Tokyo: Jichosha, 1947 and 1949). For the excellent exposition in English on the development of Tokugawa agriculture, see Thomas Smith, *The Agrarian Origins of Modern Japan* (Stanford: Stanford University Press, 1959).

[3] The Tokugawa Shogunate (Tokugawa Bakufu) means literally the military government of Supreme Commander Tokugawa.

[4] Smith, *Agrarian Origins*, pp. 67–86.

[5] Ibid.

[6] See the works of Furushima, *Nihon Hoken Nogho Shi*, and Smith, ibid, pp. 87–107.

7) The book by Smith (*Agrarian Origins*) focuses on this process. See also Shinzaburo Oishi, *Hokenteki Tochishoyu no Kaitai Katei* (The Process of Dissolution of Feudal Land Ownership), (Tokyo: Ochanomizu Shobo, 1958).

8) Ibid.

9) For the economic and political processes leading to the Meiji Restoration, see E. Herbert Norman, *Japan's Emergence as a Modern State: Political and Economic Problems of the Meiji Period* (New York: Institute of Pacific Relations, 1940).

10) The "Meiji period" refers to the period from 1868 to the death of Emperor Meiji in 1912.

11) *NNHS*, vol. 1, pp. 77–85.

12) For the process of transformation of the land-tenure system, see Kunio Niwa, *Meiji Ishin no Tochi Henkaku* (Land Reform in the Meiji Restoration), (Tokyo: Ochanomizu Shobo, 1962).

13) For references on the Land Tax Revision, see ibid; Takeo Ono, *Meiji Zenki Tochi Seido Shi Ron* (Treatise on Early Meiji Land System), (Tokyo: Yuhikaku, 1948); and Masao Fukushima, *Chiso Kaisei no Kenkyu* (Study on Land Tax Revision), (Tokyo: Yuhikaku, 1970). Also, see *NNHS*, vol. 1, pp. 53–106.

14) The tax revision on cultivated farmland was completed by 1876, but not before 1881 on forest and wild land.

15) Gustav Ranis, "Financing of Japanese Economic Development," *Economic History Review* 11 (April 1959): 440–454.

16) *NNHS*, vol. 1, pp. 70–76.

17) The deflation was named after Finance Minister Matsukata Masayoshi (1835–1924), who intended to stop inflation by withdrawing inconvertible paper currencies issued during the revolt of ex-*samurai* in southern Kyushu.

18) For the development of landlordism, see Toshio Furushima, ed., *Nihon Jinushi Seido Shi Kenkyu* (Study on the Development of Landlordism in Japan), (Tokyo: Iwanami, 1958).

19) The report of the Iwakata mission was published as *Tokumei Zenken Taishi Beio Kairan Zikki* (The Real Record of American-European Tour of the Ambassador Omnipotent) (Tokyo: Hakubunsha, 1878).

20) Ibid., vol. 91, pp. 190–214.

21) Toshimichi Okubo (1830–1878) was a top leader in the early Meiji government. He was a member of the Iwakata mission, and, upon returning home, laid the foundation for industrial development in Japan as minister of the interior.

22) For those early efforts of transplanting foreign technology, see *NNHS*, vol. 2, pp. 110–118; and Ogura, *Agricultural Development*, pp. 299–301.

23) *NNHS*, vol. 2, p. 114.

24) For the comprehensive study on the development of agricultural science in the Meiji period, see Yukio Saito, *Nihon Nogakushi* (The History of Agricultural Science in Japan), 2 vols. (Tokyo: National Research Institute of Agriculture, 1968 and 1970). Another useful reference is Toshio Furushima (ed.), *Nogaku* (Agricultural Science), vols. 22 and 23 of *Nihon Kagaku Gijutsushi Taikei* (The Comprehensive History of Science and Technology in Japan), (Tokyo: Daiichi Hoki Shuppan, 1967 and 1970).

25) Among others, Oskar Kellner, in the field of plant and animal nutrition, and Max Fesca, in the field of soil science, made important contributions in establishing modern agricultural science in Japan. See also fn. 24.

26) Reduction of the tax burden was one of the slogans of the political movement demanding constitution and parliamentary democracy.

27) Reprinted in Ministry of Agriculture and Foresty, ed., *Meiji Zenki Kannojiseki Shuroku* (The Compilation of Measures to Encourage Agriculture), (Tokyo:

Dainihon Nokai, 1939), vol., 2, pp. 1765–1779.

[28] Saito, *Nihon Nogakushi*, vol. 2, pp. 126–134 and 161–164.

[29] *NNHS*, vol. 1, pp. 107–118. For the role of landlords in irrigation and drainage improvements, see Akira Baba, *Suiri Jigyo no Tenkai to Jinushisei* (Development of Water Utilization Projects and Landlordism), (Tokyo: Ochanomizu Shobo, 1965).

[30] *NNHS*, vol. 3, pp. 262–277.

[31] Yajiro Shinagawa (1843–1900), who later became minister of interior, is known for his contribution to agricultural association and agricultural cooperative movements. He was an ideologue for the advantage of small-scale farms in opposition to the opinion that Japanese agriculture should be reorganized into large-scale farming according to the Western model.

[32] The Agricultural Association Law was enacted in 1899; its revision in 1905 authorized compulsory participation, and the 1922 revision authorized compulsory fee collection.

[33] For the development of this agricultural association, see *NNHS*, vol. 3, pp. 262–386; vol. 5, pp. 309–415; and vol. 7, pp. 149–255.

[34] For the comprehensive history of the agricultural cooperative association, see Nogyo Kumiai Kenkyujo (Institute for Cooperative Association Study), *Nogyo Kumiai Seido Shi* (History of Agricultural Cooperative Association System), 7 vols. (Tokyo, 1967–1969).

[35] For the practice of fertilizer application in the Tokugawa period, see Furushima, *Nihon Nogyo Gijutsu Shi*, and Smith, *Agrarian Origins*, pp. 87–107.

[36] Ogura, *Agricultural Development*, pp. 365–387.

[37] *NNHS*, vol. 4, pp. 159–196.

[38] Ibid, vol. 1, pp. 119–152; and vol. 4, pp. 117–158.

[39] Ibid, vol. 4, pp. 197–232.

[40] For the development of the agricultural credit system, see Ogura, *Agricultural Development*, pp. 247–285.

[41] For more details, see Hayami and Ruttan, *Agricultural Development*, pp. 300–302.

[42] Ibid.

[43] For a lively description of this process, see Seiichi Tobata, *Nihon Nogyo no Ninaite* (Carriers of Japanese Agriculture), *NNHS*, vol. 9, pp. 561–604.

[44] For the history of rice price and trade policy, see Yujiro Hayami, "Rice Policy in Japan's Economic Development," *American Journal of Agricultural Economics* 54 (February 1972): 19–31.

[45] Yujiro Hayami, "Elements of Induced Innovation: A Historical Perspective for the Green Revolution," *Explorations in Economic History* 8 (Summer 1971): 445–472.

[46] For a quantitative analysis of the impact of colonial rice import on rice prices in Japan, see Yujiro Hayami and Vernon Ruttan, "Korean Rice, Taiwan Rice, and Japanese Agricultural Stagnation: An Economic Consequence of Colonialism," *Quarterly Journal of Economics* 84 (November 1970): 562–589; and Hayami and Ruttan, *Agricultural Development*, pp. 218–227.

[47] See Hayami, "Rice Policy."

[48] Tsutomu Ouchi called these policies "Social-policy-like agricultural policy": *Nogyo Shi* (History of Agriculture), (Tokyo: Toyokeizai Shimposha, 1960), pp. 225–240.

[49] The number of tenancy disputes in a year rose from 408 in 1920 to 2,478 in 1930 and 6,824 in 1935. Ibid., p. 211.

[50] Ibid., p. 236.

[51] The number of extension workers employed by the agricultural associations grew to 5,200 in 1914, 10,000 in 1924, and 14,000 in 1933; see *Nogyo Hyakka Jiten* (Encyclopedia of Agriculture), (Tokyo: Nosei Chosa Iinkai, 1965), vol. 6, p. 721.

[52] For the history of crop-breeding research, see *NNHS*, vol. 9, pp. 85–161.

[53] Takamine Matsuo, *Suito Hinshu Kairyo Shijo no Shomondai* (Problems in the History of Rice Variety Improvement), (Tokyo: Nogyo Hattatsushi Chosakai, Data No. 42, 1951), mimeo.

[54] For official documentation of the land reform in postwar Japan, see Laurence I. Hewes, *Japanese Land Reform Program* (Tokyo: General Headquarters of the Supreme Commander of Allied Powers Natural Resources Section Report No. 127, 1950). Also, see Ronald P. Dore, *Land Reform in Japan* (London: Oxford University Press, 1958); and Ogura, *Agricultural Development*, pp. 138–148.

[55] For the period 1945–1950 the producer's price of rice (the government procurement price) rose by as much as 20 times, from 300 yen per 150 kilograms of brown rice to 6047 yen.

[56] Shigeto Kawano, "Effects of the Land Reform on Consumption and Investment of Farmers," in *Agriculture and Economic Growth: Japan's Experience*, eds. Kazushi Ohkawa, B. F. Johnston, and Hiromitsu Kaneda (Tokyo: University of Tokyo Press, 1969), pp. 374–397.

[57] For radical criticism on cooperative associations, see Yasuo Kondo, *Zoku Mazushisa karano Kaiho* (Liberation from Poverty, Book II), (Tokyo: Chuokoronsha, 1954).

[58] Ouchi, *Nogyo Shi*, p. 361.

[59] For the process of small-scale tractorization, see Hayami and Ruttan, *Agricultural Development*, pp. 181–182.

[60] Ibid.

[61] Ogura, *Agricultural Development*, pp. 286–296.

[62] See Hayami, "Rice Policy."

[63] Based on the exchange rate of 360 yen per U.S. dollar, which prevailed in the years concerned.

Part 2 Accounting for Growth

Chapter 4

Sources of Long-Term
Productivity Growth[1]

From observations of long-term trends in agricultural output, inputs, and productivities, as measured in Chapter 2, it was found that about one-half of the growth in aggregate output in Japanese agriculture from the early Meiji period until recently is left unexplained by inputs of "conventional" factors, which include labor, land, capital, and such current inputs as fertilizer. In this chapter we will attempt to reduce our ignorance as to the sources of agricultural output growth, measured by the increase in total productivity, within the framework of the aggregate production function.

From our review in chapter 3 of the history of agricultural development it is reasonable to identify the following as sources of agricultural productivity growth: (*a*) the ability of farm producers to allocate resources effectively in response to changes in prices and technology, either individually or in groups, such as agricultural associations and cooperatives; and (*b*) the provision by the government of necessary infrastructure for agricultural production, such as irrigation and agricultural-research systems. These "nonconventional" factors may be considered the shifters of the agricultural production function; and a part of the growth in total productivity may be identified as an error due to the neglect of those relevant variables.[2]

Another possible source of measured productivity growth is the error due to employing factor-share weights for the aggregation of inputs of conventional factors.[3] As discussed in chapter 2, the factor shares coincide with the production elasticities at the equilibrium of the factor market. In equilibrium the factor shares represent the appropriate weights for the aggregation of inputs, as they reflect accurately the relative contributions of respective factors to output. However, it is highly unlikely that the dynamic process of agricultural development was not accompanied by substantial disequilibrium.

In order to reduce these errors, we employ the technique of growth accounting in the tradition of Zvi Griliches.[4] First, we measure the major shifters of the aggregate agricultural production function by: (a) the education of farmers who increase their ability to allocate resources more efficiently; (b) public investments in agricultural research and extension that contribute to the creation and propagation of a more productive technology; and (c) improvements in land infrastructure, such as irrigation and drainage, that have the effect of augmenting land for agricultural production. Second, we estimate the aggregate agricultural production function on the basis of forty-six cross-prefectural data. Production functions were estimated for two pre-World War II periods, 1930 (1928–1932 averages) and 1935 (1933–1937 averages); and for two postwar periods, 1960 (1958–1962 averages) and 1965 (1963–1967 averages). Finally, using as weights for aggregation the production elasticities from estimates of the production function, the growth in agricultural output is accounted for by changes in four conventional inputs—land, labor, capital, and current inputs—and in two nonconventional inputs—farmers' education and agricultural research and extension.

Land infrastructure in the form of irrigation and drainage facilities is not introduced explicitly as a variable in the cross-prefectural production function because of data limitation. However, its contribution to growth in agricultural output over time is taken into account by adjusting land for quality changes due to investments in land infrastructure.

4-1 Cross-Prefectural Production Function

In this section we estimate the aggregate production function of Japanese agriculture on the basis of forty-six cross-prefectural data in order to obtain estimates of production elasticities that will be used for the growth-accounting analysis.

Specification of production function

In the growth-accounting approach it has been customary to employ the production function of the Cobb-Douglas or log-linear form, primarily for its ease in manipulation. It has been argued that the constant production elasticities implied in the Cobb-Douglas production function are not a critical limitation for the short- to the medium-range analysis.[5] In this study we have also adopted the Cobb-Douglas production function for the postwar period, 1955 to 1965.

However, the constancy of production elasticities is clearly not a sufficient approximation for analysis of long-term growth in the prewar period, which extends over a half-century and involves major technological changes. The constant elasticities cause no problem if we can estimate them for different technological epochs, but sufficient cross-prefectural data for estimating the aggregate agricultural production function are unavailable before 1930.

It is especially difficult to assume the constancy of the elasticities of land and current inputs (of which fertilizer was the dominant factor). In agriculture in prewar Japan, because land was relatively scarce and labor relatively abundant, efforts for technological improvements concentrated on saving land or increasing the output per unit of limited land areas, primarily through the development of fertilizer-responsive high-yielding varieties and related cultural practices. Such technological improvements imply innovations facilitating the substitution of fertilizer and other current inputs, such as pesticides, for arable land. Such bias in technological change is also reflected in the decrease in the share of land and the corresponding increase in the share of current inputs in the total cost of agricultural production, especially before 1920 (see Chapter 2, Section 3).

Another critical aspect should be the constancy of the production elasticity for research and extension. Theodore Schultz has argued that agricultural research is characterized by scale economies.[6] The Schultz hypothesis has been supported empirically by Robert Evenson.[7] Between 1880 and 1930 Japan established a modern system of agricultural research and extension. Public expenditures for research and extension rose more than twenty times during this period. Given the scale economies of the technology-producing sector, especially in its infant stage, it is highly unlikely that the production elasticity of research and extension remained constant for the sixty prewar years.

For those considerations we estimated not only the ordinary Cobb-Douglas production function but also its modified form, since the coefficients of land, fertilizer, and research and extension vary correspondingly with changes in their input levels. While the ordinary Cobb-Douglas function in logarithmic transformation is specified as

$$\log (Y/A)_i = \alpha_0 + \alpha_L \log (L/A)_i + \alpha_K \log (K/A)_i + \alpha_F \log (F/A)_i$$

$$+ \alpha_E \log E_i + \alpha_R \log R_i + \sum_{j=0}^{5} \delta_j D_j + U_i \qquad (1)$$

the modified form is

$$\log (Y/A)_i = \alpha_0 + \alpha_L \log (L/A)_i + \alpha_K \log (K/A)_i + \beta_F \sqrt{(F/A)_i}$$

$$+ \alpha_E \log E_i + \beta_R \sqrt{R_i} + \sum_{j=0}^{5} \delta_j D_j + U_i \qquad (2)$$

Where

Y = output E = education
A = land R = research and extension
L = labor D_j = regional dummy ($j = 0...5$)
K = capital U = error term
F = fertilizer

and the subscript i's denote prefectures.

In both equations (1) and (2) output and conventional inputs are expressed in per-unit-of-land terms, and the production elasticity of land (α_A) is obtained as one minus the sum of production elasticities of labor (α_L), of capital (α_K), and of fertilizer (α_F), assuming linear homogeneity $(\alpha_L+\alpha_K+\alpha_F+\alpha_A=1)$. While the coefficients of equation (1) are themselves the production elasticities, in equation (2) the production elasticities of fertilizer and of research and extension are derived as

$$\alpha_F = \frac{1}{2}\beta_F\sqrt{\frac{F}{A}} \quad \text{and} \quad \alpha_R = \frac{1}{2}\beta_R\sqrt{R}$$

In other words, the production elasticities of F and R in equation (2) are specified as the increasing functions (at decreasing rates) of (F/A) and R, respectively, for the positive values of β_F and β_R.

For the positive estimate of β_F the production elasticity of fertilizer (α_F) increases, and the implicit coefficient of land (α_L), which can be obtained from the linear homogeneity assumption, decreases correspondingly as the inputs of fertilizer per unit of arable land area rise. This specification is consistent with the pattern of land-saving and fertilizer-using technological progress in prewar Japan. Also, the production elasticity of research and extension in equation (2) increases at a declining rate, consistent with the pattern expected in a period of rapid evolution from an infant stage to a mature stage of the national system of research and extension in agriculture.

The problem is whether such a bias in technical progress in agriculture and scale economies in research investment over time was reflected in the cross-prefectural data of the 1930's. Of course, the validity of extrapolating cross-sectional estimates into a time-series dimension is always open to question. However, it seems reasonable to expect that cross-prefectural variations in the effects of scale economies of research and extension in agricultural production in Japan in the 1930's were sufficient to estimate the scale economies. Evenson successfully estimated scale economies for research and extension in the United States using interstate cross-sectional data for the 1950's.[8]

It is even more reasonable to assume wide interregional variations in agricultural technology with respect to factor-saving bias. In this period northeastern districts (particularly Tohoku) were still agriculturally backward relative to southwestern districts (particularly Kinki and Northern Kyushu), though the interregional technology gap had been reduced since the early Meiji period. The 1930–1935 average fertilizer input per hectare of arable land in paddy-field units in the Kinki district was about 100 percent higher than in the Tohoku district. In the same period it is estimated that the difference in the price of fertilizer between Kinki and Tohoku was, at most, only 20 percent. Since the long-run price elasticity of fertilizer demand was estimated as about unity,[9] only 20 percent of the difference in the input of fertilizer per hectare can be explained by the difference in prices. A major part of the remaining 80 percent should be explained by differences in the level of fertilizer-using technology. This evidence seems to support the presumption that the cross-prefectural data in the 1930's reflect, to a significant extent, differences in the fertilizer-using and land-saving technical progress over time.

As discussed in chapter 3 a condition for the development and diffusion of fertilizer-responsive high-yielding varieties from the early period of modern economic growth in Japan was the relatively well developed irrigation infrastructure inherited from the feudal regime. The irrigation and drainage systems were more highly developed in advanced agricultural regions, such as Kinki, than in backward regions, such as Tohoku. The interregional differences in the levels of fertilizer-using and land-saving technology should have been more or less parallel with the differences in the levels of agricultural land infrastructure. Since our cross-prefectural production function does not include land infrastructure, due to the lack of data, the estimates of the production elasticity of fertilizer might reflect the contribution of land infrastructure to agricultural production in addition to the net effect of fertilizer input per se.

Both equations (1) and (2), because the variables are expressed in per-land-unit terms, have a limitation in that it is not possible to test the scale economies of conventional inputs. This specification is to avoid the strong multi-collinearity between land and labor. This limitation does not seem critical for the prewar analysis, since micro-production function estimates using farm survey data invariably indicate that constant returns prevailed before World War II and even until 1955.[10] Although the evidence is not conclusive, there is some sign that scale economies have emerged in Japanese agriculture since the late 1950's with the development of mechanical technology.[11] We do not deny a possibility that the specification of linear, homogeneous production functions might have caused some bias in our growth accounting, especially for the postwar period.

Data

Here we will explain the cross-prefectural data for the variables included in the specified production function.[12] In principle the data are five-year averages centering on 1930, 1935, 1960, and 1965.

The output variable (Y) is measured in terms of gross agricultural output, measured in 1934–1936 constant prices for the prewar period and in 1960 constant prices for the postwar period. The unusually bad crop years of 1929 and 1934 were excluded from averaging as they do not seem to reflect the "normal" production capacity.

Land (A) is measured in paddy-field units, which are equivalent to a *chō* (0.9917 hectare) of lowland paddy field; upland-field areas are converted into areas in paddy-field equivalents by applying the ratio of the price of upland field to the price of lowland paddy field.

Labor (L) is the number of farm workers in terms of number of male equivalents: the sum of the numbers of gainful male workers and of female workers converted into man equivalents by applying the ratio of male wage rate to female wage rate.

Fertilizer (F) for the prewar period represents the purchased current inputs in agriculture measured in terms of 1934–1936 constant prices. For the postwar period the aggregates of farm expenditures for current inputs, including fertilizer, pesticides, insecticides, and others, are adopted as the series for F.

As the capital variable (K), we adopted for the prewar period the stock of livestock capital as representing the total capital stock in agriculture. For the postwar period we took the stock of farm machinery and implements representing farm capital in the 1960's.

The education variable (E) is measured in terms of average years of schooling of farm workers.[13]

The variable for research and extension (R) is the accumulation of annual expenditures for agricultural research and extension activities both by central and by local governments for the past fifteen years, ending in the year of analysis, divided by the number of farms in each prefecture. The annual expenditures are accumulated after being deflated by the consumer price index. For the prewar period the research and extension expenditures are measured independently for each prefecture. For the postwar

Table 4-1. Estimates of Agricultural Production Function on Cross-Prefectural

Explanatory Variables		Regression Number,	
		1 1930 46	2 1930 46
Labor	$(\log L/A)$	.465 (.108)	.457 (.104)
Livestock capital	$(\log K/A)$	.145 (.058)	.187 (.055)
Fertilizer	$(\log F/A)$	.241 (.059)	.249 (.053)
	$(\sqrt{F/A})$		
Education	$(\log E)$		.169 (.138)
Res. and ext.	$(\log R)$		.210 (.069)
	$(\sqrt{R})$		
Regional dummies:			
D_1 (Hokkaido, Tohoku, Northern Kanto)		−.038 (.031)	−.052 (.028)
D_2 (Southern Kanto, Hokuriku)		.017 (.036)	−.005 (.034)
D_3 (Tozan, Tokai)		−.007 (.036)	−.049 (.035)
D_4 (Kinki)		.067 (.033)	.049 (.031)
D_5 (Chugoku, Shikoku)		−.010 (.027)	−.003 (.025)
Time Dummy: T_{35}			
Constant term		1.489	1.231
Coef. of det. (adj.)		.819	.854
S. E. of est.		.053	.048
Implicit Coef. of land		.149	.107

Equations are estimated by ordinary least squares. The standard errors of period those expenditures are pooled and averaged among pre-fectures within each of eleven ecological regions. The data pre-pared in this way brought about better results for the postwar analysis. The analysis implies that the spill-over effects of research among prefectures in the same ecological region became domi-nant in the 1960's with the progress in communication systems.

Five regional dummy variables (D_j's) are adopted in order to

Data, 1930 (1928–1932 averages) and 1935 (1933–1937 averages)

Year, and Sample Size				
3 1935 46	4 1935 46	5 1930–1935 92	6 1930–1935 92	7 1930–1935 92
.344 (.098)	.337 (.095)	.404 (.071)	.396 (.067)	.423 (.064)
.119 (.054)	.176 (.054)	.136 (.038)	.188 (.037)	.165 (.036)
.323 (.058)	.323 (.052)	.280 (.039)	.284 (.035)	
				.0357 (.0042)
	.144 (.102)		.156 (.078)	.140 (.077)
	.138 (.054)		.167 (.040)	
				.0692 (.0183)
−.046 (.029)	−.048 (.027)	−.042 (.020)	−.049 (.018)	−.057 (.018)
.029 (.034)	.024 (.031)	.023 (.024)	.011 (.022)	.007 (.022)
−.021 (.034)	−.039 (.032)	−.014 (.024)	−.042 (.022)	−.052 (.022)
.050 (.031)	.041 (.029)	.058 (.022)	.045 (.020)	.041 (.020)
−.010 (.026)	−.0002 (.024)	−.011 (.018)	−.002 (.016)	−.008 (.016)
		.014 (.011)	−.034 (.014)	−.029 (.014)
1.589	1.308	1.531	1.282	1.480
.828	.855	.835	.867	.869
.052	.047	.051	.045	.045
.214	.164	.180	.132	.112

coefficients are in parentheses.

adjust for the effects of differences in climate and other environmental conditions on agricultural production.

Results of estimation of production function

The main results of estimates for the prewar and the postwar periods of the cross-prefectural agricultural production function,

Table 4-2. Estimates of Agricultural Production Function on Cross-Prefectural Data, 1960 (1958–1962 averages) and 1965 (1963–1967 averages)

Explanatory Variables	Regression Number, Year, and Sample Size					
	8 1960 46	9 1960 46	10 1965 46	11 1965 46	12 1960–1965 92	13 1960–1965 92
Labor (log L/A)	.287 (.105)	.292 (.106)	.250 (.069)	.294 (.059)	.277 (.059)	.285 (.060)
Machinery capital (log K/A)	.284 (.113)	.199 (.116)	.357 (.079)	.303 (.060)	.305 (.064)	.259 (.061)
Current inputs (log F/A)	.243 (.074)	.224 (.078)	.274 (.043)	.218 (.040)	.260 (.039)	.226 (.038)
Education (log E)		.236 (.921)		.731 (.552)		.508 (.581)
Res. and ext. (log R)		.046 (.041)		.063 (.050)		.055 (.031)
Regional dummies:						
D_1 (Hokkaido, Tohoku, Northern Kanto)	.044 (.025)	.040 (.024)	.035 (.016)	.033 (.014)	.040 (.014)	.038 (.013)
D_2 (Southern Kanto, Hokuriku)	.025 (.030)	.032 (.030)	.036 (.017)	.040 (.015)	.030 (.016)	.034 (.015)
D_3 (Tozan, Tokai)	.026 (.027)	.035 (.028)	.007 (.019)	.013 (.016)	.017 (.016)	.019 (.014)
D_4 (Kinki)	.019 (.031)	.032 (.031)	.009 (.021)	.016 (.018)	.015 (.018)	.021 (.017)
D_5 (Chugoku, Shikoku)	−.003 (.025)	.020 (.026)	−.013 (.016)	.008 (.014)	−.008 (.014)	.012 (.014)
Time Dummy: T_{65}					−.037 (.022)	−.032 (.020)
Constant term	1.486	1.401	1.234	1.203	1.371	1.323
Coef. of det. (adj.)	.771	.770	.899	.901	.870	.869
S. E. of est.	.044	.044	.031	.030	.037	.037
Implicit Coef. of land	.186	.285	.119	.185	.158	.230

Equations are estimated by ordinary least squares. The standard errors of coefficients are in parentheses.

based on data for forty-six prefectures, are summarized in Tables 4–1 and 4–2. Each column reports the results of a least-squares regression of gross agricultural output per hectare of paddy-field-equivalent land area (in logarithm) on a different set of specified variables, including estimates of the production coefficients and their standard errors (in parentheses), the standard error of estimate (S.E.), and the coefficient of determination adjusted for the degree of freedom. Except Regression (7), which is the estimate of equation (2), they represent the estimates of the ordinary Cobb-Douglas production function.

Considering the crudeness of the data, the levels of statistical significance of the estimated coefficients seem satisfactory in most cases, except for the coefficients of education in the postwar regressions. The coefficients stay fairly stable when nonconventional variables are added or subtracted. Comparisons of the estimates with data of different time points and with the pooled data indicate the stability of the production function over time both within the prewar period and within the postwar period.[14]

In terms of the goodness of fit to data, as measured by the coefficient of determination, Regression (7) is slightly better than Regression (6), which may be taken as supporting evidence for specifying equation (2) for the prewar analysis.

Estimates of production elasticities in Tables 4–1 and 4–2 can be compared with the factor-share estimates in Table 2–11 (chapter 2).

Modal values of the estimates of production elasticities and the estimates of factor shares in the comparable periods are, roughly, as follows:

	Production Elasticities	*Factor Shares*
Prewar (1930–1935):		
Labor	0.4	0.5
Capital	0.15	0.1
Fertilizer	0.3	0.1
Land	0.15	0.3
Postwar (1960–1965):		
Labor	0.3	0.5
Capital	0.3	0.1
Fertilizer	0.2	0.2
Land	0.2	0.2

A clear contrast exists between the 1930–1935 and the 1960–1965 periods in the way that the production elasticities differ from the factor shares. For the 1930–1935 period the production elasticity of fertilizer is estimated to be much larger than fertilizer's distributive share, and the production elasticity of land to be much smaller than land's share. In contrast, for the 1960–1965 period the production elasticities of capital and labor differ significantly from their factor shares; production elasticities are larger for capital and smaller for labor, respectively, relative to their factor shares.

Differences between the 1930–1935 and the 1960–1965 periods, in the way that production elasticities diverge from the factor shares, seem to reflect the differences in the pattern of technological progress in agriculture in Japan between the prewar and the postwar periods. As previously explained, technical innovations in the prewar period were motivated primarily at overcoming the constraints of land endowment on agricultural production, by developing such technologies as fertilizer-responsive high-yielding varieties, which facilitate the substitution of fertilizer and other current inputs for land. It was hypothesized that those land-saving and fertilizer-using innovations were, to a large extent, induced by the rapid decline in the price of fertilizer relative to the price of land (see chapters 2 and 3).

We can hypothesize that there had emerged disequilibria in the levels of inputs of fertilizer and land due to a lag in the farmers' adjustment to rapidly changing equilibrium levels, corresponding to a rapid decline in the relative prices of fertilizer and land and the rapid progress in land-saving and fertilizer-using technology.[15] This hypothesis is consistent with Griliches' finding—in his cross-regional analysis of the agricultural production function—that a disequilibrium in the form of a gap between a production elasticity and a factor share existed in the United States during a period that was also characterized by a rapid decline in the price of fertilizer.[16]

In the postwar period the situation began to change drastically with the dramatic spurt in industrial development since the mid-1950's. The labor force in agriculture began to decline and the wage rates to rise rapidly, especially after 1960. Also, industry in Japan had increased its capacity to supply sophisticated farm machinery and implements to the agricultural sector. In response to rapid rises in the wage rates relative to machinery prices, the substitution of power and machinery for labor became a major concern of farm producers. The primary motivation for innovations in agriculture began to shift from saving land to saving labor.

In such a situation it is reasonable to expect that disequilibria, reflected in a gap between production elasticities and factor shares, have emerged with respect to labor and machinery capital due to a lag in farmers' adjustment to changes in technology and relative prices. It is entirely consistent to have disequilibria in the levels of inputs closely related with rapid technological changes—land and fertilizer in the prewar period, and labor and machinery capital in the postwar period.

Comparison with previous estimates

The results of our estimation may be checked with the earlier studies of the agricultural production function.

A classical study by Kazushi Ohkawa, based on production-cost survey data for 1937–1939 in the eastern part of Japan, resulted in estimates of the elasticities of rice production as 0.2 to 0.3 for labor; 0.4 to 0.5 for land; and 0.3 for current inputs (which Ohkawa called " working capital ").[17] Ohkawa found those estimates consistent with the factor shares in rice production. Keizo Tsuchiya estimated the same model as Ohkawa, using production-cost survey data from Shizuoka prefecture, for 1951, when the prewar pattern of land scarcity and labor abundance still prevailed.[18] His estimates of rice-production elasticities are not significantly different from Ohkawa's. Their estimates of rice-production elasticities are smaller for labor and larger for land than our estimates of aggregate production elasticities.

We do not consider these estimates by Ohkawa and Tsuchiya inconsistent with ours. Their estimates are of rice production, while ours are of aggregate agricultural production, including livestock and sericulture, which are less dependent on land.[19] Also, their estimates are for relatively homogeneous regions. As explained previously, interregional variations in the level of agricultural technology, especially between western and eastern

Japan, were significant. The estimates by both Ohkawa and Tsuchiya for relatively more homogeneous regions, based on farm survey data, can be considered estimates of the micro-production function of the neoclassical tradition. In contrast, our estimates for the whole nation, including technically heterogeneous regions and based on prefectural aggregates, should be the estimate of the envelope of the micro-production functions—an innovation possibility curve or the meta-production function in the Hayami-Ruttan sense.[20] It seems reasonable to infer that disequilibria in the factor inputs, as reflected in the gap between production elasticities and factor shares, are more likely to appear along the surface of a meta-production function involving technical changes.

Masahiko Shintani has attempted to estimate an aggregate agricultural production function in value-added terms, based on the farm household economy survey data for 1925–1936.[21] His estimates of production elasticities are 0.3 to 0.5 for labor and 0.1 to 0.2 for capital, which are consistent with ours, but 0.3 to 0.5 for land, which is much larger than our estimate. It appears that the large value of the elasticity estimate for land was a result of specifying the production function in value-added terms, subtracting current inputs from gross output. This specification is based on the assumption that current inputs, such as fertilizer, are paid in the market equal to their marginal value products. It appears possible that, when this equilibrium assumption does not hold, a specification bias emerges in the coefficient of land, which is a close substitute for current inputs.

There have been a number of attempts to estimate aggregate agricultural production functions for the postwar period. A study by Yasuhiko Torii in gross output terms, based on farm-economy survey data for 1957-1960, is characterized by unstable and somewhat implausible results, probably due to excess disaggregation of inputs.[22] However, his estimate of the production elasticity of labor in the range of 0.2 to 0.3 is consistent with our estimate.

Yasuhiko Yuize's estimates of aggregate production elasticities in value-added terms, based on farm-household economy survey data for 1960 and 1962, are in the ranges of 0.4 to 0.6 for labor, 0.2 to 0.4 for land, and 0.2 to 0.5 for capital.[23] His estimates are, on the whole, consistent with ours, considering that the ratio of value added to gross output in agriculture is about 0.7 in this period.

Ryoshin Minami has estimated the aggregate production function in value-added terms by pooling the time-series and the cross-regional data from the 1953–1965 farm-household economy surveys, resulting in estimates of production elasticities ranging from 0.4 to 1.0 for labor, 0.2 to 0.3 for capital, and 0.5 to −0.1 for land, for different farm-size classes.[24] Judging from estimates for typical farm-size classes (1.0–1.5 and 1.5–2.0 hectares), his estimates of the labor elasticity (0.8 and 1.0) appear too high. More implausible is his zero estimate of the land elasticity for the same classes, considering the fact that a "black market" rent of 50 percent of produce has often been reported.[25]

Finally, we will examine the production elasticities of rural education and of agricultural research and extension for which no previous estimates are available for Japanese agriculture. Both the U.S. cross-regional estimates of the aggregate agricultural production function by Griliches and the cross-country study by Hayami and Ruttan have found that the production elasticity of education is equivalent to that of labor, implying that a given percentage increase in education that improves the quality of labor has the same output effect as an equal percentage increase in labor itself.[26] The present estimates for postwar Japan do not reject this hypothesis, although they represent very weak evidence because of relatively large standard deviations in the coefficients of education. However, estimates of the production elasticity of education for the prewar period are clearly smaller than those of labor.

A significant increase in the production elasticity of education from the 1930–1935 to the 1960–1965 periods appears reasonable. Since the late 1950's, agricultural producers in Japan have been experiencing dramatic technical and economic changes. As wage rates have risen, they have shifted from a traditional land-saving technology to a new labor-saving technology. At the same time the producers have adjusted their product mix in favor of commodities characterized by high income elasticities, such as livestock products, vegetables, and fruits, in response to rapid rises in per-capita income. In this situation there is a higher premium on capacity for efficient resource reallocation in response to changes in prices and technology. As a result it seems reasonable that the effects of education on agricultural output should have risen significantly.[27]

In contrast, the interwar period was characterized by relative

stagnation in agricultural technology. Moreover, technical progress, if any, was of a traditional land-saving nature to which
farmers had been accustomed for several generations. Under these
conditions, we will find significantly lower estimates of the
production elasticity for education for 1930–1935 than for 1960–
1965. Also, the 1930–1935 elasticities for Japan are lower than the
elasticities estimated by Griliches for the United States in the
1940's and the 1950's because of the dramatic changes in agricultural technology in the United States during this period.

It is interesting to observe that our estimates of the production
elasticity of research and extension for 1930–1935 are similar to the
Hayami-Ruttan estimates based on the cross-country data and
those for 1960–1965 similar to the Griliches estimates based on the
U.S. cross-regional data. A signicant reduction in the elasticity of
research and extension from the 1930–1935 to the 1960–1965
periods seems to be explained by a lag in the output effect of
agricultural-research investment. The real growth in public expenditure for agricultural research in Japan has been accelerated
in the postwar period, an annual rate of more than 10 percent as
compared with the prewar (1900–1935) rate of 5 percent. Investment in research is, by nature, characterized by a substantial
lag in the realization of its output effect, as it generally involves
a long gestation period. It appears possible that the return on
research investment may be characterized by short-run decreasing returns during a period of rapid accumulation of research
capital even if research activities are characterized by increasing
returns in the long run. In terms of this hypothesis the decline
in the coefficient of research and extension from the prewar
to the postwar period may not be unreasonable. It might be
that the Griliches estimates for the United States reflect a similar
situation.

4-2 Accounting for Growth

On the basis of the estimates of the aggregate agricultural
production function in the previous section we will attempt to
account for growth in agricultural output in Japan. Since our

production function is assumed to be linear homogeneous, the rate of growth in output can be expressed as the sum of growth rates in inputs weighted by the relevant production elasticities.

A set of production elasticities based primarily on Regression (7) for the prewar period and on Regression (13) for the postwar period is adopted, as shown in Table 4–3. The choice of the elasticity for education for the postwar period was made on the basis of the previous discussion of the equivalence of labor and education.

Growth rates of output and inputs

The growth rates of total output and of factor inputs estimated in Tables 2–1 and 2–9 are adopted here for growth accounting. The number of workers in male equivalents and the area of cultivated land in paddy-field equivalents are used as labor and land variables instead of the number of workdays and the crop area. This is partly because of the statistical weakness in labor flow data but, more fundamentally, because of the consistency with the definitions of the labor and land variables used for the cross-prefectural production function. Research, extension, and land-infrastructure improvement were identified in chapter 3 as the major factors underlying the diffusion of double cropping and summer-fall cocoon culture, which contributed to the increase in the rate of utilization of labor and land. Therefore, we will make a double accounting of the effects of increases in the utilization rates of labor and land, if we use the labor and land inputs measured in flow terms in addition to including agricultural research, extension, and land-infrastructure improvement in the growth accounting.

The growth rates of education measured in terms of the average number of school years per male farm worker and of research and extension in terms of the public expenditures (by both the national and the prefectural governments) at 1955 prices are calculated from data in the Appendix.[28]

The contribution of improvements in land infrastructure, such as irrigation and drainage, is incorporated into the growth accounting by treating them as a factor that improves the quality of

Table 4-3.   Weights for Aggregation of Inputs

	Labor	Capital	Ferti-lizer	Land	Educa-tion	Research and Extension
Production elasticities :[a]	(α_L)	(α_K)	(α_F)	(α_A)	(α_E)	(α_R)
1880–1900	0.40	0.15	0.08	0.37	0.15	0.03
1900–1920	0.40	0.15	0.14	0.31	0.15	0.08
1920–1935	0.40	0.15	0.20	0.25	0.15	0.12
1955–1965	0.30	0.25	0.20	0.25	0.30	0.05
Factor shares :[b]	(δ_L)	(δ_K)	(δ_F)	(δ_A)		
1880–1900	0.51	0.10	0.08	0.31		
1900–1920	0.50	0.10	0.10	0.30		
1920–1935	0.51	0.11	0.12	0.26		
1955–1965	0.51	0.12	0.15	0.22		

[a] Based on estimates of production function in Tables 4-1 and 4-2:

$$\alpha_F = \frac{1}{2}\times 0.035\sqrt{\frac{F}{A}}, \qquad \alpha_R = \frac{1}{2}\times 0.06\sqrt{R},$$
$$\alpha_A = 1-(\alpha_L+\alpha_K+\alpha_F).$$

[b] Based on the estimates in Table 2-11.

land, thereby augmenting land measured in physical units. It is assumed that quality change in land can be adjusted by multiplying the land variable by the land-quality index. This index is calculated from the data on the area covered by the land-improvement projects, assuming that the area improved by those projects became 10 percent more productive. The growth rate of the land-quality index is weighted by the production elasticity of land in order to measure the contribution of land-infrastructure improvement to the growth rate of agricultural output.

The abnormal periods of war devastation and recovery (periods IV and V in the time demarcation of chapter 2) are excluded from the present analysis. The growth rates for the whole period are calculated as weighted averages of the rates for the periods 1880–1935 and 1955–1965.

Major findings

Results of the growth accounting are summarized in Table 4–4, which may be compared with the conventional accounting of total input and total productivity in Table 4–5. Each row compares for

Table 4-4. Accounting for Growth in Agricultural Output, Based on Estimates of Production Elasticities, in Terms of Annual Compound Rates of Growth (%)

| | Output ($\dot{Y}/Y$) | Conventional Inputs | | | | | Contribution to Output Growth Rates of | | | |
		Labor (Male equivalents) $\alpha_L(\dot{L}/L)$	Land (Paddy-field equivalents) $\alpha_A(\dot{A}/A)$	Capital $\alpha_K(\dot{K}/K)$	Current Inputs $\alpha_F(\dot{F}/F)$	Total	Education $\alpha_E(\dot{E}/E)$	Res. and Ext. $\alpha_R(\dot{R}/R)$	Land Improvement $\alpha_A(\dot{I}/I)$	Residual
Prewar period: 1880–1935	1.6 (100)	−0.08 (−5)	0.13 (8)	0.16 (10)	0.48 (30)	0.69 (43)	0.44 (28)	0.44 (28)	0.05 (3)	−0.02 (−1)
Phase 1: 1880–1920	1.8 (100)	−0.10 (−6)	0.17 (9)	0.17 (9)	0.42 (23)	0.66 (37)	0.45 (25)	0.38 (21)	0.04 (2)	0.27 (15)
I. 1880–1900	1.6 (100)	0.04 (3)	0.14 (9)	0.14 (9)	0.18 (11)	0.50 (31)	0.45 (28)	0.25 (16)	0.03 (2)	0.37 (23)
II. 1900–1920	2.0 (100)	−0.24 (−12)	0.19 (10)	0.20 (10)	0.66 (33)	0.81 (41)	0.44 (22)	0.51 (25)	0.05 (3)	0.19 (10)
Phase 2: 1920–1935	0.9 (100)	−0.04 (−4)	0.05 (6)	0.14 (16)	0.64 (71)	0.79 (88)	0.42 (47)	0.60 (67)	0.09 (10)	−1.00 (−111)
Postwar period: 1955–1965	3.6 (100)	−0.93 (−26)	0.05 (1)	1.95 (54)	1.70 (47)	2.77 (77)	0.12 (3)	0.68 (19)	0.13 (4)	−0.10 (−3)
Whole period: 1880–1935 and 1955–1965	1.9 (100)	−0.21 (−11)	0.12 (6)	0.43 (23)	0.67 (35)	1.01 (53)	0.39 (21)	0.47 (25)	0.06 (3)	−0.03 (−2)

NOTE: Inside parentheses are percentages with growth rate of output set equal to 100. Production elasticities (α's) are from Table 4-3. Growth rates of conventional inputs are from Table 2-9. Growth rates of land improvement, education, and research and extension are calculated from the data in Appendix Table A-10 (7) and Table A-11 (3) and (6).

Table 4-5. Accounting for Growth in Agricultural Output, Based on Factor Share Weights, in Terms of Annual Compound Rates of Growth (%)

| | | Output ($\dot{Y}/Y$) | Contribution to Output Growth Rates of | | | | | Residual = Total Productivity ($\dot{Y}/Y$)−($\dot{X}/X$) |
| | | | Conventional Inputs | | | | | |
			Labor (Male equivalent) $\delta_L(\dot{L}/L)$	Land (Paddy-field equivalent) $\delta_A(\dot{A}/A)$	Capital $\delta_K(\dot{K}/K)$	Current Inputs $\delta_F(\dot{F}/F)$	Total Input ($\dot{X}/X$)	
Prewar period:	1880–1935	1.6 (100)	−0.10 (−6)	0.12 (8)	0.11 (7)	0.33 (21)	0.46 (29)	1.14 (71)
Phase 1:	1880–1920	1.8 (100)	−0.13 (−7)	0.15 (8)	0.11 (6)	0.31 (17)	0.44 (24)	1.36 (76)
I.	1880–1900	1.6 (100)	0.05 (3)	0.12 (8)	0.09 (6)	0.14 (9)	0.40 (25)	1.20 (75)
II.	1900–1920	2.0 (100)	−0.30 (−15)	0.18 (9)	0.13 (7)	0.47 (24)	0.48 (24)	1.52 (76)
Phase 2:	1920–1935	0.9 (100)	−0.05 (−6)	0.05 (6)	0.10 (11)	0.38 (42)	0.48 (53)	0.42 (47)
Postwar period:	1955–1965	3.6 (100)	−1.58 (−44)	0.04 (1)	0.94 (26)	1.28 (36)	0.68 (19)	2.92 (81)
Whole period:	1880–1935 and 1955–1965	1.9 (100)	−0.33 (−17)	0.11 (6)	0.24 (13)	0.47 (25)	0.49 (26)	1.41 (74)

NOTE: Inside parentheses are percentages with growth rate of output set equal to 100.
Factor shares (δ's) are from Table 4-3.
Growth rates of conventional inputs are from Table 2-9.

each period the growth rate in total output in agriculture with the rates of growth in inputs weighted by the production elasticities and factor shares specified in Table 4–3. Inside parentheses appears the index with the output growth rate set equal to 100.

In a long-term analysis Table 4–4 is successful in reducing the residual in the growth in agricultural output unexplained by the growth in inputs. For the whole period of analysis from 1880 to 1965—excluding the period of war devastation and recovery—as well as for the entire prewar period 1880–1935, the rate of output growth is almost completely explained by changes in the four conventional inputs, in education, and in research and extension. As summarized in Table 4–6, the three major sources for the whole period are: (a) changes in weights for input aggregation from factor shares to production elasticities; (b) the contribution of rural education; and (c) the contribution of agricultural research and extension, which are of roughly equal importance in accounting for the growth in the total productivity index. For the prewar period the contribution of education is slightly larger, and the effect of changes in weights smaller. The contribution of land improvement accounts for only 4 percent of the total productivity growth.

Although we are reasonably successful in accounting for long-term growth, our approach proves inadequate in explaining the variations in the rate of growth in agricultural output and productivity among different phases or " technical epochs." Significant residuals, either positive or negative, remain for the subperiods. Period 1 (1880–1920), which was characterized by rapid growth in output and the total productivity index, has a positive residual; and period 2 (1920–1935), which was characterized by a relative stagnation in agricultural growth, has a large negative residual. Again, the postwar period of rapid growth is marked by a positive residual.

Another problem with the present approach is related to the contribution of land-infrastructure improvement. In Table 4–6 it is estimated that the improvement in land infrastructure accounted for only a minor fraction of total productivity growth. However, we should not be beguiled by this result to derive the conclusion that the land-infrastructure improvement played a minor role in agricultural development in Japan. The slow speed with which the

Table 4-6.   Sources of Long-Term Growth Rates in Total Productivity
in Agriculture

	Annual Compound Rates of Growth (%)	
	Prewar Period (1880–1935)	Whole Period (1880–1935 and 1955–1965)
Total productivity[a]	1.14 (100)	1.41 (100)
Sources explained :		
Change in input weights[b]	0.23 (20)	0.52 (37)
Contribution of education[c]	0.44 (39)	0.39 (28)
Contribution of res. and ext.[c]	0.44 (39)	0.47 (33)
Contribution of land improvement[c]	0.05 (4)	0.06 (4)
Unexplained residual	−0.02 (−2)	−0.03 (2)

Inside parentheses are percentages with the growth rate of total productivity set equal to 100.
   [a] From Table 4-5.
   [b] Column (Total) in Table 4-4 minus Column (Total input) in Table 4-5.
   [c] From Table 4-4.

land-quality index grew during the period of analysis resulted partly from the relatively high initial stock of irrigation capital inherited from the feudal period. A more critical reason for the low rate of measured improvement in land quality is to assume a modest 10 percent increase in land productivity due to the land-improvement projects. This figure was based on comparisons of yields per hectare between improved and unimproved areas planted with the same varieties at the same level of fertilizer application.

As discussed previously, the irrigation and drainage systems that improved water control represented a necessary condition for introducing fertilizer-using and land-saving technology. Without the adequate land infrastructure, the capacity of the high-yielding seed varieties would not have been realized, and the increased application of fertilizers would not have been duly rewarded. Such basic complementarity between the land infrastructure and the biological and chemical technology in agriculture is not considered in the construction of our land-quality index. The key role of land infrastructure as a basic factor in facilitating the development of fertilizer-using and land-saving technology is not properly evaluated in this growth-accounting analysis.

4-3 Major Unsolved Problems

In this chapter, by estimating the aggregate agricultural production function using cross-prefectural data, factors have been identified that could influence the level of agricultural output. With the estimates of production elasticities, the major portion of growth in agricultural output and productivity for 1880–1965 has been explained by four conventional factors—land, labor, capital, and fertilizer—and the three categories of nonconventional inputs—rural education, agricultural research and extension, and land infrastructure.

Overall, about half of the long-term rate of growth in agricultural output has been accounted for by changes in the four conventional inputs; one-quarter by an increase in the level of education; and another one-quarter by an increase in public expenditures for agricultural research and extension. A large gap between the growth in output and the growth in conventional inputs, as measured by the total productivity index, has been closed and accounted for in roughly equal magnitudes by (a) adoption of the estimates of production elasticities for input aggregation; (b) the contribution of education; and (c) the contribution of research and extension. The divergence between the production elasticities and the factor shares has been interpreted as arising from a lag in the adjustment of farmers to a factor-saving bias in technical progress corresponding to changes in relative factor prices.

Our approach has proved insufficient for explaining the emergence of distinct phases or technological epochs in the modern agricultural development of Japan. Significant residuals in the growth accounting remain for subperiods. The sequences in which positive and negative residuals appear for different phases remain one of the major unsolved problems, and will be the subject of analysis in the next chapter.

It must be emphasized that our approach is a very rough first approximation and that we should be cautious in deriving any theory and policy implications from the results of this study. In addition to problems involved in data and estimation procedures, the present approach has an intrinsic weakness in that interactions among factors cannot be properly analyzed, because the factors in the production function are specified as independent and separable.

In reality, the pay-off to investment in education is not independent of the speed of technical progress, and the productivity of high-yielding seed varieties is dependent on levels of fertilizer application. Above all, the present approach is not adequate for analyzing properly the key role of land-infrastructure investments in agricultural development in Japan as the basis for the development and the diffusion of seed-fertilizer technology. The complementarity between improvement in land infrastructure and development of land-saving and fertilizer-using technology will be focused on in the analysis of chapter 7.

Notes to Chapter 4

[1] This chapter draws heavily on Masakatsu Akino and Yujiro Hayami, "Sources of Agricultural Growth in Japan, 1880–1965," *Quarterly Journal of Economics* 88 (August 1974): 454–479.

[2] It is T. W. Schultz who has contributed most to the emergence of the new consensus in the field of agricultural development economics that the " nonconventional " inputs, such as investments in the education of farm people and in agricultural research, are critical variables that must be introduced explicitly into the analysis of modern agricultural growth. For a clear and provocative statement of his perspective, see T. W. Schultz, "Reflections on Agricultural Production, Output and Supply," *Journal of Farm Economics* 38 (August 1956): 748–762; and "Output-input Relationships Revisited," *Journal of Farm Economics* 40 (November 1958): 924–932.

[3] For detailed discussions on the sources of measured productivity growth, see D. W. Jorgenson and Zvi Griliches, "The Explanation of Productivity Change," *Review of Economic Studies* 34 (July 1967): 249–283.

[4] Zvi Griliches, "Research Expenditures, Education, and the Aggregate Agricultural Production Function," *American Economic Review* 54 (December 1964): 961–974. A number of empirical studies on growth accounting of agriculture have appeared that employed the methodology of Griliches; see Willis Peterson and Yujiro Hayami, *Technical Change in Agriculture*, paper prepared for the American Agricultural Economics Association Literature Review Committee (St. Paul: University of Minnesota, Department of Agricultural and Applied Economics, 1973). For an alternative approach to the sources of total productivity growth in agriculture, see A. M. Tang, "Research and Education in Japanese Agricultural Development, 1880–1938," *Economic Studies Quarterly* 13 (February–May 1963): 27–41 and 91–99.

[5] R. R. Nelson, "Aggregate Production Functions and Medium Range Growth Projections," *American Economic Review* 54 (September 1964): 575–606.

[6] T. W. Schultz, *Transforming Traditional Agriculture* (New Haven, Conn.: Yale University Press, 1964), pp. 145–153..

[7] R. E. Evenson, "Economic Aspects of the Organization of Agricultural Re-

search," in *Resource Allocation in Agricultural Research*, ed. W. L. Fishel (Minneapolis: University of Minnesota Press, 1971), pp. 103–182.

[8] Ibid.

[9] Yujiro Hayami, "Hiryo Jyuyo Kozo no Henka to Nogyo Hatten no Nikyoku-men" (Structural Changes in Fertilizer Demand and the Two Phases of Japanese Agricultural Development), *Economic Studies Quarterly* 17 (March 1967): 27–35.

[10] See the surveys by Keizo Tsuchiya, "Nihon Nogyo no Keiryoteki Bunseki: Tenbo" (Econometric Analysis of Japanese Agriculture: Survey), *Economic Studies Quarterly* 17 (March 1967): 50–64; and *Nogyo Keizai no Keiryo Bunseki* (Econometric Analysis of Agricultural Economy), (Tokyo: Keiso Shobo, 1962), pp. 14–25.

[11] Yasuhiko Yuize, "Nogyo ni okeru Kyoshiteki Seisankansu no Keisoku" (The Aggregate Production Function in Agriculture), *Nogyo Sogo Kenkyu* 18 (October 1964): 1–54, estimates increasing returns; whereas, Yasuhiko Torii, "Nogyo Bumon no Genkaiseisanryoku Sokutei" (Measurement of Agricultural Marginal Productivity), *Economic Studies Quarterly* 16 (June 1966): 52–66, indicates constant returns prevailing.

[12] More detailed explanations of data are available in Masakatsu Akino, "Nogyo Seisan Kansu no Keisoku" (Estimation of Agricultural Production Function), *Nogyo Sogo Kenkyu* 26 (April 1972): 163–200.

[13] It is estimated by the following formula:

$$E_i = \bar{E} + 8(k_i - \bar{k})$$

where E_i denotes the average number of school years per worker in Prefecture i; $\bar{E}$ the national average of school years per worker; k_i and $\bar{k}$ are, respectively, the ratio in Prefecture i and the national average ratio of the farm workers who had had the secondary and third levels of agricultural education.

[14] The null hypotheses of the equality of the production parameters between 1930 and 1935, and between 1960 and 1965, are accepted according to the results of analysis of variance: the F-statistics are calculated as 0.80 between Regressions (1) and (3); as 1.09 between Regressions (2) and (4); as 0.98 between Regressions (8) and (10); and as 1.10 between Regressions (9) and (11).

[15] According to an estimate by Akino based on experimental data, the level of nitrogen input in an average farm in Japan in the 1930's was 50 to 100 percent lower than the optimum level. See Akino, "Nogyo Seisan Kansu no Keisoku."

[16] Griliches, "Research Expenditure, Education, and the Aggregate Agricultural Production Function."

[17] Kazushi Ohkawa, *Shokuryo Keizai no Riron to Keisoku* (Theory and Measurement of Food Economy), (Tokyo: Nihonhyoronsha, 1945), pp. 145–163.

[18] Tsuchiya, "Nihon Nogyo no Keiryoteki Bunseki: Tenbo," pp. 29–40.

[19] Ohkawa's estimates for 1940–1941 suggest lower production elasticities of land even for such winter crops as wheat, barley, and naked barley. Ohkawa, *Shokuryo Keizai no Riron to Keisoku*, pp. 164–197.

[20] For the concept of the meta-production function, see Yujiro Hayami and V. W. Ruttan, *Agricultural Development: An International Perspective* (Baltimore and London: Johns Hopkins University Press, 1971), pp. 82–85 and 122–128.

[21] Masahiko Shintani, *Senzen Nihon Nogyo no Gijutsu Shimpo to Fukyu ni Kansuru Bunseki* (Technological Innovation and Its Diffusion in Prewar Japanese Agriculture), paper resented at the Annual Meeting of the Japanese Association of Theoretical Economics in 1971, Tokyo.

[22] Torii, "Nogyo Bumon no Genkaiseisanryoku Sokutei."

[23] Yuize, "Nogyo ni okeru Kyoshiteki Seisankansu no Keisoku."

[24] Ryoshin Minami, *The Turning Point in Economic Development: Japan's Experience* (Tokyo: Kinokuniya, 1973), pp. 179–204.

25) Official rents under the regulations of the land reform laws cannot be considered to reflect the marginal productivity of land in agriculture.

26) Griliches, "Research Expenditure, Education and the Aggregate Production Function"; and Hayami and Ruttan, *Agricultural Development*, pp. 86–107.

27) For discussions on the dependency of returns to schooling on technical progress, see Finis Welch, "Education in Production," *Journal of Political Economy* 78 (January–February 1970): 35–57.

28) The growth rate of research and extension for 1955–1965 is substituted by the growth rate for 1955–1960 because of the lack of data for 1965.

Chapter 5 Technology Diffusion and
Growth Phases[1]

The growth-accounting analysis used in the preceding chapter
was successful in reducing the residual in long-term growth in
aggregate agricultural output that was unexplained by changes
in inputs of both conventional and nonconventional factors.
However, it failed to identify the causes for the formation of distinct growth phases in Japanese agriculture. Significant positive
residuals remain for the initial growth phase (1880–1920) and
for the postwar growth phase (1955–1965), while the interwar
stagnation phase (1920–1935) was characterized by a large negative residual.

In this chapter we will attempt to explore the sources of such
positive and negative residuals in different phases. First, the
hypothesis will be postulated that the sequences in the phases of
relatively rapid growth and stagnation resulted from the time lag
between the accumulation and the diffusion of technological
potential in agriculture. Then, the hypothesis will be tested on
the time-series data of average rice yields per hectare in forty-six
perfectures.

5-1 Accumulation and Diffusion of
Technological Potential: A Hypothesis

Here we will try to postulate a hypothesis with which we may
adequately explain the sequences of positive and negative re-

siduals in the growth accounting of Japanese agriculture. These sequences are primarily responsible for the distinct shifts from the initial phase of relatively rapid growth in agricultural output and productivity until about 1920, to the stagnation phase during the interwar period, and, then, to the new phase of rapid growth after World War II.

It appears that proper specification of the dynamic process of technical change is the key to understanding such sequences in major growth phases in agriculture. Technical progress, defined as the upward shifting of the aggregate production function, can be viewed according to the Schumpeterian tradition as the combined effect of two processes: invention and diffusion.[2] We define s_t as the actual shift and u_t as the potential shift in the aggregate production function. The latter is the shift that should be realized by year t if all producers have accepted and efficiently practiced all the best techniques currently available. The best techniques will continue to diffuse among producers and, with a lapse of time, s_t will approach u_t if no new techniques are invented along the way. Most simply, we may specify the process as

$$s_{t+1}-s_t = \lambda_t(u_t-s_t), \quad 0 \leqq \lambda_t \leqq 1 \qquad (1)$$

where λ_t is the parameter that determines the rate of diffusion. The above equation implies that the actual shift in the aggregate production function is a certain proportion of the discrepancy between the potential and actual shifts in the previous period. If u and λ are constant, s will approach u. In the actual world, however, those values are functions of nonconventional inputs, such as education and research, and will vary as technical, social, and institutional conditions vary.

As discussed in chapter 3, during the three hundred years of the feudal Tokugawa period preceding the Meiji Restoration, agricultural techniques advanced slowly in raising u. By the end of the Tokugawa period several advanced techniques were already practiced in various districts in the nation. But restraints of the feudal system had suppressed the diffusion of new techniques, so that the actual shift in the aggregate production function should have been much slower than the potential shift.

To reiterate the discussion in chapter 3, under the feudal system peasants were bound to their land and were, in principle, not allowed to leave their villages except for pilgrimages to the Ise Grand Shrine or the Zenkoji Temple.[3] Nor were they free to choose what crops to plant or what varieties of seeds to sow. Barriers that divided the nation into feudal territories interrupted nation-wide communications. Though feudal lords were anxious to raise agricultural productivity within their own territories, in many cases they prohibited the export of improved techniques from their territorial boundaries. Even within the territory of a lord, diffusion was not quite free. It is recorded that a village called Maesawa in Toyama prefecture placed a guard at its border to prevent exportation of a variety of rice seeds selected in the village.[4] Although those restraints on innovation were gradually undermined as the market economy developed, they persisted as a principal feature of the feudal society until the Meiji Restoration.

It is not difficult to imagine how such institutional restraints suppressed λ. The rate of increase in u had been slow under the feudal regime, but λ had been so low that the discrepancy between u and s had widened cumulatively. Abolition of such feudal restraints at the time of the Meiji Restoration and the subsequent modernization measures, including the introduction of railway and postal services, brought a jump in λ. With the wide gap opened between u and s, the jump in λ resulted in a rapid increase in s.

It is the potential accumulated in the form of $(u-s)$ that has been neglected in the analysis in the preceding chapter. Certainly, nonconventional factors included in the growth-accounting analysis should have contributed to technological progress. Extension activities by the government and the agricultural associations as well as the spread of compulsory education should have vast effects on λ. Introduction of Western techniques and the establishment of agricultural experiment stations also helped to raise u. But all those current activities cannot fully explain the increase in s during the phase of initial growth.

The discussions in chapter 3 have identified the $r\bar{o}n\bar{o}$ techniques (veteran farmers' techniques) as a basis for development in agricultural technology in the Meiji period. When the imported techniques failed to take root in Japanese soil and research in the agricultural experiment stations was in its infancy, it was the technological potential embodied in the practices of the veteran farmers that provided the basis for technological progress. The process by which the *rōnō* techniques were replaced with the techniques developed in the experiment stations toward the end of the initial growth phase should have paralleled the process of exhaustion of indigenous technological potential inherited from the Tokugawa period. Without considering this process, the rapid initial growth contrasted with the succeeding stagnation cannot be really understood.

Another question now arises. What explains the postwar spurt? It may be explained partly by the increase in research and extension expenditures of the government, pressed by the acute food shortage immediately after the war. Also, the increased aspiration of farmers due to the land reform must not be ignored. But, a more basic cause may be identified as the new potential in agricultural technology accumulated under the Assigned Experiment System (see chapter 3), which was deferred from diffusion due to the shortage of such complementary inputs as fertilizers during the war.

Another major factor may be the backlog of scientific knowledge and technology accumulated during the war as the result of gigantic research investments, domestic and foreign, for military purposes. As is well documented by Nelson,[5] a wide spectrum of scientific activity exists, ranging from applied science at the one end to basic science at the other. It is often the latter that produces a major breakthrough for practical problems, as is the case with the development of hybrid corn in the United States. While most of the research done during the war was not for agricultural purposes, it formed a backlog for advancements in agricultural techniques. A notable example is the practice of protecting nursery beds by using vinyl cover, which has contributed greatly to the stabilization of rice yields in northern Japan. This innovation was greatly facilitated by advancements in synthetic chemistry.

Our basic hypothesis explains the major phases of technological progress in Japanese agriculture in terms of the accumulation and diffusion of technological potential.

5-2   Interregional Diffusion of Rice Technology

We will now try to test the hypothesis postulated in the previous section. Materials for the analysis are the average rice yields per unit of planted area for forty-six prefectures for the period 1885–1965.[6] The rice yield is used as a proxy for technical progress or the shift in aggregate production in agriculture.

Since land has been the major limiting factor of agricultural production in Japan, especially during the prewar period, efforts in technological development have been directed toward saving land or increasing output per unit of land area. Rice is by far the most important single crop, comprising 40–60 percent of the total agricultural production in value terms. Farmers, as well as the government, have placed their major efforts on raising rice yields. Increases in rice yield per hectare have been almost synonymous with technological progress in Japanese agriculture. In-

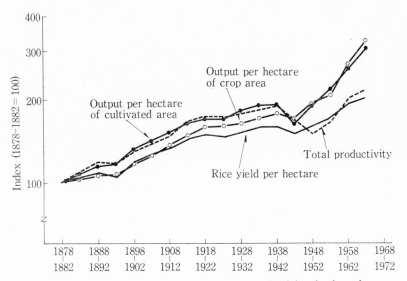

Figure 5–1.   Comparison of indices of total productivity, land productivity, and rice yield per hectare of planted area, five-year averages, semi-log scale.

SOURCE: Table 5–1; and Appendix Tables A-5 and A-9.

deed, the movements in the rice-yield index are closely associated with movements in total productivity as well as land productivities (Figure 5–1). They have in common the same major growth phases: (*a*) initial growth ending around 1920; (*b*) interwar stagnation; and (*c*) rapid growth after World War II. The adoption of the average rice yield per unit of planted area as the proxy for technical progress in agriculture in this study can be justified both in terms of the dominant weight of rice in the total agricultural output and in terms of the close association of its movements with those of other productivity measures.

Statistical findings

Figure 5–2 (data in Table 5–1) includes the series of averages (*Y*), advanced levels (*U*), and coefficients of variations (*V*) of the average rice yields per unit of planted area for (*a*) all prefectures, (*b*) eighteen eastern prefectures (excluding Hokkaido), and (*c*) twenty-seven western prefectures.[7] We will use for *U* the average of the average rice yields of the upper five prefectures in the case of all prefectures and of the upper three prefectures in the case of eastern and western prefectures.[8] The coefficient of variation (*V*) is the unweighted standard deviation divided by the simple mean.

Statistically, *U*, *Y*, and *V* are parameters of distribution. Assuming a form of the distribution, *Y* will be determined by *U* and *V*.[9] It will increase as *U* increases, for a given *V*, or, as *V* decreases, for a given *U*. Economic interpretations may well be possible. *Y* corresponds to *s*, *U* to *u*, and *V* to (*u*−*s*) in Equation (1). The national or regional average level of technology will advance as the backward districts catch up with the advanced. The former process implies an increase in *u* and the latter a decrease in (*u*−*s*). Naturally, a discrepancy always exists between *U* and *u*, as it is inconceivable that all farmers in the advanced prefectures are operating at the very frontiers of current technology. As the potential technology *u* would diffuse within advanced prefectures, *U* would rise in closing the gap between *U* and *u*.[10] Concurrently, the advanced technology realized in the advanced prefectures would diffuse among less-advanced prefectures in raising *Y*

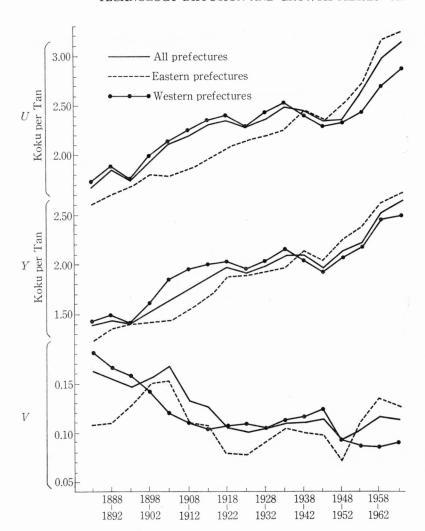

Figure 5–2. Changes in advanced levels (*U*), average (*Y*), and coefficients of variations (*V*) of rice yields.
SOURCE: Table 5–1.

(which is a proxy of *s*). In that sense, the decrease in *V* represents a fraction of the reduction in $(u-s)$.[11]

The relation of *Y* to *U* and *V* may be approximated in the following equation:

Table 5-1. Averages and Variations of Rice Yields among Prefectures

Years	Averages Y (koku/tan)[a]				Advanced Levels[b] U (koku/tan)			Coefficient of Variation[c] V		
	All Prefectures		Eastern Prefectures Simple	Western Prefectures Simple	All Prefectures	Eastern Prefectures	Western Prefectures	All Prefectures	Eastern Prefectures	Western Prefectures
	Weighted	Simple								
1883–1887	1.39	1.38	1.33	1.42	1.69	1.50	1.72	0.163	0.109	0.180
1888–1892	1.43	1.43	1.36	1.48	1.85	1.58	1.89	0.155	0.111	0.165
1893–1897	1.37	1.39	1.39	1.39	1.75	1.67	1.77	0.147	0.129	0.158
1898–1902	1.52	1.53	1.42	1.59	1.94	1.80	1.99	0.156	0.151	0.143
1903–1907	1.63	1.65	1.44	1.79	2.11	1.77	2.15	0.168	0.155	0.121
1908–1912	1.73	1.76	1.57	1.89	2.20	1.86	2.26	0.143	0.112	0.111
1913–1917	1.84	1.88	1.71	1.99	2.31	2.00	2.37	0.128	0.108	0.105
1918–1922	1.93	1.96	1.87	2.02	2.35	2.11	2.42	0.106	0.081	0.107
1923–1927	1.88	1.91	1.87	1.94	2.27	2.14	2.29	0.101	0.079	0.109
1928–1932	1.91	1.98	1.93	2.02	2.37	2.19	2.44	0.104	0.092	0.106
1933–1937	2.01	2.08	1.98	2.14	2.49	2.27	2.55	0.111	0.104	0.105
1938–1942	2.04	2.09	2.12	2.06	2.45	2.45	2.42	0.111	0.101	0.117
1943–1947	1.95	1.97	2.02	1.93	2.34	2.34	2.29	0.116	0.099	0.124
1948–1952	2.16	2.15	2.26	2.08	2.47	2.52	2.35	0.093	0.069	0.094
1953–1957	2.25	2.24	2.31	2.18	2.65	2.73	2.42	0.103	0.112	0.087
1958–1962	2.60	2.53	2.64	2.46	3.07	3.18	2.77	0.116	0.136	0.086
1963–1967	2.67	2.60	2.73	2.51	3.14	3.23	2.86	0.114	0.129	0.092

[a] In terms of brown rice. 1 koku of brown rice=150 kilogram, and 1 tan=0.099174 hectare.

[b] Advanced levels: All prefectures—Simple average of upper five prefectures. Eastern prefectures—Simple average of upper three prefectures. Western prefectures—Simple average of upper three prefectures.

[c] The unweighted standard deviation divided by the unweighted mean.

SOURCE: Data from Statistical Yearbook of the Ministry of Agriculture and Forestry (formerly the Ministry of Agriculture and Commerce), various issues, with revisions.

$$\left(\frac{\dot{Y}}{Y}\right)_t = \alpha\left(\frac{\dot{U}}{U}\right)_t + \beta\left(\frac{\dot{V}}{V}\right)_t + \gamma + \varepsilon_t \qquad (2)$$

where

$$\left(\frac{\dot{Y}}{Y}\right)_t = \frac{Y_t - Y_{t-1}}{Y_{t-1}}$$

$$\left(\frac{\dot{U}}{U}\right)_t = \frac{U_t - U_{t-1}}{U_{t-1}}$$

$$\left(\frac{\dot{V}}{V}\right)_t = \frac{V_t - V_{t-1}}{V_{t-1}}$$

$$\epsilon_t = \text{error term}$$

and α, β, and γ are parameters. The above equation is estimated by the least squares on the basis of quinquennial data in Table 5–1 with the results shown in Table 5–2. Two cases were estimated for all prefectures. One used the simple average of prefectural averages for Y, and another used a weighted average, with the planted areas taken as weights. Hardly any difference can be observed between those cases. Also, two cases were considered for eastern and western prefectures. One used U values for all prefectures, and another used the U values for eastern and western prefectures, respectively. This procedure is designed to test whether it is the nation's U or the region's U that is relevant as "best practice" technology for farmers in a region. Statistical evidence is not enough, however, to settle this problem.[12]

In all six cases, except for the eastern prefectures using U values for all prefectures, the estimates of α and β have signs consistent with theory and are significant at the 5 percent level. On the other hand, estimates of γ are not significantly different from zero, indicating that there exists no trend in Y that cannot be explained by U and V. The estimates were repeated with the restriction that $\gamma = 0$. The results are very close to the unrestricted estimates.

With the estimates of α and β, we evaluated the contributions of U and V to the growth in Y for subperiods, as shown in Table 5–3.[13] Periods I and II correspond to the phase of initial growth, period III to the phase of succeeding stagnation, period IV to

Table 5-2. Estimation Results of Equation (2)

	Intercept γ	Parameter Estimates[a] α	β	Coefficient of Determination	Standard Error of Estimate	Durbin-Watson Statistics	F-statistics[b]
All							
$Y=$ Weighted average	0.0039	0.8969 (0.1147)	-0.1326 (0.0670)	0.8257	0.0244	1.55	0.27
	0	0.9323 (0.0863)	-0.1437 (0.0613)	0.8932	0.0238	1.47	
$Y=$ Simple average	0.0044	0.8476 (0.0870)	-0.1359 (0.0508)	0.8799	0.0185	1.56	0.49
	0	0.8876 (0.0661)	-0.1483 (0.0470)	0.9283	0.0182	1.48	
Eastern							
$U=$ Advanced level of all	0.0308	0.4768 (0.1871)	-0.1041 (0.0486)	0.4038	0.0407	2.29	6.02
	0	0.7407 (0.1782)	-0.1084 (0.5666)	0.5564	0.0475	1.84	
$U=$ Advanced level of Eastern	0.0048	0.9168 (0.1103)	-0.1156 (0.0235)	0.8583	0.0199	1.76	0.49
	0	0.9699 (0.0739)	-0.1166 (0.0230)	0.9260	0.0195	1.81	
Western							
$U=$ Advanced level of all	0.0052	0.9189 (0.1118)	-0.1507 (0.0740)	0.8975	0.0222	0.98	0.53
	0	0.8791 (0.0968)	-0.1462 (0.0726)	0.9222	0.0218	0.99	
$U=$ Advanced level of Western	0.0032	0.8180 (0.1004)	-0.1880 (0.0725)	0.8960	0.0223	1.22	0.21
	0	0.8353 (0.0915)	-0.1947 (0.0693)	0.9228	0.0217	1.20	

[a] The standard errors of the coefficients are given in parentheses.

[b] F-statistics for testing the null hypothesis that $\gamma=0$. The critical points at 1 percent and 5 percent significance levels are 8.86 and 4.60, respectively.

the recovery from the devastation of the war, and period V to the phase of postwar growth.

Table 5-3. Contributions of Changes in U and V to the Growth in Y

		Period[a]	Growth Rates of Y ($\dot{Y}/Y$)	Contributions[b]		
				$\alpha(\dot{U}/U)$	$\beta(\dot{V}/V)$	Residual
All	$Y=$ Weighted average	I	0.80	1.04	−0.02	−0.22
		II	1.13	0.67	0.43	0.03
		III	0.27	0.36	−0.04	−0.05
		V	1.44	1.17	0.17	0.10
		VI	1.73	1.59	−0.15	0.29
	$Y=$ Simple average	I	0.90	0.99	0.02	−0.07
		II	1.15	0.64	0.45	0.06
		III	0.40	0.35	−0.05	0.10
		V	1.29	1.11	0.17	0.01
		VI	1.50	1.52	−0.15	0.13
Eastern	$U=$ Advanced level of all	I	0.40	0.83	−0.19	−0.24
		II	1.76	0.53	0.46	0.77
		III	0.38	0.29	−0.18	0.27
		V	1.35	0.93	−0.13	0.55
		VI	1.69	1.27	−0.15	0.57
	$U=$ Advanced level of Eastern	I	0.40	0.81	−0.21	−0.20
		II	1.76	1.14	0.49	0.13
		III	0.38	0.48	−0.20	0.10
		V	1.35	1.50	−0.14	−0.01
		VI	1.69	1.64	−0.17	0.22
Western	$U=$ Advanced level of all	I	1.16	0.98	0.29	−0.11
		II	0.81	0.63	0.12	0.06
		III	0.38	0.34	0.02	0.02
		V	1.23	1.10	0.51	−0.38
		VI	1.42	1.50	−0.08	0.00
	$U=$ Advanced level of Western	I	1.16	0.94	0.37	−0.15
		II	0.81	0.66	0.16	−0.01
		III	0.38	0.29	0.03	0.06
		V	1.23	0.46	0.68	0.09
		VI	1.42	1.41	−0.11	0.12

[a] Period I: 1883–1887 to 1903–1907   II: 1903–1907 to 1918–1922
III: 1918–1922 to 1933–1937   V: 1943–1947 to 1953–1957
VI: 1953–1957 to 1963–1967

[b] Estimates of α and β used here are those obtained under the restriction that $\gamma=0$ in Table 5-2.

Interpretations of results

Figure 5–2 and Table 5–3 provide evidence for our hypothesis. First, let us examine the case of all prefectures. Y had grown rapidly until it turned stagnant in the period 1918–1922, the end of period II.[14] The growth path of U seems similar to that of Y, but it differs at a crucial point. While Y rose linearly until the end of period II, U began to decelerate in 1903–1907, the end of period I. The linear rise in Y for period II, in spite of the deceleration in U, can be explained in terms of V, which began to fall in 1903–1907. The decline in V ended in 1918–1922 with the resulting stagnation in Y for the succeeding period. In fact, the contribution of V to the growth in Y increased from I to II, and declined from II to III.

The above observations seem to suggest that, before 1903–1907, the prime factor in the rapid progress of technology was a rise in the potential of technology rather than a spread of the existing potential. This finding is not consistent with our hypothesis postulating that technological progress in the initial growth phase was primarily due to the backlog inherited from the feudal age. This inconsistency can be explained, however, by examining the cases of eastern and western prefectures.

In period I, the Y value of the western prefectures (Y_W) had grown much faster than the Y value of all prefectures, but it began to decelerate in 1903–1907. In contrast, the Y value of eastern prefectures (Y_E) rose more rapidly from 1903–1907. To a large extent, this difference is attributable to the difference in movements of V. While the V value for western prefectures (V_W) had fallen until 1903–1907, when it became stagnant, the V value for eastern prefectures (V_E) had risen until 1903–1907, when it began to fall.

This contrast in the ways Y_E and Y_W had grown seems to reflect what we may call "the eastward movement in rice-farming technology." This refers to the process in which the backward districts caught up with and surpassed the traditionally advanced western districts. The backlog of traditional technology had been concentrated among the veteran farmers in such advanced districts as North Kyushu and Kinki. With the Meiji reforms the

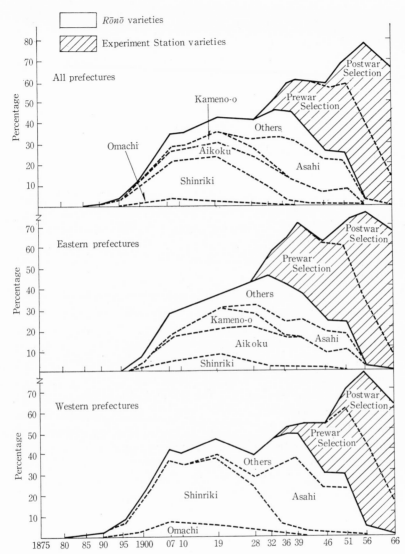

Figure 5-3.   Changes in percentage of area planted in improved varieties
to total area planted in rice, Japan, 1875–1963.

SOURCE: Yujiro Hayami and Saburo Yamada, "Technical Progress in
Agriculture," in Lawrence Klein and Kazushi Ohkawa, eds., *Economic
Growth: The Japanese Experience since the Meiji Period* (Homewood, Ill.:
Richard D. Irwin, 1968), p. 152.

accumulated potential started to diffuse among the surrounding districts, which must have reduced V_W and raised Y_W. The diffusion toward the distant eastern districts lagged, however. At the beginning only pioneering farmers in the relatively advanced districts in the east tried to transplant the advanced techniques. In other words, the diffusion of the advanced technology was not uniform among the eastern prefectures in the earlier periods, resulting in the rise in V_E. It was approximately 1903–1907 when diffusion among eastern prefectures had reached a stage at which V_E began to fall.

More concrete evidence is available. Figure 5–3 shows the changes in the percentage of total rice area planted in the form of major improved varieties. It clearly indicates that the linear growth in Y for 1890–1920 coincides with the rise in the area planted in the improved varieties selected by rōnō, which we may call rōnō varieties.[15]

Regional patterns in the spread of rōnō varieties are also consistent with movements in Y and V. In western prefectures, rōnō varieties had been selected earlier and spread very rapidly until the end of period I, at which time they became stagnant. By contrast, in the eastern prefectures their percentage continued to grow until they were replaced by the varieties selected in the experiment stations.

It must be emphasized that the "eastward movement of rice-farming technology" was not a simple diffusion of seeds or practices but rather the diffusion of concepts and methods of improving seed varieties and cultural practices suited for different local environments. Also, it involved the process of assimilating environmental conditions for rice production in the east to those in the west by improving the irrigation and drainages systems.

In period III, the area planted in improved varieties (rōnō varieties and experiment-station varieties combined) began to show another rapid growth. Nevertheless, Y did not show a similar rise, due, no doubt, to the exhaustion of the initial backlog. In order to raise Y when the backlog is used up, it is necessary to raise U by investing in research and development. The spread of the experiment-station varieties represents the fruits of this kind of investment. But, the return to R and D investments, which had seemed very high when the backlog had existed, must have been found rather meager when it disappeared. The initial backlog included such practices as the selection of seeds in salt water and checkrow planting, besides the use of improved seeds. When the backlog was used up, the improvement in seeds (which was the product of current research expenditures) did not assure as fast a rise in productivity as it did when the backlog existed.

We will now turn to the phase of postwar growth. The remarkable features of the growth in Y from 1950 to 1960 are the growth accompanying a rise in U faster than Y and the increase in V at the same time as there was a rise in Y, indicating that the leading factors are different between the initial growth and the postwar spurt. While the leading factor in the former period is diffusion, in the latter it is growth in technological potential emerging from the application of scientific knowledge accumulated during the war to the development of agricultural technology. This finding is consistent with the hypothesis postulated in the previous section. However, V began to decline in 1960 indicating, perhaps, that Japanese agriculture has recently been moving toward the exhaustion of technological potential.

5-3 Summary and Conclusions

The analysis in this chapter represents an attempt to identify the sources of variations in the rate of growth in agricultural output and productivity among different growth phases or "technological epochs." The analysis was motivated in search for an answer to the question raised in the growth-accounting analysis in the preceding chapter: Why in accounting for agricultural growth do significant positive residuals remain both for the initial growth phase and for the postwar growth phase, while a large negative residual remains for the interwar stagnation phase?

It was hypothesized that these sequences in which positive and negative residuals appear resulted from sequences in the accumulation and diffusion of the potential in agricultural technology. This hypothesis was tested on the data of average rice yield per unit of area planted for forty-six prefectures. The major findings are summarized as follows.

The rapid growth in the initial growth phase was supported

by a backlog of technological potential accumulated during the feudal Tokugawa period. Superior methods and advanced knowledge embodied in practices of veteran farmers (rōnō) in various localities, which had hitherto been dammed by feudal constraints until they were removed by the Meiji reforms, were diffused on a nation-wide scale. Exploitation and diffusion of the backlog of indigenous technology were also facilitated by the government's agricultural-research and extension activities and by the introduction of a modern communication and transportation system, including postal service and railway.

Stagnation during the interwar period resulted from exhaustion of this technological potential as the result of its diffusion before the modern agricultural-research system began to supply new potential in sufficient amounts. The postwar spurt is considered to be a process of realization of technological potential that had accumulated during the war period, resulting from massive research investments, domestic and foreign, for military purposes. Most of the research conducted during the war was not for agricultural purposes, but it formed a backlog for advancements in agricultural techniques.

When technological potential has accumulated, agricultural research tends to have a high pay-off by exploiting the existing potential. When the potential is exhausted, research investment is likely to yield lower returns, at least in the short run, until it produces major breakthroughs. Also, returns from formal education would be higher for a period of faster technical progress, as evidenced from the estimation of the production function in the preceding chapter.

We are not denying the importance of investment in agricultural research, extension, and rural education. Without them, the potential might, to a large extent, have remained as mere potential. But, without the potential, those investments would have turned out to be far less fruitful.

Does all this imply a dark prospect for agricultural development in developing nations that do not seem to possess such potential? On the contrary, the backlog of those nations is the vast amount of knowledge and techniques accumulated in the advanced nations. For the past several decades agricultural technology has been carried on primarily by the developed countries in temperate zones so as to be efficient in these environmental conditions, in addition to being consistent with the relative factor- and product-price relationship specific to those countries. While its direct transfer to the developing countries located in tropical and subtropical zones has been limited by the difference in environmental conditions, the productivity difference between the developed and the developing countries has increased cumulatively.[16]

It should be possible for developing countries to attain rapid growth in agricultural productivity by closing this productivity gap, if the transfer of agricultural technology among the different ecological zones can be successfully implemented.[17] The first requirement for such interregional transfer of agricultural technology must be research and development designed to adapt location-specific technology to different environmental conditions. Simultaneously, efforts should be made to modify the environments by investment in land infrastructure, such as irrigation and drainage. Once the new advanced technology has become available for practical application by farmers, the need for education, which increases their ability to use resource allocations, including the ability of decoding technical information, will be increased.

It seems reasonable to hypothesize that the large agricultural productivity differences among countries represent the backlog of technological potential for the present world in the same way as the interregional productivity differences did for Meiji Japan. The backlog, if properly exploited by research, education, and land-infrastructure improvement, should provide the basis for very rapid growth in agricultural productivity in the developing countries.

Research, education, and land infrastructure are characterized by indivisibility, externality, and jointness in supply and utilization. It can hardly be expected that goods and services having such attributes are supplied at socially optimum levels when left to market mechanism. Public investments are required to correct for such market failures. The need for public institutions to conduct adaptive research and to build and coordinate the use of irrigation systems is especially critical in Asian agriculture where the possibility for small producers to conduct such activities by themselves, individually, are limited. In the next two chapters we will try to analyze the Japanese experience with regard to those public factors critical for agricultural development.

Notes to Chapter 5

[1] This chapter draws heavily on Yujiro Hayami and Saburo Yamada, "Technological Progress in Agriculture," in *Economic Growth: The Japanese Experience since the Meiji Era*, eds. Lawrence Klein and Kazushi Ohkawa (Homewood, Illinois: Richard D. Irwin, 1968), pp. 135–161, although the statistical analysis has been revised using a new set of data.

[2] J. A. Schumpeter, *The Theory of Economic Development* (New York: Oxford University Press Galaxy Book, 1961).

[3] The fact that varieties of rice originating along the pilgrimage routes were planted widely over the nation shows that such pilgrimages worked as an important medium for the diffusion of technology in the premodern period.

[4] Seizo Yasuda, ed., *Meiji Iko ni Okeru Nogyo Gijutsu no Hatten* (Agricultural Development since Meiji), (Tokyo: Nogyo Gijutsu Kyokai, 1952), p. 3.

[5] R. R. Nelson, "The Simple Economics of Basic Scientific Research," *Journal of Political Economy* 67 (June 1959): 297–306.

[6] The data pertain only to the lowland paddy-field rice. The weight of upland rice is negligible in Japan.

[7] *Eastern prefectures* include: Aomori, Iwate, Miyagi, Akita, Yamagata, Fukushima, Ibaragi, Tochigi, Gunma, Chiba, Saitama, Tokyo, Kanagawa, Niigata, Nagano, Yamanashi, Shizuoka, Aichi. *Western prefectures* include: Toyama, Ishikawa, Fukui, Gifu, Mie, Shiga, Kyoto, Osaka, Hyogo, Nara, Wakayama, Tottori, Shimane, Okayama, Hiroshima, Yamaguchi, Tokushima, Kagawa, Ehime, Kochi, Fukuoka, Saga, Nagasaki, Kumamoto, Oita, Miyazaki, Kagoshima. *All prefectures* include Hokkaido in addition to the eastern and western prefectures.

[8] The upper five or upper three prefectures varied in the course of agricultural development.

[9] While V is a parameter of dispersion, U is a parameter of the location of the upper tail of distribution. If we assume that the average yield of the i-th prefecture, y_i, is subject to the distribution function determined by the two parameters, $f(y_i/U, V)$, the national average yield, Y, can be expressed as a function of U and V:

$$Y = \sum_i y_i f(y_i/U, V)$$

$$= F(U, V).$$

[10] The following relation is assumed:

$$U_{t+1} - U_t = \gamma_t(u_t - U_t), \quad 0 \leqq \gamma_t \leqq 1$$

Take, as an example, Osaka prefecture, which belonged to the upper five prefectures continuously for 1883–1947. For the period 1890–1935, the average rice yield per *tan* in Osaka rose by 11 percent, from 2.19 *koku* to 2.43 *koku*, while the average of the upper three countries in the prefecture rose by only 4.7 percent, from 2.47 *koku* to 2.58 *koku*. For the same period, the coefficient of variation of the county averages declined by 30.5 percent, from 0.095 to 0.066. This seems to suggest that the rise in U was affected by the diffusion of u within the advanced prefectures. Again, the levels of productivity in the advanced counties in the advanced prefectures would have been affected by the diffusion of u.

[11] Therefore, the analysis in this section will substantiate only a part of the relation specified in general terms in the previous section.

[12] Probably the truth lies somewhere between the extremes.

[13] The demarcation between period I and period II is drawn at 1903–1907 instead of 1898–1902, because it represents a turning point in the movements in *V*, as explained in the text.

[14] The drop in the average yield in 1893–1897 is due to the severe drought that hit the western part of Japan in 1897.

[15] This is not to deny that those varieties were improved and publicized by the experiment stations. The later the period, the greater were the contributions of research and development at the experiment stations to the improvement and diffusion of varieties selected by the *rōnō*. It is somewhat arbitrary to draw a demarcation between the *rōnō* varieties and the experiment-station varieties.

[16] For the data of intercountry differences in agricultural productivity, see Yujiro Hayami and V. W. Ruttan, *Agricultural Development: An International Perspective* (Baltimore and London: Johns Hopkins University Press, 1971), pp. 67–107.

[17] For the conditions of the international transfer of agricultural technology, see ibid., pp. 169–190.

^{Part}3 Public Factors in Growth

6   Public Investments and Social Returns to Agricultural Research[1]

Both the historical review of agricultural development (chapter 3) and the growth-accounting analysis (chapter 4) have identified research in agricultural science and technology as a critical factor contributing to growth in agricultural output and productivity. In fact, research on biological technology in agriculture, resulting in the successful breeding of fertilizer-responsive high-yielding seed varieties, has been identified as the key to the development of Japanese agriculture against the constraint of scarce land resources.

This key factor has been provided primarily by the public sector, although the innovative efforts by farmers and landlords have underlaid the high productivity of public research. Recent data on the public-private mix in agricultural research appears in Table 6-1. In terms of the amount of research expenditure as well as the number of research staff, about 60 percent of agricultural research is conducted at governmental institutions, nearly 40 percent at universities, and only 3 percent is shared by the private sector. This structure contrasts greatly wtih the organization of nonagricultural research as shown in Table 6-1. Also, the organizational pattern of agricultural research in Japan is distinct from that in the United States where roughly half the expenditures for agricultural research are shared by private firms.[2]

In chapter 3 we reviewed the historical process by which government leaders and agricultural scientists established the agricultural-research infrastructure in response to farmer and land-

Table 6-1. Compositions of Expenditures and Research Staff of Agricultural and Nonagricultural Institutions in Japan, 1972 (in percentage terms)

	Research expenditure[a]		Number of Research Staff	
	Agriculture[c]	Nonagriculture[d]	Agriculture[c]	Nonagriculture[d]
	............................%........................			
Universities[b]	35	14	40	24
Public research				
National government	17	4	17	3
Local government	44	2	40	2
Private research	4	80	3	71
Total	100	100	100	100

[a] Including both current and capital expenditures.
[b] Including both public and private universities.
[c] Including forestry and fishery research.
[d] Excluding medical research.
SOURCE: Bureau of Statistics, Office of the Prime Minister, *Kagaku Gijutsu Kenkyu Chosa Hokoku* (Report on the Survey of Research and Development in Japan, 1972), pp. 62, 150, and 166.

lord demands for better technology. The question now arises as to how profitable public investments in agricultural research have been to society. Can those investments be justified in terms of the returns as well as the distribution of gains from research?

In this chapter we attempt to answer this question by estimating the social returns of rice-breeding research in the course of Japan's economic development to public investments.

6-1   Conditions of Public Resource Allocations to Agricultural Research

Before proceeding to the case study of rice-breeding research, we discuss the general conditions that have given rise to the predominance of the public sector in agricultural-research activities.[3]

Agricultural research is an activity that produces information, perhaps embodied in material inputs, and that contributes to an increase in agricultural output for a given level of conventional inputs. It is an activity of producing an input for agricultural production. In this respect there is no difference between research and the production of other inputs, such as fertilizers, that are traded in market places. However, both the special attributes of the product of research and the unique characteristics of agriculture have required public support for the efficient supply of information about agricultural science and technology.

Attributes of the product of research

New information or knowledge produced from research is typically endowed with the attributes of the "public good" in the Samuelson-Musgrave definition; it is characterized by (a) *nonrivalness*, or jointness in supply and utilization, and (b) *nonexcludability*, or external economies.[4] The first attribute implies that the good can be equally available to all. The latter implies that it is impossible for private producers to appropriate, through pricing in market, the full social benefits arising directly from the production (and consumption) of the good; in short, it is difficult to exclude from the utilization of that good those who do not pay for it. Socially, the optimum supply level of such a good cannot be expected if it is left to private firms.

Nonrivalness belongs to the very nature of information. The use of information about a new farming practice (contour ploughing, for example) by a farmer is by no means hindered by the adoption of the same practice by other farmers; there is no capacity limit to its utilization.

Nonexcludability is not a natural attribute of information, but it is determined by institutional arrangements. In fact, patent laws are institutional arrangements that make a certain kind of information (called "invention") excludable, thereby creating the profit incentives for private inventive activities. Also, it is common practice for big firms to keep secret the "know-how" that they produce. However, present institutional arrangements are such that the information produced from basic research is nonexcludable; here we find the rationale for basic scientific research being conducted primarily at non-profit institutions.[5]

A unique aspect of agricultural research, particularly in biological technology, is that even the products of research at the applied end are characterized by *nonexcludability*. Protection by patent laws is either unavailable or insufficient. The nature of agricultural production, conducted in an open space, makes it difficult to keep the know-how secret. Moreover, the gain to small-scale farmers from secret know-how is hardly sufficient to reward their producing such know-how.

It is no wonder that private research activities in agriculture have been directed primarily toward developing mechanical technology for which patent protection is established. Since it is difficult for private firms to capture the social benefits arising from research in the biological technology of agriculture, the optimum supply of biological-research products cannot be expected without the participation of public agencies. It is not surprising that the private-sector share in agricultural research has been very small in Japan where primary research efforts have been, because of the conditions of factor endowments, on the development of biological technology.

Research resources and research production function

Research resources for producing useful information are scarce. Among these resources human capital in the form of competent research workers represents the critical limiting factor.[6] The supply of this form of human capital is highly inelastic, at least in the short run. In order to increase the supply of this factor the institutions of advanced education and training have to be expanded, which, however, cannot be accomplished within a short period of time.[7] The capacity of agricultural research at a given point in time is conditioned by the historical accumulation of agricultural scientists and technicians. In organizing agricultural research, highest priority must be placed on considering how to economize on the use of this critical limiting factor.

The form of the production function in agricultural research is conditioned by the fact that it includes as a critical factor scientific research personnel. A hypothesis has been established that agricultural research is characterized by scale economies.[8] To some extent buildings and equipment for research can be utilized more efficiently for large-size operations. But, more importantly, the productivity of scientists increases through interactions with other scientists. A basic feature of intellectual activity is the production of new ideas through the mutual stimulation among participants in the same activity. In the research production function of an individual scientist, his colleagues are included as an input with a positive marginal product. This production externality among individual scientists should be the primary cause for the scale economies in the "aggregate" research production function. By all means, private farm firms are too small a unit to exploit the merits of such scale economies.

Another important attribute of the research production function is its stochastic form. The research is, by nature, characterized by risk and uncertainty. Success in a research project is like hitting a "successful oil well" after a number of dry holes. As Richard Nelson has pointed out, this stochastic nature of the research production function, which is especially strong in the case of basic research, contributes to the "failure of market" in attaining optimum resource allocations over time:

> The very large variance of the profit probability distribution from a basic research project will tend to cause a risk-avoiding firm, without the economic resources to spread the risk by running a number of basic-research projects at once, to value a basic-research at significantly less than its expected profit, and hence, . . . at less than its social value.[9]

Public investments are required for correcting such market failure.

Industrial organization of agriculture

The "public good" attributes of the agricultural-research product, together with the production externality and the stochastic nature of the research production function, make the public support of agricultural research socially desirable. It does not necessarily follow, however, that agricultural research should be conducted in governmental institutions financed by tax revenue. Social benefits produced from agricultural research can be measured by the sum of increases in consumers' and producers' surpluses due to the downward shift in the supply function of the agricultural product. If the benefit consists primarily of producers' surplus, agricultural research may be left to the cooperative activities of agricultural producers (i.e., to the activities of such institutions as farm bureaus and agricultural cooperatives).

The share of the producers' surplus in the social benefits from research depends on (a) the organization of the industry that uses the product of research as an input and (b) the price elasticity of demand for the product of that industry. Assuming the profit maximization of firms under the monopolistic structure of industry, the lower the demand elasticity, the larger the share of gains by producers.

The organization of agricultural production is unique in its closeness to the model of perfect competition, having a large number of small producers who have no power over monopolistic pricing. Also, agricultural commodities, except those for export, are mostly characterized by the low price elasticity of demand. As a result the major share of social benefits produced from research tends to go to consumers. In such a situation the cost of agricultural research should be borne by the general public or consumers. The predominance of public institutions in agricultural research in Japan may be justified on this ground.

Contributions to national economic development

The above discussion has identified public support to agricultural research as critical for the efficient allocation of resources to the activities of developing agricultural technology. However, it does not necessarily mean that the central government must take the responsibility. Rather it appears that local governments are more appropriate agents for allocating resources to agricultural research because agricultural technology produced from research is, by nature, highly location-specific or constrained by local ecologies.[10] Although basic principles and methods (e.g., plant-type concepts and the method of artificial crossbreeding) are more universally applicable, the technologies of actual farm use (e.g., improved seed varieties) are limited to specific ecological conditions. If the final product of agricultural research is primarily for the joint consumption of local people, it would be fair, as well as more effective, to have the local government take charge of its supply.

Since the products of agricultural research are not subject to market-pricing, the allocation of research resources among various research projects must be left to the perception of research administrators and scientists who supposedly know the demands of farmers for techniques that can be developed potentially. In fact, it is the process of dialectic interaction among farmers, research administrators, and scientists that leads research in a socially desirable direction. It is clear that the allocation of resources among various research projects can be more efficient when the information linkage between farmers and research administrators and staff is more closely established.

In this respect a decentralized system is more effective in research-resource allocation, because in this system agricultural scientists have a better perception of the needs of farmers while working closely with them. The pressure or lobbying of farmers' associations can work as an effective channel of information, especially in a decentralized system. Agricultural research in its applied end is more like local police than national defense. It can work more efficiently in a decentralized system for satisfying local demand.

Yet, in the history of agricultural development in Japan it was the central government rather than the local governments that took the initiative in establishing agricultural-research infrastructure (see chapter 3). The major share of public expenditures for agricultural research before 1900 were borne by the national government (Table 6–2). Only after the enactment of the Law of State Subsidy for Prefectural Agricultural Experiment Stations in 1899 did the share of the prefectural governments rise above 50 percent. Even after 1900 the national government continued to take leadership in developing agricultural-research systems by bearing the responsibility for conducting more basic research at the national experiment stations and by assisting and coordinating the activities at the prefectural stations.

This positive involvement of the national government in establishing agricultural-research infrastructure cannot be explained

Table 6-2. Composition of Expenditures for Agricultural Research by National and Prefectural Governments

	Expenditures in 1,000 yen (1934–1936 prices)			Percentage Compositions		
	Total	National[a]	Prefectural	Total	National[a]	Prefectural
1897	616	367	249[b]	100	60	40[b]
1902	2,044	930	1,114[b]	100	46	55[b]
1907	2,032	718	1,314[b]	100	35	65[b]
1912	3,044	822	2,222[b]	100	27	73[b]
1918	2,521	849	1,672[b]	100	34	66[b]
1923	5,385	1,286	4,099[b]	100	24	76[b]
1927	6,561	1,251	5,310[b]	100	19	81[b]
1932	8,196	1,686	6,510[b]	100	21	79[b]
1955	9,478	4,190	5,288[c]	100	44	56[c]
1960	12,300	4,661	7,639[c]	100	38	62[c]
1965	38,814	12,257	26,557[a]	100	32	68[a]
1970	60,093	17,257	42,836[a]	100	29	71[a]

[a] Five-year averages ending in the years shown, except for the 1918 and 1923 figures, which are five-year averages ending in 1917 and 1922.

[b] Single-year figures of the years shown.

[c] Estimations: (1) Changes in percentage compositions between 1951–1955 and 1956–1960 were assumed to be the same as between 1956–1960 and 1961–1965. (2) The percentage composition in 1958 was applied for 1956–1960.

SOURCE: National government expenditures—Ministry of Agriculture and Forestry, *Norinsho Yosan Kessan Hennenshi* (Annual Budget and Expenditure Accounts of the Ministry of Agriculture and Forestry), 1954; Ministry of Agriculture and Forestry, *Norinsho Yosansho* (Annual Budget of the Ministry of Agriculture and Forestry), various issues; and Agriculture, Forestry, and Fishery Research Council, *Todofuken Norinsuisan Kankei Shikenkenkyu Kikan no Gaiyo* (Outline of Agriculture, Forestry, and Fishery Research Institutions in Prefectures), 1963–1972.

Local government expenditures—Ministry of Agriculture and Forestry (formerly Ministry of Agriculture and Commerce), *Norinsho Tokei Hyo* (Statistical Yearbook of the Ministry of Agriculture and Forestry), various issues; Nogyo Gijutsu Kyokai, *Todofuken Nogyokankei Shikenjo Yoran* (Outline of Agricultural Experiment Stations in Prefectures), 1959; and Agriculture, Forestry, and Fishery Research Council, *Todofuken Norinsuisan Kankei Shikenkenkyu Kikan no Gaiyo* (Outline of Agriculture, Forestry, and Fishery Research Institutions in Prefectures), 1963–1972.

Deflator—The general price index from Kazushi Ohkawa et. al. (eds.), *Estimates of Long-term Economic Statistics of Japan since 1868*, vol. 8 (Tokyo: Toyokeizaishinposha, 1967), p. 134; and the implicit deflator from Economic Planning Agency, *Annual Report of National Income Statistics*, 1972, pp. 24–29.

without considering the contribution of such infrastructure to national economic development. As discussed in chapter 3, it was the major national goal of Meiji Japan to catch up with the Western powers through industrial development. An increase in the surplus in agriculture, the dominant sector of the economy, was essential for financing industrialization and other modernization measures. The agricultural surplus, exploited either directly by government taxation or indirectly through market mechanisms, represented the major sources of the wage good—food—for industrial workers and of the foreign-exchange earnings for the import of capital goods and technical know-how. The development of agricultural technology, through investment in research, was considered a critical means of increasing productivity and a surplus in agriculture.

From the above discussion we can hypothesize that the establishment of an agricultural-research infrastructure under the leadership of the central government was stimulated by expected gains from research in the form of growth in agricultural productivity and surpluses, required for national economic development.

6-2 Approach to Social Returns from Rice-breeding Research

In order to demonstrate the gains to society from public investment in agricultural research, we will try to estimate the social rate of returns to rice-breeding research. In this section, we will first summarize the history of rice-breeding research in Japan, so as to define the scope of our analysis, and, then, we will develop the methodology of estimating the social benefits from rice research.

History of rice-breeding research

The rice crop has dominated agricultural production in Japan. No less important has been the role of rice in food consumption. Before World War II it was the source of more than 60 percent of the total caloric intake of the Japanese people. Only in the late 1960's did the share of rice in the total caloric intake drop below 40 percent. The share of rice in consumption expenditures of urban blue-collar workers continued to be as high as 30 percent until 1930. Despite rapid postwar economic growth the share of rice in consumption expenditures of urban-worker households did not drop below 10 percent until after 1960.

Given this predominance of rice in the consumption expenditure of urban workers, a rise in the price of rice should have contributed significantly to the rise in the cost of living, particularly for those at the lower income levels. As a result, higher rice prices added to the pressure for wage-rate increases and general inflationary tendencies. The increase in the supply of rice to meet the growing demand from the urban sector was not only critical for the welfare of urban dwellers, but also important for the industrial development of Japan, especially in its early stages when labor-intensive light industries (such as textiles) predominated and rises in wage rates had a significant impact on returns to capital.

Since the national goal was one of industrial development, it is plausible that the rice policy was designed to increase the supply of rice, which would hold down the rise in the cost of living of urban workers.[11] Of cource, the rice supply may be augmented by imports from abroad. In fact, since Japan became a net importer of rice at the beginning of this century, the government has manipulated tariffs of rice prices. However, reliance on rice imports would have resulted in a drain on foreign exchange critical for development.

Thus, a requisite for industrialization and economic growth in Japan was an increase in the domestic supply of rice consistent with the expansion of demand. The basic approach to the increase in rice yield was to develop and diffuse high-yielding varieties of rice responsive to heavier application of fertilizers. Responding to this need, the government began in the 1880's to organize rice research by establishing agricultural experiment stations.

The history of rice-breeding research since the establishment of the National Agricultural Experiment Station in 1893 may be demarcated into four periods: (a) 1893 to 1903, (b) 1904 to

1925, (c) 1926 to 1949, and (d) 1950 to the present. The first covers the period before the start of scientific rice-breeding programs. During this period the experiment station was in its infant stage, and simple field experiments that compared yield performances of different varieties of crops or cultural practices were conducted.

The second period was characterized by rice-breeding research based on the method of pure line selection. The scientific rice-breeding program began with the application of the crossbreeding technique in 1904, but it took almost two decades before new varieties of major practical significance were developed by this method. In contrast, the rice-breeding programs that applied the method of pure line selection brought about quicker practical results. However, the potential of yield increase by this technique was exhausted as the purity of strains was raised to a limit.

Meanwhile, as experience and knowledge of the crossbreeding method were accumulated, the area planted in the varieties developed by this method increased sharply after 1920 (Figure 6–1). The major problem in applying this method was the shortage of expert breeders able to handle the initial crossing, which required particularly high-quality work. In order to solve this bottleneck a nation-wide coordinated crop-breeding program, called the "Assigned Experiment System," was established in 1926. This marked the beginning of the third period. Under the Assigned Experiment System the National Experiment Station was given the responsibility for conducting the initial crossing up to the selection of the first several filial generations. The regional breeding centers, in each of eight regions, conducted further selections under different ecological conditions. The varieties selected at the regional stations were then sent to prefectural stations for local testing. The varieties developed by this system were called *Norin* varieties. As shown in Figure 6–1, the *Norin* varieties spread rapidly, especially after 1935.

The experiment-station system was modified again in 1950. Now local experiment stations began to conduct independent crop-breeding programs from the first step of artificial crossing. This change reflected the increase in the capacity of local agricultural experiment stations and enabled them to breed varieties more specifically designed to satisfy local demand.

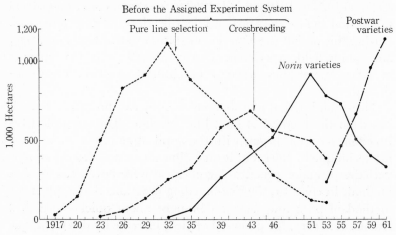

Figure 6–1.   Changes in area planted in improved varieties of rice, 1917–1961.

The rice-breeding research that we analyze here is limited to research for the period 1904–1950. It was in 1904 when the scientific crop-breeding program was initiated. Rice research since 1950, based on a new system, is excluded because its impact has not yet been fully realized. We conduct separate analyses for the periods before and after the start of the Assigned Experiment System, in order to evaluate the impact of the organizational innovation on social productivity.

Theoretical framework for estimating social returns

We now move to develop the theory and method of estimating social benefits from rice-breeding research and the distribution of these benefits in society. We will assume a market equilibrium in a closed economy. Later, we will try to incorporate into the model the implications of rice imports and government policy.

Using the Marshallian concepts of social welfare and cost, social returns to rice-breeding research are measured in terms of changes in consumers' and producers' surpluses that resulted from the shift in the rice-supply curve corresponding to a shift in the rice-production function.[12] This relation is shown in Figure 6–2

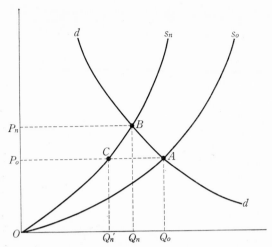

Figure 6–2. Model of social welfare and cost in demand and supply of rice.

in which d and s_0 represent the actual market demand and supply curves, whereas s_n represents the supply curve that would have existed if the improved rice varieties were not developed. Assuming market equilibrium and no rice imports, the shift in the supply curve from s_n to s_0 would increase the consumers' surplus by (*area ABC+area BP_nP_0C*); the producers' surplus by (*area ACO —area BP_nP_0C*); and the social benefit by (*area ABC+area ACO*).

In reality, however, Japan remained a net importer of rice during the period of analysis. The rice import was regulated by the government through tariffs and quotas. As discussed previously, the basic motive behind government policy was to maintain a stable price level for rice so as to prevent a rise in the living cost of urban workers. In fact, a stable trend in the price of rice relative to the general price index was maintained in the course of modern economic growth in Japan until around 1960 when it began to rise sharply after the dramatic change in rice policy that aimed at protecting producers (Figure 6–3, lower portion). In spite of occasional price-support operations, the actual level of rice prices in Japan before 1960 should have been below the market equilibrium in autarky.

Assuming the basic policy motivation of securing a sufficient

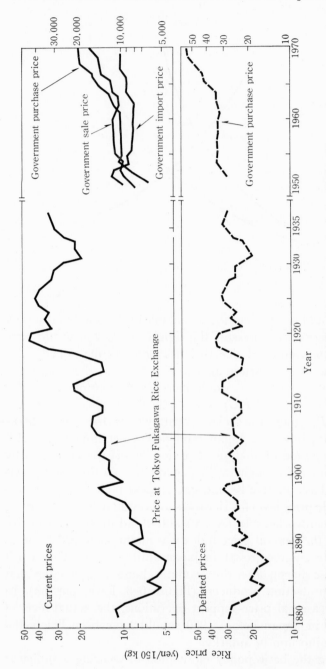

Figure 6–3. Changes in rice prices, both current and deflated by general price index (1934–1936 = 100), in Japan (log scale in brown rice term), 1880–1937 and 1951–1970.
SOURCE: Yujiro Hayami, "Rice Policy in Japan's Economic Development," *American Journal of Agricultural Economics* 54 (February 1972): 19–31.

supply of rice in order to prevent a rise in the cost of living of urban workers, if an increase in domestic rice production through varietal improvement and other means could not meet the increasing demand requirement, the gap would have been filled by imports. Let P_0 in Figure 6–2 be the price of rice that the government determined to maintain. If the domestic supply schedule did not shift from s_n to s_0, the government would have manipulated policy instruments to increase rice imports by $Q'_n Q_0$. Then, the producers' surplus would have been reduced by *area BP_nP_0C* without being compensated for by *area ACO*. In this case, the foreign exchange would have been reduced by *area $ACQ'_n Q_0$*.

If there had been no breeding program to shift the domestic supply from s_n to s_0, the producers' surplus would have been smaller by *area ACO*. This area may be defined as the producers' gain, in economic welfare, from the rice-breeding research, assuming a price-stabilization policy by means of rice imports. Since the consumers' surplus would remain unchanged under this assumption, the producers' gain would be equivalent to the total social benefit produced from the rice-breeding programs. Another contribution of breeding research to the national economy in the open economy case would be the gain in foreign exchange by *area $ACQ'_n Q_0$*.

In reality, in spite of the efforts to shift the rice-production function upward, the domestic supply could not keep up with the expansion in demand, resulting in rice imports in the order of 5 to 20 percent of the domestic production. Therefore, s_0 in Figure 6–2 would have been located somewhere to the left of A if we define A as the point of equilibrium of the total market supply and demand. However, this does not require modification of our model.

Model for quantitative estimation

The first step in estimating the changes in consumers' and producers' surpluses is to specify demand and supply schedules.

In this study a constant elasticity demand function is assumed as

$$q = Hp^{-\eta}$$

where q and p are the quantity and the price of rice, respectively, and η the price elasticity of demand. Similarly, a constant elasticity supply function is assumed as

$$q = Gp^\gamma$$

where γ is the price elasticity of the rice supply. We assume a hypothetical supply curve that would have existed in the absence of improved varieties as

$$q = (1-h)Gp^\gamma$$

where h represents the rate of shift in the supply function due to varietal improvement. In competitive equilibrium the supply function is equivalent to the marginal cost function derived from the production function. Since the relation between the rate of shift in the marginal cost function (h) and the rate of shift in the production function (k) can be approximated by

$$h \cong (1+\gamma)k$$

the following approximation formulas hold in equilibrium:

$$\text{area } ABC \cong \frac{1}{2}p_0 q_0 \frac{[k(1+\gamma)]^2}{\gamma+\eta}$$

$$\text{area } ACO \cong kp_0 q_0$$

$$\text{area } BP_n P_0 C \cong \frac{p_0 q_0 k(1+\gamma)}{\gamma+\eta}\left[1 - \frac{1}{2}\frac{k(1+\gamma)\eta}{\gamma+\eta} - \frac{1}{2}k(1+\gamma)\right]$$

and

$$\text{area } ACQ'_n Q_0 \cong (1+\gamma)kp_0 q_0$$

For the derivation of the above formula, see the mathematical supplement to this chapter.

6-3   Parameters and Data

In order to estimate social returns from rice-breeding research by the model developed in the previous section, we have to specify the data for the price elasticities of demand and supply (η and γ), the data for the rate of shift in the production function (k), and the value of rice output ($p_0 q_0$). In addition, we need the data for research costs in order to calculate the social rate of returns to rice-breeding research.

Demand and supply parameters

The estimate of the price elasticity of demand for rice (η) is available from Kazushi Ohkawa's classic study.[13] His estimates are based on 1931–1938 household survey data for the urban population and on 1920–1938 market data for the rural population. The estimates differ for different occupational, regional, and income groups, but they cluster around 0.2. We will adopt 0.2 for η.

The price elasticity of the rice supply (γ) was estimated by Yujiro Hayami and Vernon Ruttan on the basis of 1890–1937 time-series data,[14] and by Yasuhiko Yuize on 1952–1962 time series.[15] The results of the former study indicate that γ was in the vicinity of 0.2, and those of the latter in a range of from 0.2 to 0.3. Here we will adopt 0.2 for γ.

Although the relative magnitudes of the changes in consumers' and producers' surpluses are critically dependent on the choice of specific values for η and γ, the social benefit defined as the change in total economic surplus (*area ABC+area ACO*) is not so sensitive to the choice of those parameters so far as k is a small fraction of output (which is, in fact, smaller than 4 percent, as will be shown later). For $k=0.04$ and $\eta=0.2$, (*area ABC+area ACO*)/$kp_0 q_0$ is calculated as 1.10 for $\gamma=0$, 1.07 for $\gamma=0.2$, and 0.99 for $\gamma=\infty$; and for $k=0.04$ and $\gamma=0.2$, it is 1.14 for $\eta=0$, 1.07 for $\eta=0.2$, and 1 for $\eta=\infty$. Therefore, a possible error in the estimate of the social benefits would be within the range of 8 percent for both the positive and the negative directions.

Shift in rice production function

We estimated the rate of shift in the aggregate rice production function (k) by averaging the yield differences between the improved and the unimproved varieties for the same level of inputs, using the areas planted in the improved varieties as weights. The data for yield differences between improved varieties and varieties that were replaced by improved varieties at the same level of inputs are based on results of comparative yield tests at various agricultural experiment stations.

A good collection of results of comparative rice-yield tests for varieties developed before the period of the Assigned Experiment System is available in the reports of a survey conducted by the Ministry of Agriculture and Forestry (Table 6–3). In these reports the results of three years of tests for the 130 improved varieties in comparison with the varieties that they replaced are collected. Based on these data we calculated the rate of shift in the aggregate rice production function in the t-th year due to varietal improvement (k_t) by the following formula:

$$k_t = \sum_i \sum_j k_{ij} \frac{A_{ijt}}{A_t}$$

where k_{ij} is the ratio of the increase in rice yield of the i-th variety in the j-th region over the variety that it replaced; and A_t, and A_{ijt} are, respectively, the total rice area in the nation and the rice area planted in the i-th variety in the j-th region.[16]

Because of data limitations a more crude method is applied

Table 6–3. Estimates in the Rate of Shift in the Rice Production Function Due to Varietal Improvement

Before the Assigned Experiment System		Under the Assigned Experiment System	
Year	k_t (%)	Year	k_t (%)
1915	0.01	1932	0.02
1916	0.01	1933	0.06
1917	0.06	1934	0.11
1918	0.14	1935	0.15
1919	0.23	1936	0.20
1920	0.36	1937	0.30
1921	0.52	1938	0.42
1922	0.79	1939	0.52
1923	1.11	1940	0.60
1924	1.48	1941	0.66
1925	1.89	1942	0.74

Table 6-3.   (Continued)

Before the Assigned Experiment System		Under the Assigned Experiment System	
Year	k_t (%)	Year	k_t (%)
1926	1.91	1943	0.82
1927	1.97	1944	0.93
1928	2.08	1945	1.02
1929	2.20	1946	1.13
1930	2.41	1947	1.26
1931	2.73	1948	1.40
1932	3.17	1949	1.56
1933	2.70	1950	1.72
1934	2.77	1951	1.89
1935	2.80	1952	1.75
1936	2.87	1953	1.62
1937	2.94	1954	1.55
1938	2.94	1955	1.49
1939	3.01	1956	1.20
1940	2.94	1957	0.96
1941	2.87	1958	0.86
1942	2.80	1959	0.76
1943	2.72	1960	0.70
1944	2.58	1961	0.63
1945	2.44		
1946	2.22		
1947	2.08		
1948	1.93		
1949	1.79		
1950	1.65		
1951	1.50		
1952	1.36		
1953	1.22		

SOURCE :   Ministry of Agriculture and Forestry, *Dohuken ni okeru Beibaku Hinshukairyo Jigyo Seiseki Gaiyo* (Summary Report on the Results of the Varietal Improvement Projects of Rice and *Muji* in Respective Prefectures), 1926 ; *Dohuken ni okeru Shuyo Syokuryo Nosanbutsu Hinshu Kairyojigyo narabini Keikaku Gaiyo* (Summary Report on the Varietal Improvement Projects of Major Staples in Respective Prefectures), 1935 ; *Suito hinshu no Hensen to Ikuseihinshu no Tokusei narabini Fukyujokyo no Gaiyo* (Summary Report on Changes in Rice Varieties and the Characteristics and Diffusions of Improved Varieties), 1953 ; and *Beikoku no Hinshubetsu Sakuzuke Jokyo* (Annual Report on Area Planted in Respective Rice Varieties), 1954–1961 issues ; Nogyo Hattatsushi Chosakai, *Meiji Iko ni okeru Suitohinshu no Hensen* (Changes in Rice Varieties since the Meiji Era), 1955.

for estimating the rate of the production-function shift due to varieties developed by the Assigned Experiment System. Judging from a limited number of results of comparative yield tests we adopted 6 percent as the average rate of yield increases of the *Norin* varieties over the varieties they replaced. This rate was multiplied by the ratio of the area planted in the *Norin* varieties, in order to calculate the rates of shift in aggregate rice production due to breeding research under the Assigned Experiment System. The results of the estimation of the k_t's are as shown in Table 6–3.[17]

It must be recognized that the k_t's thus calculated involve an underestimation bias in figuring the contribution of breeding research to rice production. The assumption that underlies our method of calculating the k_t's is the neutrality in the shift of the rice production function. However, the improved varieties are usually more responsive to fertilizers, and their yield margins over the unimproved varieties increase for the higher levels of fertilizer application. The assumption of neutral technical progress would result in a bias in the estimation of the shift in the production function to the extent that the positive-interaction effects between varietal improvement and fertilizer application were neglected.

Value of rice output

Data for the value of rice output ($p_0 q_0$) are obtained by valuing the physical outputs of rice by the 1934–1936 average price in order to estimate the stream of social benefits in real terms. The years 1934–1936 are generally used as the basis of index construction because it is considered that "normal" price relations prevailed during this period. The price of rice relative to the prices of other commodities was somewhat lower during this period, for this period was characterized by a large inflow of rice from overseas territories, Korea and Taiwan, although the government tried to support the price of rice by increasing the government inventory. The valuation of output by the 1934–1936 average price might result in an understimation of the stream of social benefits.

Cost of rice-breeding research

Data for expenditures on rice-breeding research before the Assigned Experiment System are not readily available. One estimate is that the ratio of expenditures on crop-breeding programs to the total expenditures of agricultural experiment stations in 1927 was 43 percent for the national experiment stations and 45 percent for the prefectural experiment stations.[18] We estimated the annual expenditures for rice-breeding research by multiplying these ratios by the total expenditures of the national and prefectural stations.

All expenditures for research under the Assigned Experiment were paid for from the budget of the central government, and these data are readily available. In addition to the expenditures covered by the central government, prefectural governments paid for tests of local adaptability of the *Norin* varieties and of the multiplication of improved seeds. Those expenditures by local governments were estimated by multiplying the expenditures for crop-breeding programs in the prefectural experiment stations by the ratios of area planted in the *Norin* varieties to area planted in the total improved varieties.[19]

The time series of expenditures on crop-breeding programs, thus estimated, were deflated by the consumer price index with 1934–1936=100, as shown in Table 6–4. It must be emphasized that those estimates of expenditures on crop-breeding programs include not only the cost of research and development but also the cost for extension, such as the multiplication of seeds. Also, our cost data would be overestimating the cost of rice-breeding research, because the breeding programs include not only the projects on rice but also those on *mugi* (wheat, barley, and naked barley), although the weight of rice research in the programs should have been predominant.

The allocation of costs between the programs before and after the Assigned Experiment System is somewhat arbitrary. Some of the pre-AES costs might well be attributed to the realization of AES benefits. This problem of "pervasiveness" or "spill-over effects" represents a difficulty inherent in estimating the social rate of returns to research investment.

Table 6-4. Expenditures on Rice-breeding Programs by National and Prefectural Governments (thousand *yen* in 1934–1936 constant prices)

Before the Assigned Experiment System				Under the Assigned Experiment System			
Year	National	Prefectural	Total	Year	National	Prefectural	Total
1904	135	330	465	1927	97		97
1905	136	327	463	1928	83		83
1906	137	362	499	1929	87		87
1907	130	365	495	1930	94		94
1908	162	445	607	1931	98		98
1909	158	439	597	1932	86	11	97
1910	160	489	649	1933	79	29	108
1911	185	502	687	1934	70	58	128
1912	142	465	607	1935	65	86	151
1913	113	402	515	1936	58	116	174
1914	121	468	589	1937	49	166	215
1915	134	520	654	1938	44	198	242
1916	142	541	683	1939	36	205	241
1917	106	483	589	1940	32	192	224
1918	94	499	593	1941	32	193	225
1919	100	538	638	1942	30	187	217
1920	98	657	755	1943	41	178	219
1921	130	923	1,053	1944	37	167	204
1922	119	834	953	1945	25	131	156
1923	150	877	1,027	1946		108	108
1924	182	785	967	1947		194	194
1925	112	818	930	1948		298	298
1926	135	1,035	1,170	1949		417	417
1927	126	1,180	1,306	1950		479	479
1928	139	1,265	1,404	1951		624	624
1929	147	1,140	1,287	1952		652	652
1930	163	1,297	1,460	1953		685	685
1931	175	1,350	1,525	1954		729	729
1932	320	1,450	1,770	1955		642	642
1933	243	1,456	1,699	1956		588	588
1934	252	1,454	1,706	1957		527	527
1935	261	1,536	1,797	1958		505	505
1936		1,323	1,323	1959		480	480
1937		1,257	1,257	1960		419	419
1938		1,150	1,150	1961		403	403
1939		1,075	1,075				
1940		791	791				
1941		690	690				

Table 6-4. (Continued)

	Before the Assigned Experiment System				Under the Assigned Experiment System		
Year	National	Prefec-tural	Total	Year	National	Prefec-tural	Total
1942		593	593				
1943		500	500				
1944		401	401				
1945		265	265				
1946		186	186				
1947		268	268				
1948		337	337				
1949		394	394				
1950		382	382				
1951		409	409				
1952		424	424				
1953		427	427				

SOURCE: Masaji Hara and Naoo Kawabe, "Nogyo Shiken Kenkyuhi no Bunseki" (Analysis of Agricultural Research Expenditures), *Nogyo Gijutsu* 4 (October 1950): 36–40; Ministry of Agriculture and Forestry, *Norinsho Tokeihyo* (Statistical Yearbook of the Ministry of Agriculture and Forestry), 1893–1938 issues; *Shitei Shiken Seido Jigyo ni kansuru Sanko Shiryo* (References on the Assigned Experiment System), 1953; *Todo Fuken Nogyo Kankei Shiken Kenkyu Kikan no Gaiyo* (Summary Report on Prefectural Agricultural Experiment Stations), 1963; Zenkoku Nogyo Shikenjocho Kai, *Todo Fuken Nogyo Kankei Shikenjo Yoran* (Directory of Prefectural Agricultural Experiment Stations), 1959.

6-4 Quantitative Findings

Distribution of social benefits

Estimation of the social benefits was conducted separately for pre-Assigned Experiment System programs and for the programs under that system. The results are summarized in Tables 6–5 and 6–6.

In the autarky case, the most remarkable aspect in the results of estimation is that the social benefits produced from the research were more than totally captured by the consumers and that the producers were made worse off. Such results were derived from applying low price elasticities of demand and supply. In

Table 6-5. Estimates of Social Benefits from Rice-breeding Research and Its Distribution, before the Assigned Experiment System (million *yen* in 1934–1936 prices)

Year	Autarky Case			Open Economy Case	
	Producers' Gain (1)	Consumers' Gain (2)	Total Social Benefits (3)=(1)+(2)	Producers' Gain (=Total benefits) (4)	Saving in Foreign Exchange (5)
1915	−0.30	0.45	0.15	0.15	0.18
1916	−0.32	0.48	0.16	0.16	0.19
1917	−1.80	2.70	0.90	0.90	1.08
1918	−4.20	6.30	2.11	2.10	2.52
1919	−7.68	11.52	3.85	3.84	4.60
1920	−12.47	18.75	6.28	6.25	7.50
1921	−15.69	23.64	7.95	7.88	9.45
1922	−26.21	39.51	13.30	13.17	15.80
1923	−33.49	50.73	17.24	16.91	20.29
1924	−45.90	69.75	23.85	23.25	27.90
1925	−60.97	93.03	32.06	31.01	37.21
1926	−57.37	87.54	30.17	29.18	35.01
1927	−66.07	100.86	34.79	33.62	40.34
1928	−67.65	103.38	35.73	34.46	41.35
1929	−70.68	108.12	37.44	36.04	43.24
1930	−86.68	132.87	46.19	44.29	53.14
1931	−80.80	124.23	43.43	41.41	49.69
1932	−102.25	157.86	55.61	52.62	63.14
1933	−102.56	157.62	55.06	52.54	63.04
1934	−77.01	118.41	41.40	39.47	47.36
1935	−86.21	132.63	46.42	44.21	53.05
1936	−103.53	159.35	55.82	53.12	63.74
1937	−104.33	160.67	56.34	53.56	64.27
1938	−103.65	159.62	55.97	53.21	63.85
1939	−110.97	171.07	60.10	57.03	68.43
1940	−95.79	147.52	51.73	49.18	59.01
1941	−84.69	130.35	45.66	43.45	52.14
1942	−100.18	154.12	53.94	51.38	61.65
1943	−91.07	139.95	48.88	46.65	55.98
1944	−81.11	124.52	43.41	41.51	49.81
1945	−78.69	120.62	41.93	40.21	48.25
1946	−73.44	112.35	38.91	37.45	44.94
1947	−65.79	100.55	34.76	33.52	40.22
1948	−69.27	105.70	36.43	35.24	42.28
1949	−52.91	80.62	27.71	26.88	32.25
1950	−57.49	87.50	30.01	29.17	35.00
1951	−48.99	74.50	25.51	24.84	29.80
1952	−48.84	74.15	25.31	24.72	29.66
1953	−36.42	55.20	18.78	18.40	22.08

Table 6-6. Estimates of Social Benefits from Rice-breeding Research and Its Distribution, under the Assigned Experiment System (million *yen* in 1934–1936 prices)

Year	Autarky Case			Open Economy Case	
	Producers' Gain (1)	Consumers' Gain (2)	Total Social Benefits (3)=(1)+(2)	Producers' Gain (=Total benefits) (4)	Saving in Foreign Exchange (5)
1932	−0.66	0.99	0.33	0.33	0.39
1933	−2.32	3.48	1.16	1.16	1.39
1934	−3.12	4.68	1.56	1.56	1.87
1935	−4.72	7.08	2.36	2.36	2.83
1936	−7.40	11.10	3.71	3.70	4.44
1937	−10.90	16.38	5.48	5.46	6.55
1938	−15.15	22.80	7.65	7.60	9.12
1939	−19.61	29.55	9.94	9.85	11.82
1940	−19.96	30.09	10.13	10.03	12.03
1941	−19.86	29.94	10.08	9.98	11.97
1942	−26.97	40.71	13.74	13.57	16.28
1943	−28.13	42.48	14.35	14.16	16.99
1944	−29.69	44.88	15.19	14.96	17.95
1945	−33.30	50.40	17.10	16.80	20.16
1946	−37.74	57.18	19.44	19.06	22.87
1947	−40.18	60.93	20.75	20.31	24.37
1948	−50.49	76.68	26.19	25.56	30.67
1949	−47.81	72.72	24.91	24.24	29.08
1950	−59.86	91.20	31.34	30.40	36.48
1951	−61.52	93.87	32.35	31.29	37.54
1952	−62.64	95.43	32.79	31.81	38.17
1953	−48.18	73.32	25.14	24.44	29.32
1954	−51.04	77.64	26.60	25.88	31.05
1955	−66.73	101.40	34.67	33.80	40.56
1956	−47.42	71.88	24.46	23.96	28.75
1957	−39.98	60.48	20.50	20.16	24.19
1958	−37.64	56.88	19.24	18.96	22.75
1959	−34.58	52.20	17.62	17.40	20.88
1960	−32.79	49.47	16.68	16.49	19.78
1961	−28.51	42.99	14.48	14.33	17.19

particular, the demand elasticity plays a decisive role in the distribution of benefits among consumers and producers.

If the price elasticity of demand is infinitely elastic, the social gain from a shift in supply would be totally captured by producers as long as supply is competitive. If the producers have the power of monopolistic pricing, they would be able to capture the major share of the welfare gain by taking advantage of the inelastic demand. However, such a possibility does not exist in the case of agriculture characterized by proximity to perfect competition with a mass of small producers.

In reality, however, Japan did not operate in the condition of rice autarky during the period of this analysis. Assuming the basic method of government policy for stabilizing rice prices was to import rice, producers would have been made worse off by *area ACO* as measured in Tables 6–5 and 6–6, if there were no program for rice-breeding research. Thus, rice research preserved a larger share of the Japanese rice market for domestic producers. Without the research the Japanese economy would have lost foreign exchange by *area* $ACQ'_n Q_0$.

In fact, as the estimates in Tables 6–5 and 6–6 indicate, the possible loss in foreign exchange due to the shortage of domestic rice supply during the 1930's would have amounted to about 5 percent of the total import of Japan. Considering the chronic shortage of foreign exchange in the course of industrialization in Japan, the contribution of rice-breeding research to economic growth should have been quite significant.[20]

In the open economy case, the producers were made better off by the rice-breeding research, while the consumers continued to enjoy the same level of economic welfare without causing a drain on foreign exchange.

In reality, however, it does not appear that the same level of consumer welfare could have been secured in the absence of the shift in the domestic rice supply schedule, brought about by the breeding research, since the constraint of foreign exchange would not have allowed additional rice imports on such a large scale. The autarky and the open-economy cases in our analysis represent the polar cases within which reality lies.

The social rate of returns

In order to assess the efficiency in resource allocations to rice-breeding research, both the external and the internal rates of returns are calculated by relating the research costs in Table 6–4 with the estimates of social benefits shown in Tables 6–5 and 6–6.

The external rate of returns (r_e) is defined as the rate calculated from the following formula:

$$r_e = \frac{100(iP+F)}{C}$$

where i is the external rate of interest, P the accumulation of past returns, F the annual future returns, and C the accumulation of past research expenditures. The external rate of interest (i) is applied to the accumulation of both returns and expenditures. In this study 10 percent is assumed for the interest rate.

The internal rate of returns (r_i) is the rate that results in

$$\sum_{t=0}^{T} \frac{R_t - C_t}{(1+r_i)^t} = 0$$

where R_t is the social benefit in year t, C_t the research cost in year t, and T the year that research ceases to produce returns.

The social rates of returns for breeding programs before the Assigned Experiment System are calculated for two alternative cases: Case A, which assumes that the net returns (R_t-C_t) in 1935 would have been maintained forever from that year; and Case B, which assumes that the net returns would become zero after 1935. Case A represents a polar case in which the knowledge and experience accumulated in a breeding program would continue to be utilized even after the varieties developed by the program were replaced by varieties developed by subsequent breeding programs, whereas Case B assumes that the life of the varieties ends when they are replaced by new ones.

In calculating the rates of returns in the programs under the Assigned Experiment System, two alternative assumptions about the stream of returns were made: Case A assumes that the net returns would have continued to be maintained forever at the level of 1951 since that represented the year when the area planted in the *Norin* varieties reached a peak; and Case B assumes that the net returns would have become zero after 1961.

The results of estimating the social rates of return, for both the

Table 6-7. Estimates of Social Rates of Returns to Rice-breeding Research (million *yen* in 1934–1936 constant prices)

	Autarky Case		Open Economy Case	
	Case A	Case B	Case A	Case B
Before the Assigned Experiment System				
External rate				
(1) Net cumulated past returns	985.88	7,660.95	952.52	7,392.64
(2) Past returns expressed as annual flow	98.58	766.09	95.25	739.26
(3) Net annual future returns	44.63	0	42.41	0
(4) Total net annual returns, (2)+(3)	143.21	766.09	137.66	739.26
(5) Cumulated past research expenditures	123.39	783.47	123.39	783.47
(6) Rate of return, 100 (4)/(5)	116%	98%	112%	94%
Internal rate	27%	25%	26%	25%
Under the Assigned Experiment System				
External rate				
(1) Net cumulated past returns	487.98	1,639.77	480.11	1,610.65
(2) Past returns expressed as annual flow	48.79	163.97	48.01	161.06
(3) Net annual future returns	31.73	0	30.67	0
(4) Total net annual returns, (2)+(3)	80.52	163.97	78.68	161.06
(5) Cumulated past research expenditures	14.51	46.78	14.51	46.78
(6) Rate of return, 100 (4)/(5)	554%	350%	542%	344%
Internal rate	75%	73%	75%	73%

autarky and the open-economy cases, are reported in Table 6–7. In terms of the magnitude of the social rates of return there are only small differences between the two cases. Both results indicate that crop-breeding research represents a lucrative public-investment opportunity.

Estimates for pre-Assigned Experiment System programs are comparable with those for the hybrid-corn research in the United States by Zvi Griliches (about 35 percent of the internal rate and 700 percent of the external rate), and for the poultry research in the United States reported by Willis Peterson (about 20 percent of the internal rate and 140 percent of the external rate).[21] Estimates of the rate of returns for rice research under the Assigned Experiment System are comparable in magnitude with those for cotton research in Sao Paulo, Brazil, by Harry Ayer and G. Edward Schuh (about 90 percent of the internal rate), and for wheat research in Mexico by L. Ardito Barletta (about 75 percent of the internal rate).[22] Judging from these estimates, gross underinvestment in varietal improvement research has been pervasive in the world. It appears, therefore, that the allocation of resources to such research has been less than optimum.

The results in Table 6–7 show that the social rate of return was increased after the crop-breeding programs were reorganized into the Assigned Experiment System. Thus, efficiency in research was improved by institutional innovation: the conflict between the constraint of research resources and the need for location-specific breeding research was solved by organizing a division of labor among the national and the prefectural experiment stations. We do not deny the possibility that the increase in the rate of return over time reflects the scale economies inherent in the process of research in producing knowledge and information. However, if there had been no organizational improvements that enabled the better coordination of an enlarged research complex, the increase in the efficiency of rice-breeding research would not have been as dramatic as that measured in this study.

6-5 Implications

Finally, we will discuss the implications of the results of the case study on the social returns to rice-breeding research to the problem of public resource allocation. We will keep in mind economic development in the developing countries.

As discussed previously, because of the public-good attributes of the product of research, public support should be required in order to attain a socially optimum level of investment in research. This study of rice breeding in Japan adds to the evidence the fact that underinvestments prevail in research. If underinvestments in agricultural research were the case for Japan as well as for the United States, as suggested by Griliches and others —both being characterized by a relatively well established agricultural experiment system—the potential benefits from research for the developing countries, in which the public research system is in an infant stage, should be extremely large. This inference is consistent with the findings of the very high rates of social returns to cotton research in Brazil and wheat research in Mexico. Public planners and policy-makers should be constantly reminded that there is a tendency to underestimate the social productivity of research.

The fact that the product of research is endowed with the attributes of public good does not necessarily mean that the investment in research should be financed out of government tax revenue. If the major share of the gain were captured by producers, it might be more appropriate in terms of equity criteria to let that group finance the investment. However, as the results of our analysis suggest in the assumption of autarky, investment in research on such commodities as rice, characterized by the low price elasticities of demand and supply, tends to result in an increase in the consumers' welfare and a sacrifice in the producers' benefit. In such a case it should be more than fair to pay for the research cost from the government budget.

The results based on the autarky assumption, though unrealistic in the case of Japan, should be relevant to developing countries, such as Taiwan, characterized by a self-sufficiency of food staples.

In fact, as the study by T. H. Lee shows, a major source of resource outflow from agriculture to nonagriculture in Taiwan was the deterioration of internal terms of trade against agriculture corresponding to a remarkable increase in agricultural productivity.[23] Agricultural research and extension can be utilized as a system of resource transfer from agriculture to nonagriculture for financing industrial development. To some extent, the above discussion would also hold for countries with food exports such as Thailand, which face relatively inelastic world demand.

If we assume a food policy of controlling food imports in order to keep food prices low for urban workers and facilitate industrial capital accumulation and development, research that shifts the food production function upward would partially compensate for the decline in the producers' surplus due to import. In addition, it would contribute to the national economy as it enables the saving of foreign exchange needed for the import of technical know-how and capital goods. These appeared to be the critical contributions of rice-breeding research to the modern economic growth of Japan. Japan's experience should be highly relevant to such developing countries as India that have to rely on the import of food staples from abroad in the process of economic development.

Finally, the experience of Japan is also relevant with respect to the increase in the social rate of return to research investment corresponding to the reorganization of the rice-breeding system. Public funds for economic development are scarce in developing countries. More scarce are competent scientists and technicians who can carry out significant research programs. How to economize the scarce research resources is a problem especially serious for the design of research organizations in the developing countries. Institutional innovations, such as the Assigned Experiment System in Japan, should be critical in meeting the extremely large potential demand for research resources with the limited endowments in those countries.

6-6 Mathematical Supplement

A. The relation between h and k

The actual and the hypothetical supply functions that would have existed in the absence of improved varieties are assumed, respectively, as

$$q = Gp^\gamma \tag{A-1}$$

$$q = (1-h)Gp^\gamma \tag{A-2}$$

Assuming that the supply curves are equivalent to the marginal cost curves, the marginal costs $\left(\dfrac{dc}{dq}\right)$ are

$$\frac{dc}{dq} = p = G^{-1/\gamma}q^{1/\gamma} \tag{A-3}$$

$$\frac{dc}{dq} = p = (1-h)^{-1/\gamma}G^{-1/\gamma}q^{1/\gamma} \tag{A-4}$$

Total cost curves derived by taking the integrals of the marginal cost curves, which are assumed to pass through the origin are

$$C = \frac{\gamma}{(1+\gamma)}G^{-1/\gamma}q^{(1+\gamma)/\gamma} \tag{A-5}$$

$$C = \frac{\gamma}{(1+\gamma)}G^{-1/\gamma}(1-h)^{-1/\gamma}q^{(1+\gamma)/\gamma} \tag{A-6}$$

Let q_0 and q'_n represent, respectively, the output levels for a given cost in equations (A–5) and (A–6). Then, the relation between q_0 and q'_n is represented approximately for a sufficiently small value of h as

$$(q'_n/q_0) \cong 1-h/(1+\gamma) \tag{A-7}$$

Since k is denoted $(q_0-q'_n)/q_0$, the relation between h and k can be shown approximately as

$$h \cong (1+\gamma)k \tag{A-8}$$

The above formula implies that h becomes infinite when $\gamma = \infty$.

This is due to the approximate nature of the formula. Actually, h is equal to $k/(1-k)$ when $\gamma=\infty$.

B. The formulas of social returns, changes in consumers' surplus and producers' surplus

Area ABC is derived as follows:

p_0 and p_n in Figure 6–2 are represented, respectively, as

$$p_0 = (H/G)^{1/(\gamma+\eta)} \tag{B-1}$$

$$p_n = (H/G)^{1/(\gamma+\eta)}(1-h)^{-1/(\gamma+\eta)} \tag{B-2}$$

Hence, $(p_n-p_0) \cong p_0 h/(\gamma+\eta)$ for a sufficiently small value of h.

Thus, *area* $ABC \cong \frac{1}{2}p_0 q_0 h^2/(\gamma+\eta)=\frac{1}{2}p_0 q_0 [k(1+\gamma)]^2/(\gamma+\eta)$.

Area ACO is derived as follows:

$$area\ ACO = \int_0^{p_0} hGp^\gamma dp = p_0 q_0 h/(1+\gamma) \cong k p_0 q_0$$

Area BP_nP_0C is derived as follows:

$$area\ BP_n P_0 C \cong (p_n - p_0)q_0 - \frac{1}{2}(p_n - p_0)(q_0 - q_n) - area\ ABC$$

Since (p_n-p_0) is approximately equal to $p_0 h/(\gamma+\eta)$, and (q_0-q_n) to $q_0 h\eta/(\gamma+\eta)$:

$$area\ BP_n P_0 C \cong \frac{p_0 q_0 k(1+\gamma)}{\gamma+\eta}\left[1-\frac{1}{2}\frac{k(1+\gamma)\eta}{\gamma+\eta}-\frac{1}{2}k(1+\gamma)\right]$$

Notes to Chapter 6

[1] This chapter draws heavily on Masakatsu Akino and Yujiro Hayami, "Efficiency and Equity in Public Research: Rice Breeding in Japan's Economic Development," *American Journal of Agricultural Economics* 57 (February 1975): 1-10; and Yujiro Hayami and Saburo Yamada, "Agricultural Research Organization in Economic Development: A Review of the Japanese Experience," paper prepared for the conference on "Agriculture in Development Theory" held at Bellagio, Italy, May 23–28, 1973.

[2] Yujiro Hayami and V. W. Ruttan, *Agricultural Development: An International Perspective* (Baltimore and London: Johns Hopkins University Press, 1971), p. 144.

[3] For the references on the research resource allocations, see ibid.; and W. L.

Fishel, ed., *Resource Allocation in Agricultural Research* (Minneapolis: University of Minnesota Press, 1971), pp. 90–120.

[4] P. A. Samuelson, "The Pure Theory of Public Expenditure," *Review of Economics and Statistics* 36 (November 1954): 387–389; "Diagramatic Exposition of a Theory of Public Expenditures," *Review of Economic Statistics* 37 (November 1955): 350–356; and "Aspects of Public Expenditure Theories," *Review of Economics and Statistics* 40 (November 1958): 332–338. R. A. Musgrave, *The Theory of Public Finance* (New York: McGraw-Hill, 1959).

[5] R. R. Nelson, "The Simple Economics of Basic Scientific Research," *Journal of Political Economy* 67 (June 1959): 297–306.

[6] This point was emphasized by T. W. Schultz, "The Allocation of Resources to Research," in *Resource Allocation in Agricultural Research*, ed. W. L. Fishel, pp. 90–120.

[7] The supply of this form of human capital to a specific field, such as agricultural science, may be more elastic since it is possible to draw away the scientists of neighboring disciplines like biology and engineering. Yet, the possibility of such transfer is probably limited.

[8] This hypothesis was suggested by T. W. Schultz, *Transforming Traditional Agriculture* (New Haven: Yale University Press, 1964), pp. 150–152, and was empirically supported by R. E. Evenson, "Economic Aspects of Organization of Agricultural Research," in *Resource Allocation*, ed. W. L. Fishel, pp. 163–182.

[9] Nelson, "Simple Economics," p. 304.

[10] This aspect was emphasized by A. H. Moseman, *Building Agricultural Research Systems in the Developing Nations* (New York: Agricultural Development Council, 1970); and by Hayami and Ruttan, *Agricultural Development*.

[11] For a historical review of rice policy in Japan, see Yujiro Hayami, "Rice Policy in Japan's Economic Development," *American Journal of Agricultural Economics* 54 (February 1972): 19–31.

[12] In this study producers' surplus is defined as the total value output in agriculture minus the payment to the inputs applied to agricultural production that are supplied from nonagriculture; it includes not only the entrepreneurial profit of farmers but also land rent, wages to family labor, and returns to farm capital.

[13] Kazushi Ohkawa, *Shokuryo Keizai no Riron to Keisoku* (Theory and Measurement of Food Economy), (Tokyo: Nihon Hyoronsha, 1945).

[14] Yujiro Hayami and V. W. Ruttan, "Korean Rice, Taiwan Rice, and Japanese Agricultural Stagnation: An Economic Consequence of Colonialism," *Quarterly Journal of Economics* 84 (November 1970): 562–589.

[15] Yasuhiko Yuize, "Nogyo Seisan ni Okeru Kakaku Hanno" (On the Price Responses in Agricultural Production), *Nogyo Sogo Kenkyu* 19 (January 1965): 107–142.

[16] The nation is divided into ten regions according to ecological conditions.

[17] To a large extent k_t depends on the ratio of area planted in improved varieties developed by the rice-breeding programs. Declines in k_t since 1932 in the case of the pre-Assigned Experiment System and since 1951 in the case of the Assigned Experiment System reflect the replacement of varieties developed in those systems by those developed in succeeding ones.

[18] Takeichi Oda, "Honpo ni okeru Beibaku Hinshu Kairyo Jigyo no Taiko" (Summary of the Rice and Mugi Varietal Improvement Programs in Japan), *Dainihon Nokai-ho* (November 1929): 14–28.

[19] This procedure might involve some bias because the expenditures on testing *Norin* varieties preceded the adoption of the varieties.

[20] However, it is difficult to estimate the gain in national economic welfare due

to the saving of foreign exchange in a term comparable with consumers' or producers' surplus.

21) Zvi Griliches, "Research Costs and Social Returns: Hybrid Corn and Related Innovations," *Journal of Political Economy* 66 (October 1958): 419–431; W. L. Peterson, "Return to Poultry Research in the United States," *Journal of Farm Economics* 49 (August 1967): 656–669.

22) H. W. Ayer and G. E. Schuh, "Social Rates of Return and Other Aspects of Agricultural Research: The Case of Cotton Research in Sao Paulo, Brazil," *American Journal of Agricultural Economics* 54 (November 1972): 557–569; L. A. Barletta, " Costs and Social Returns of Agricultural Research in Mexico," Ph. D. dissertation, University of Chicago, 1967.

23) T. H. Lee, *Intersectoral Capital Flows in the Economic Development of Taiwan, 1895–1960* (Ithaca: Cornell University Press, 1971).

Chapter 7 Role of Land Infrastructure in Agricultural Development

The role of land infrastructure, such as irrigation and drainage, has been emphasized in previous chapters (especially chapters 3 and 5). It represents a basic condition in the development and diffusion of seed-fertilizer technology that facilitates the substitution of fertilizers and other current inputs for land, thereby breaking the constraint of scarce land resources on agricultural production.

The basis of the development of the seed-fertilizer technology from the early Meiji period has been identified as the relatively well developed irrigation system inherited from the feudal Tokugawa period. However, according to the growth-accounting analysis in chapter 4, the contribution of land-infrastructure improvements to agricultural growth in Japan since the Meiji Restoration was relatively minor. It was therefore hypothesized that the apparent minor role of land infrastructure resulted partly from the large initial stock of irrigation capital, reducing the rate of improvement in the quality of land due to current investments in land infrastructure.

Another reason for the low estimate of the contribution of land-infrastructure improvement was to assume independence and separability among the factors of agricultural production, on which the growth-accounting analysis was based. In reality, however, without adequate land infrastructure the capacity of the high-yielding varieties could not have been realized and the application of fertilizers in increasing amounts would have been poorly rewarded. Without taking such basic complementarity into consideration, it was inevitable that the contribution of land-infrastructure improvement was underestimated.

In this chapter we attempt to put into proper perspective the role of land infrastructure in Japanese agricultural development in terms of its basic complementarity with seed-fertilizer technology. We also try to demonstrate the significance of the feudal heritage of irrigation infrastructure compared with construction of such infrastructure since the Meiji Restoration.

Similar to the products of agricultural research, land infrastructure should be considered endowed with the attributes of public goods, such as indivisibility, externality, and jointness in supply and utilization. However, the public-goods characteristics are weaker in the case of land infrastructure. There are capacity limits in the irrigation and drainage systems, which limit the scope of joint utilization. Also, it is easier to exclude from the use of the facilities those who do not share the costs. Therefore, group action of farm producers plays a more important role in the provision of land infrastructure. In order to analyze the process of land-infrastructure improvement, it is critical to understand the processes by which farmers and landlords were organized and interacted with various governments in the mobilization of resources for construction of irrigation and drainage facilities.

7-1   Trends in Land-Infrastructure Improvement

First, let us observe the historical process of progress in land-infrastructure improvement. Figure 7–1 shows the trends in the areas covered by the land-improvement projects, including the construction of irrigation and drainage systems and the replotment of cultivated land.

The feudal heritage of land infrastructure was large. It is estimated that the area already improved before the Meiji Restoration, either by reservoir or by river irrigation systems, amounted to 1.8 million hectares, about 40 percent of the total cultivated land area or more than 60 percent of the lowland paddy-field area on which the irrigation projects had been con-

Table 7–1.   Areas Covered by Land-Infrastructure Improvement Projects

| | Improved Area | | Cultivated Land Area | | Ratio of Improved Area to Cultivated Land | |
	Since Meiji Restoration (1)	Total[a] (2)	Paddy Field (3)	Total (4)	(2)/(3)	(2)/(4)
	·················· 1,000 hectares ··················				········%········	
1880	186	1,799	2,802	4,749	64	38
1885	263	1,875	2,824	4,814	66	39
1890	304	1,917	2,858	4,922	67	39
1895	332	1,945	2,877	5,034	68	39
1900	358	1,971	2,905	5,200	68	38
1905	389	2,001	2,936	5,300	68	38
1910	460	2,073	3,007	5,579	69	37
1915	595	2,208	3,072	5,777	72	38
1920	733	2,345	3,136	5,998	75	39
1925	903	2,516	3,199	5,914	79	43
1930	1,199	2,812	3,274	5,962	86	47
1935	1,474	3,086	3,290	6,104	94	51
1940	1,777	3,390	3,277	6,122	103	55
1950	2,335	3,947	3,231	5,858	122	67
1955	3,140	4,750	3,302	5,982	144	79
1960	3,833	5,446	3,382	6,072	161	90
1965	4,539	6,152	3,391	6,005	181	102

[a] Includes areas improved before and after the Meiji Restoration.
SOURCE :   Appendix Table A–10.

centrated (Table 7–1).[1] Although there had been active movements for land-infrastructure improvements among the *gōnō* class during the early Meiji period, the area improved since the Restoration was only a minor fraction of the initial stock of improved area and thereby had no significant impact on the trend in total improved area until the end of the nineteenth century.

The increase in total improved area began to accelerate in the 1910's. From Figure 7–1 it is clear that the acceleration was brought about by projects under the Arable Land Replotment Law. As explained in chapter 3, the major constraint on land-improvement projects undertaken under the initiative of landlords was the difficulty in getting the consent of the farmers and landlords involved in the project area. The Arable Land Replotment Law was designed to remove this constraint by authorizing the compulsory participation of those who would be involved if the consent of two-thirds of landlords who owned two-thirds of

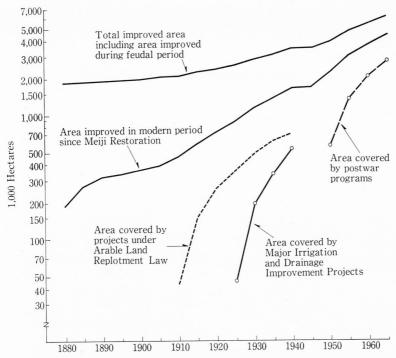

Figure 7–1.   Changes in areas covered by land-infrastructure improvement projects, semi-log scale.

SOURCE: Appendix Table A-10.

the area to be covered by the projects was obtained. By nature, it represents an institutional innovation similar to the Enclosure Acts in England.

The Arable Land Replotment Law, as enacted in 1899, was concerned primarily with the replotment of irregular small-sized fields into more efficient units. The revisions in 1905 and 1909 changed the major focus of the law to irrigation and drainage projects. In fact, the majority of the projects enforced by the law (about 80 percent of the area covered) had the purpose of improving the water-control systems.[2]

Projects under the Arable Land Replotment Law were carried out by the land-improvement associations organized under the leadership of landlords. The scale of the projects usually covered about 30 to 40 hectares. The government encouraged the activities of those associations by granting subsidies and advancing low-interest loans.

However, such relatively small associations had neither sufficient power nor resources to undertake larger-scale projects involving major canals and reservoirs. Without the construction of major systems, profitable opportunities for smaller projects would have been exhausted soon. In order to fill this gap the Rules of Subsidization of Irrigation and Drainage Projects was promulgated in 1923. The Rules authorized the central government to give a 50 percent subsidy to the prefectural governments that would agree to undertake projects for improving major irrigation and drainage systems on a scale of more than 500 hectares. The progress of the large-scale public projects under this rule, which is usually called the " Major Irrigation and Drainage Improvement Projects," is shown in Figure 7–1.

In order to meet the rising demand for food during World War II, the government's efforts toward infrastructure-improvement were strengthened. The Farmland Development Corporation was established in 1941 to carry out major land-improvement projects. A ten-year plan was drafted to improve 1.5 million hectares, in addition to developing a half million hectares of new land for cultivation. However, the growing shortage of manpower and materials brought the progress of the projects to a stop.

After the war, the government's efforts were further strengthened under the keen food shortage. The Farmland Development Corporation was abolished and its function was transferred to the Ministry of Agriculture and Forestry. The land-improvement projects promoted by the government, directly or indirectly by means of subsidy and credit, covered as much as 1.6 million hectares of paddy-field area from 1946 to 1957.

7-2 Mechanisms for Inducing Investment in Land Infrastructure

We will now investigate the economic and political forces underlying the trend in the progress of land-infrastructure improvement observed in the previous section.

The first question to be raised is why the investment in land infrastructure was accelerated in the 1910's. It is true that the acceleration was facilitated by an institutional innovation in the form of the Arable Land Replotment Law. What, then, were the factors that induced this institutional innovation? The immediate cause for the enactment of the law in 1899 was public concern about national security arising from the fact that Japan had become a net importer of rice since the Sino-Japanese War (1894–1895). However, it appears that more basic was the growing recognition of the fact that land infrastructure had become the major constraint on the growth of rice yields.

As observed in previous chapters (especially chapters 2 and 5), the development and diffusion of the seed-fertilizer technology had begun more than two decades earlier than the acceleration of the land-infrastructure investment. Figure 7–2 shows that, while both the ratio of the rice area planted in improved varieties and the

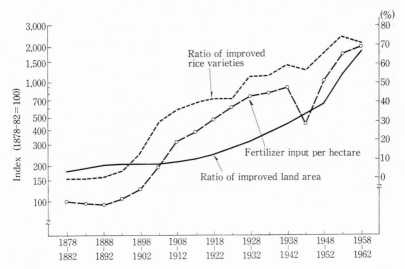

Figure 7–2. Trends in index of fertilizer input per hectare of arable land (1878–1887 = 100), semi-log scale, compared with those in the ratio of area planted in improved rice varieties to total area planted in rice and the ratio of improved land area in total arable land (%), five-year averages.

SOURCE: Table 7–1; and Yujiro Hayami and V. W. Ruttan, *Agricultural Development: An International Perspective* (Baltimore and London: Johns Hopkins University Press, 1971), p. 341.

fertilizer input per hectare began to rise parallel around 1890, the ratio of improved land area to total arable land area stayed more or less stable until the 1910's.

The lag of land-infrastructure investment behind the development of the seed-fertilizer technology can be explained by the feudal heritage of land infrastructure. It appears that by the beginning of the modern era the irrigation and drainage systems in the advanced areas in Japan, such as Kinki and North Kyushu, had been developed sufficiently to introduce high-yielding fertilizer-responsive varieties. Land infrastructure was not a factor that seriously impeded development of seed-fertilizer technology. However, it was inevitable that land infrastructure became the major constraint on rice production as the diffusion of the technology approached the limit of area endowed with adequate water-control facilities. When land infrastructure became the bottleneck in rice production, the anxiety for food self-sufficiency (in terms of national security considerations) worked as an effective device for focusing public attention on the need for public investments and institutional innovations to mitigate the constraint. This represents a case of dynamic sequences in inducing technical and institutional changes through imbalance or disequilibrium inherent in the process of economic development.[3]

Perhaps an even more basic factor underlying the acceleration in the investment in land infrastructure was the increasing relative scarcity of arable land. Although Japan was densely populated by the beginning of modern economic growth, there still remained a little room for expansion of the area for cultivation, mainly in Hokkaido and Tohoku. But, such a slack had been exhausted by the 1910's, as shown in Figure 7–3. It is interesting to note that the acceleration in land-infrastructure improvement coincided with the halt of expansion in cultivated land area. This fact seems to imply that the acceleration in land-infrastructure investment following the Arable Land Replotment Law represented a response of both private and public agents to the increasing scarcity of land.

The Arable Land Replotment Law was designed to facilitate the cooperation of farmers and landlords in mobilizing their resources for the construction of land infrastructure by whip (compulsion) and carrot (subsidy and low-interest loans). On the

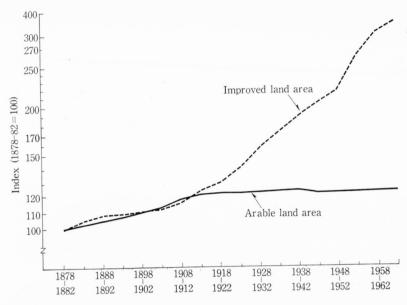

Figure 7–3. Trends in indices of arable land area and improved land area, five-year averages, semi-log scale.

SOURCE: Appendix Tables A-4 and A-10.

other hand, the Rules of Subsidization of Irrigation and Drainage Projects was designed to counteract the decreasing returns to small-scale local projects by public investments on large-scale overhead projects.

The inducement effect of such institutional innovations and public investments on the mobilization of local resources and initiatives are clearly visible in the trend in the area planned for projects under the Arable Land Replotment Law (dotted line in Figure 7–4). The planned area began to rise gradually from 1900, the first year following the enactment of the law; it rose appreciably from 1905 to 1906 and, again, from 1910 to 1911, in response to revisions in the law in 1904 and 1909. After 1911 the annual increase in the planned area began to decline, presumably reflecting the gradual exhaustion of opportunities for profitable small-scale projects. But, as public investments in the major systems were increased with the promulgation of the Rules of Subsidization in 1923, annual increases in the planned area began to rise again,

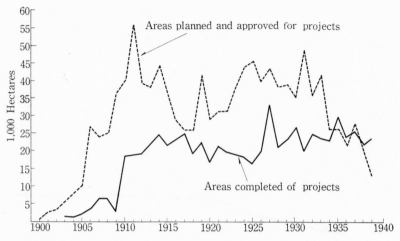

Figure 7-4. Annual changes in areas planned for and completed of land-improvement projects under Arable Land Replotment Law.
SOURCE: Ministry of Agriculture, *Dai 16-Ji Kochi Kairyo Jigyo Yoran* (16th Report on Arable Land Expansion and Improvement Projects), (Tokyo, 1941), pp. 9–10.

Table 7-2. Investments in Improvement in Land Infrastructure, 1934–1936 Constant Prices, Five-year Averages

	Investment in Land Infrastructure		Ratio of Government to Total Investment (2)/(1)
	Total (1)	Government Investment[a] (2)	
	·········million *yen*·········		%
1903–1907	23.2	5.2	22.4
1908–1912	51.6	8.7	16.9
1913–1917	72.0	10.6	14.7
1918–1922	87.8	16.2	18.5
1923–1927	135.2	26.5	19.6
1928–1932	174.8	45.0	25.7
1933–1937	158.3	49.2	31.1
1938–1942	75.0	30.4	40.5
1948–1952	568.3	358.2	63.0
1953–1957	728.5	443.2	60.8
1958–1962	979.1	671.8	68.6

[a] Includes both national and prefectural governments.
SOURCE: National Research Institute of Agriculture, *Tochi Kairyo Toshi no Suikei* (Estimates of Land Improvement Investment), Long-Term Statistics of Japanese Agriculture Series, No. 1 (Tokyo, 1967), mimeo. pp. 24–29, 32–33, and 42–44.

reflecting perhaps a process by which government investments induced group actions in the villages for mobilizing local resources in the construction of rural infrastructure.

In the course of history we observe that the role of the public sector in the formation of land infrastructure has a tendency to increase relative to the role of the private sector. This tendency is demonstrated by the increase in the government share in the total investment in land infrastructure (Table 7–2). To a large extent, the declining role of the private sector should be attributable to the decline in local entrepreneurship and initiative corresponding to the transformation from " innovative landlords " to " parasitic landlords " and, further, to the dissolution of landlordism by the postwar land reform.

However, a more basic factor underlying the increasing role of the public sector may be identified as the secular tendency of decreasing returns to small-scale projects, accompanied by the exhaustion of profitable opportunities. In such a situation, the amount of public investment in larger projects required to induce a unit of private investment should have increased. It appears that this process was parallel to the increase in the role of public-supported research in the development of agricultural technology, corresponding to the exhaustion of the backlog of indigenous technological potential embodied in the veteran farmers (see chapters 3 and 5).

7-3 Costs and Benefits of Land-Infrastructure Improvement

The process of investment-inducement for the improvement in land infrastructure, as hypothesized in the previous section, implies high rates of returns to the land-improvement projects. We will now try to estimate the costs and benefits of land-infrastructure improvements for the prewar period as a test of the investment-inducement hypothesis. In so doing we attempt to demonstrate the critical importance of complementarity between land infrastructure and seed-fertilizer technology in Japan's agricultural development.

Method and data

The approach adopted here involves the estimation of simple cost/benefit ratios, using the national aggregate time-series data for 1902–1937. The cost/benefit ratio is defined as the cost of land-infrastructure improvement required to produce one *yen* of income or value added in agriculture.

The available cost data of land-infrastructure improvement are those in the plans of the land-improvement projects that were approved by the Ministry of Agriculture and Forestry. They are not the costs actually incurred in the projects but are the estimates by engineers. It can be expected that such data are subject to both estimational errors and time lags. However, they should reflect fairly accurately the broad trends in the costs of land-improvement projects. Considering the nature of the data, we based our analysis on five-year moving averages instead of the annual observations presented in column (1) of Table 7–3.

Corresponding increases in agricultural income due to land-infrastructure improvement are estimated in Table 7–4 for different levels of rice technology. The first two of these levels assume

Table 7–3. Capital Costs of Land-Infrastructure Improvement per Hectare and Annual Flow Costs of Land Infrastructure Required to Produce one *yen* of Agricultural Income for Various Assumptions on Rice Technology, 1934–1936 Constant Prices

	Capital Cost per Hectare[a] (1)	Flow Cost per *yen* of Income[b]			
		Traditional		HYV	
		40N (2)	80N (3)	80N (4)	120N (5)
	yen/ha.	····························· *yen*/*yen* ·····························			
1902	459	0.59	0.43		
1903	490	0.63	0.45		
1904	452	0.58	0.42		
1905	410	0.53	0.38		
1906	405	0.52	0.38		
1907	499	0.64	0.46		
1908	504	0.65	0.47		
1909	548	0.70	0.51		
1910	576	0.74	0.53		

Table 7-3.   (Continued)

	Capital Cost per Hectare[a] (1)	Flow Cost per *yen* of Income[b]			
		Traditional		HYV	
		40N (2)	80N (3)	80N (4)	120N (5)
1911	596	0.76	0.55		
1912	563	0.72	0.52		
1913	607	0.78	0.56		
1914	649	0.83	0.60		
1915	648	0.83	0.60		
1916	634	0.81	0.59		
1917	599	0.77	0.55		
1918	615	0.79	0.57		
1919	646	0.83	0.60		
1920	689	0.88	0.64	0.47	0.43
1921	719	0.92	0.67	0.49	0.45
1922	732	0.94	0.68	0.49	0.45
1923	707	0.91	0.65	0.48	0.44
1924	655	0.84	0.61	0.44	0.41
1925	654	0.84	0.61	0.44	0.41
1926	680	0.87	0.63	0.46	0.42
1927	716	0.92	0.66	0.48	0.44
1928	736	0.94	0.68	0.50	0.46
1929	756	0.97	0.70	0.51	0.47
1930	770	0.99	0.71	0.52	0.48
1931	719	0.92	0.67	0.49	0.45
1932	685	0.88	0.63	0.46	0.43
1933	656	0.84	0.61	0.44	0.41
1934	707	0.91	0.65	0.48	0.44
1935	638	0.82	0.59	0.43	0.40
1936	629	0.81	0.58	0.43	0.39
1937	627	0.80	0.58	0.42	0.39

[a] Planned costs per hectare of designed area deflated by the price index of land-infrastructure construction, five-year moving averages.

[b] Annual flow costs per hectare (10 percent of capital costs) divided by increase in income per hectare (Table 7-4).

SOURCE: Capital costs per hectare in current prices are from Ministry of Agriculture and Forestry, *Dai 16-Ji Kochi Kairyo Jigyo Yoran* (16th Report on Arable Land Expansion and Improvement Projects), (Tokyo, 1941), pp. 9-11.   The deflator is from National Research Institute of Agriculture, *Tochi Kairyo Toshi no Suikei* (Estimates of Land Improvement Investment), Long-Term Statistics of Japanese Agriculture Series, No. 1 (Tokyo, 1967), mimeo, pp. 146-149.

the use of traditional varieties with the application of 40 and 80 kilograms of nitrogen per hectare, respectively. The second two levels assume the use of improved high-yielding varieties (HYV's) with the application of 80 and 120 kilograms of nitrogen, respectively.

In order to estimate the rice yield per hectare for different levels of technology, we need to specify the response curves of rice yields to nitrogen by different varieties. The most reliable estimate of the nitrogen-response curve for our purpose is the estimate by Goro Matsuki, which is based on the results of nitrogen-application tests for improved rice varieties conducted at the experiment stations in as many as thirty-seven prefectures during the 1920's. Matsuki's estimate is given as

$$Y = 2889 + 25N^2, \qquad R^2 = 0.972$$

where Y and N denote, respectively, rice yield and nitrogen input in kilograms per hectare.[4]

Considering the yield differences between experimental fields and farmers' fields, we estimated the nitrogen-response function faced by farmers who were planting HYV's in improved paddy fields, by shifting down Matsuki's response curve by 20 percent.[5] The response curve of traditional varieties in improved fields is estimated by assuming that the yield of the HYV's was the same as that of traditional varieties at zero level of N but 3 percent higher with the application of 40 kilograms of N and 6 percent higher with the application of 80 kilograms.[6] Finally, the response curve of traditional varieties in unimproved fields is estimated by assuming that it was located 10 percent below the response curve of traditional varieties planted in improved fields.[7] The nitrogen-response curves, thus specified, are shown in Table 7–4.

The rice yields derived from the response curves for different levels of nitrogen input are multiplied by the average price of rice at the farm gate for 1934–1936 to arrive at the value of the rice output. Correspondingly, the costs of intermediate current inputs are estimated as 30 percent larger than the costs of nitrogen inputs obtained by multiplying the nitrogen inputs by the average price of nitrogen for 1934–1936.[8] Improvements in irrigation and drainage facilities enable the saving of labor required for water control. Also, consolidation of small irregular fields into a large

Table 7-4. Estimates of Increase in Agricultural Income per Hectare due to Improvement in Land Infrastucture for Various Assumptions on Rice Technology, 1934–1936 Constant Prices

| Levels of Technology | Nitrogen Input N (1) | Rice Yield[a] Y (2) | Increase in Value of | | Value of Labor Saved[d] (5) | Increase in Income (6)=(3)−(4)+(5) |
			Rice Output[b] (3)	Intermediate Cost[c] (4)		
		······kg./ha.········	··yen/ha.··			
Unimproved land:						
Traditional varieties						
N=40 kg.	40	2,610	—	—	—	—
Improved land:						
Traditional varieties						
N=40 kg.	40	2,908	54	0	24	78
N=80 kg.	80	3,258	118	34	24	108
High-yielding varieties						
N= 80 kg.	80	3,476	158	24	24	148
N=120 kg.	120	3,732	205	68	24	161

[a] Derived from the response functions:

Traditional varieties in unimproved land: $Y = 2080 + 16N - 0.069N^2$

Traditional varieties in improved land: $Y = 2311 + 18N - 0.077N^2$

High-yielding varieties in improved land: $Y = 2311 + 20N - 0.068N^2$

[b] Assume: 1 kg. of rice=0.183 yen.

[c] Assume: 1 kg. of N=0.65 yen; and total intermediate cost=1.3 × nitrogen cost.

[d] Assume: Saving of labor due to land improvement=30 man-days/ha.; and 1 man-day=0.8 yen.

regular unit results in increased work efficiency in farm operations. Here we assume that the efficiency increase had, on the average, the effect of saving thirty man-days of farm labor per hectare.[9]

Increases in agricultural income due to improvement in land infrastructure were estimated by subtracting the increases in intermediate costs from the sums of increases in rice output and savings of labor, as shown in Table 7–4.[10] The gains in income due to land-infrastructure improvement in Table 7–4 may be underestimated because the effects of land-infrastructure improvement in facilitating the diffusion of double cropping and the introduction of horse ploughing are not included.

The cost/benefit ratios, defined as the costs of land-infrastructure improvement to produce one *yen* of agricultural income, are calculated in columns (2)–(5) of Table 7–3 by dividing the costs of land-infrastructure improvement in annual flow terms by the estimates of increases in agricultural income. The annual flow costs are converted from the capital costs of land-improvement projects, presented in column (1) of Table 7–3, by assuming a 10 percent interest rate. The operation and maintenance expenses are not included because of the lack of data. The resultant underestimation in the flow costs might, however, be canceled by the possible underestimation in income gains due to land-infrastructure improvements in the calculation of the cost/benefit ratios.

It must be emphasized that the cost/benefit ratios, thus calculated, represent very crude approximations and are only useful as an indicator of the broadest trends in changes in the marginal cost of land infrastructure required to produce an additional *yen* of value added in agriculture for different levels of rice technology.

Findings

The trends in the cost/benefit ratios for the different levels of rice technology estimated in Table 7–3 are plotted in Figure 7–5. The upper curve marked as " Traditional 40 N " indicates the trend of the cost of land-infrastructure improvement that would have been required to produce an additional *yen* of income in agriculture if the improved area were planted in traditional varieties with the application of 40 kilograms of nitrogen per

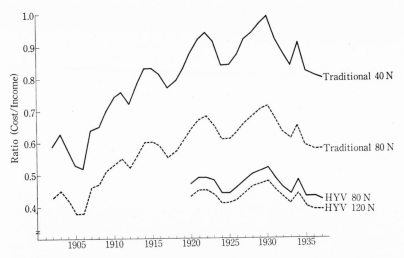

Figure 7–5.   Trends in costs of land-infrastructure improvement required
to produce one *yen* of agricultural income under alternative levels of
rice technology, five-year moving averages.
SOURCE: Table 7–3.

hectare. The lower curves designated as " Traditional 80 N,"
" HYV 80 N," and " HYV 120 N " represent the costs per *yen* of
incremental value added in agriculture for the alternative assumptions about the varieties planted and the levels of nitrogen
application.

For the first three decades of this century a dramatic rising trend
can be observed in the ratio of land-improvement cost over incremental value added for the same variety and the same fertilizer-
application level. In the case of " Traditional 40 N," the ratio
rose from about 0.5 in 1905 to almost 1 in 1930. This means
that at the beginning of the nineteenth century one *yen* spent for
improvement in land infrastructure generated an income of
nearly two *yen*, whereas in 1930 the cost of one *yen* generated an
income of only one *yen*.

The rising trend in the cost/benefit ratio or the declining trend
in the rate of returns under constant technology seems to reflect
the sharp rise in the real cost of construction of land infrastructure
corresponding to the exhaustion of relatively easy (hence inexpen-
sive) projects.

The above observations indicate that, if the variety and the fertilizer-application level had remained unchanged, the income to be generated from land-improvement projects would have declined to a level that would have barely covered cost. Then, the incentive to increase rice output by investing in irrigation and drainage systems would have been entirely lost.

In reality, however, the improvement in the water-control systems increased the profitability of applying more fertilizer and of introducing the high-yielding varieties, thereby inducing the development and diffusion of the seed-fertilizer technology. As a result, the real cost of land-infrastructure improvement required to produce an additional *yen* of income would have been lowered, as demonstrated by the shift of the " Traditional 40 N " curve down to the " HYV 120 N " curve.

However, the possibility of lowering the cost/benefit schedule would have been limited if left to the efforts of farmers alone. Corresponding to the improvements in irrigation and drainage systems, the farmers could have applied more fertilizers and introduced the better varieties available to them. However, such a dramatic cost reduction as illustrated by the shift from the " Traditional 40 N " curve to the " HYV 120 N " curve could not have been realized unless new varieties were developed that could exploit the full potential of the improved environmental conditions. For this purpose, research and development by public-supported experiment stations were required, in addition to the efforts of farmers, in the search for better varieties.

The social pay-off of conducting research for breeding varieties that would have high performance in the improved environmental conditions should have been very high. However, a substantial time lag was usually involved before such varieties were made available to farmers. Not only the breeding process itself but also redirection in the allocation of public-research resources required a large number of years.

It then appears likely that the possible increase in the rate of returns to land-infrastructure investments, due to the induced development of new varieties in the future, was beyond the scope of the planning horizon of farmers and landlords when they made the investment decisions. In such a situation it was inevitable that a gap would emerge between the expected private returns and the expected social returns to the investments in land infrastructure. The gap in the expected returns should have resulted in the divergence of private investment in land infrastructure from the socially optimum level, which would then have to be filled by the public sector.

It seems reasonable to hypothesize that the gap between the expected private and social rates of returns increased over time as the role of scientific research at the experiment stations increased beyond the experience of veteran farmers. The increasing trend in the share of government in land-infrastructure investment is explained by the increasing gap between the private and the social rates of returns, which resulted from the growing sophistication and maturity of scientific research in agriculture (see chapters 3 and 6).

With reference to Figure 7–4, we have previously hypothesized that a basic factor underlying the acceleration in land-infrastructure investment in the 1910's was a growing scarcity of land due to the exhaustion of possibilities for area expansion. The hypothesis may be restated: the investment in land infrastructure was induced because such investment began to produce higher returns than investment in the expansion of cultivated areas.

In order to test this hypothesis we have calculated the cost/benefit ratios for area expansion by the land-reclamation projects under government assistance compared to ratios of land improvement (Table 7–5). Unfortunately, data are available only for the period after the acceleration in land-infrastructure improvement.

The comparisons in Table 7–5 indicate that the cost required to produce an additional income of one *yen* was higher for land-infrastructure improvement than for land-area expansion when the traditional varieties were used. However, if the HYV's were introduced, the relative advantage would have been reversed, and it would have become more profitable to invest in increasing the quality of land than in expanding the land area.

If the development of HYV's that could fully exploit the advantage of improved irrigation and drainage systems was beyond the prediction of rice farmers and landlords, the improvement in land infrastructure would not have been as attractive to them. However, for public planners who had a longer planning horizon the improvement in land infrastructure should have represented

Table 7-5. Estimates of Costs of Arable-Land Area Expansion, Compared with Costs of Land-Infrastructure Improvement, to Produce one *yen* of Agricultural Income, 1934-1936 Constant Prices, Five-year Averages

| | Land Area Expansion | | | | | Land-Infrastructure Improvement Cost per *yen* of Income | | | |
| | Capital Cost per Hectare | Reclaimed Area | | Income per Hectare[a] | Cost per *yen* of Income[b] | Traditional | | HYV | |
		Paddy Field	Upland Field			40N	80N	80N	120N
	yen/ha.	......1000 ha.......		*yen*/ha.	....	............*yen*/*yen*............			
1918-1922	1,954	10.8	2.5	311	0.63	0.88	0.64	0.47	0.43
1923-1927	1,664	24.7	5.8	311	0.54	0.84	0.61	0.44	0.41
1928-1932	1,573	15.2	10.6	264	0.60	0.99	0.71	0.52	0.48
1933-1937	1,754	10.3	9.8	248	0.71	0.82	0.59	0.43	0.40

a Weighted averages of paddy and upland field incomes estimated by assuming that the rice yield in the reclaimed paddy fields was 15 *koku* per *chō* (2269 kg. per ha.) with the value added ratio of 0.8, and that the income from upland fields was 60 percent smaller than from paddy fields.

b Annual flow costs per ha. (10 percent of capital costs) divided by increases in income per ha.

SOURCE: Data of area expansion are from Ministry of Agriculture and Forestry, *Dai 16-Ji Kochi Kairyo Jigyo Yoran* (Tokyo, 1941), pp. 142-43. The cost/benefit ratios of land improvement are from Table 7-3.

more attractive investment opportunities than the expansion of area under cultivation. Here, there was another rationale or incentive for the public sector to assist in land-infrastructure improvement programs. Such an inference should, however, be taken with strong reservations, considering the quality of data.[11]

7-4 A Perspective on the Development of Seed-Fertilizer Technology

The analysis in this chapter indicates that the development of seed-fertilizer technology, which was the key to growth in agricultural productivity in Japan, was induced through a dynamic interaction among farmers, landlords, and public agents in solving the imbalance or disequilibrium between technology and land infrastructure.

The initial progress in seed-fertilizer technology in the early Meiji period, based primarily on the initiatives of innovative farmers and landlords in exploiting the indigenous potential, was facilitated by the feudal heritage of a relatively well developed irrigation system. However, as better varieties were diffused rapidly and fertilizer-input levels were raised, land infrastructure became the major bottleneck in rice production. The growing imbalance increased the rate of returns to investment in land infrastructure, inducing public investments as well as institutional innovations in the form of the Arable Land Replotment Law designed to facilitate the organization of farmers in the construction of land infrastructure. The progress in improvements in irrigation and drainage systems induced the development of more fertilizer-responsive higher-yielding varieties. Such varieties were effective in counteracting the rising costs of irrigation and drainage construction, thereby maintaining investment incentives. If there were no induced development in technology, the contribution of land-infrastructure improvement to agricultural growth should have been very small.

The divergence between the expected private returns and the social returns to investment in land infrastructure increased, corresponding to a rise in the role of scientific research at agricultural experiment stations. As the process of technological development became more sophisticated and round-about, it became more difficult for farmers and landlords to consider the effects of future progress in agricultural technology on the rate of returns to investments in land infrastructure. The gap between the private and the socially optimum levels of investment in land-improvement projects had to be filled by the public sector. The government investments in large-scale overhead projects were especially effective in creating profitable opportunities for small-scale projects, thereby stimulating the mobilization of private resources for improvement in land infrastructure.

Of course, it is unlikely that government administrators and planners in Japan were so perceptive as to recognize the gap between the private and the social returns as such. The immediate momentum for enacting the Arable Land Replotment Law in 1899 was the issue of public concern for food self-sufficiency, needed for national security. In the case of the Rules of Subsidization of Irrigation and Drainage Projects in 1923, the momentum was high food prices due to the boom of World War I and the Rice Riot in 1918. The extensive land-improvement programs in the early post-World War II period were introduced under the pressure of acute food shortages. However, irrespective of what the immediate focusing devices were, we should not overlook the basic economic forces operating below the surface that induced public investments and institutional changes.

The dramatic development and diffusion of high-yielding varieties in the countries of South and Southeast Asia since the mid-1960's imply that these countries have begun to follow a route of agricultural development similar to the history of Japan. It has been recognized that the lack of adequate irrigation systems in these countries represents the major constraint on current progress in seed-fertilizer technology.

Compared with developing countries in Asia today, Japanese agriculture at the beginning of modern economic growth was favored by a feudal heritage of irrigation infrastructure, which was sufficient for initial development of the seed-fertilizer technology. As a result, the resource requirements for growth in agricultural productivity were relatively minor in the early phase of industrialization and economic growth. Such experience represents a sharp contrast to the present conditions in South and Southeast Asia, where the large capital outlay required for building an adequate irrigation infrastructure is likely to cause a serious drain on scarce government funds for economic development.[12]

This condition may be aggravated by the fact that agricultural research leading to the development of high-yielding varieties in Asia today is so highly sophisticated that it is impossible for farmers to predict the future impacts of such research. Consequently, the gap between the expected private returns and the social returns to irrigation investments tends to be wide open. In such a situation, government funds required for attaining socially optimum levels of irrigation investments will be extremely large. Moreover, the tendency of public investments to concentrate on large-scale overhead projects will tend to cause a drain on foreign exchange by increasing the requirements for modern machines and materials produced in the developed countries.

The requirements of public funds and foreign exchange for providing necessary irrigation infrastructure may be so large that they will exceed the limits that governments in the developing countries might be able to mobilize under present political and administrative structures. In order to meet the requirements, the critical need seems to be for institutional innovations that facilitate the mobilization of local private resources for reducing the gap between the expected private and the social rates of returns to irrigation investments

The need for foreign aid and credit for irrigation projects will continue to rise. It is unlikely, however, that they can be a substitute for local resources. Rather, it appears that foreign resources can really be effective only when they are complemented by institutional innovations that contribute to increases in local initiatives.

Notes to Chapter 7

[1] It is likely that the initial stock of land infrastructure was larger than that suggested by this estimate, because it does not include: (*a*) minor irrigation systems based on miscellaneous water resources, such as wells and natural ponds, and (*b*) irrigation systems with dates of construction unknown. It is safe to consider that at least some sorts of irrigation facilities were built in almost all lowland paddy fields in Japan at the beginning of the Meiji period, even though many of them were highly insufficient.

[2] Nogyo Hattatsushi Chosakai, *Nihon Nogyo Hattatsushi* (History of Japanese Agricultural Development, vol. 4 (Tokyo: Chuokoronsha, 1954), p. 225.

[3] See Yujiro Hayami and V. W. Ruttan, *Agricultural Development: An International Perspective* (Baltimore and London: Johns Hopkins University Press, 1971), pp. 61–63.

[4] Goro Matsuki, *Suito no Hibai* (Fertilizer Application to Lowland Rice), (Tokyo: Tokyo Shobo, 1943), p. 61.

[5] We assume that the average rice yields per hectare on farms were about 20 to 30 percent lower than the average yields at the experiment stations. See Table 3 of Yujiro Hayami and Saburo Yamada, "Agricultural Productivity at the Beginning of Industrialization," in *Agriculture and Economic Development: Japan's Experience*, eds. Kazushi Ohkawa, B. F. Johnston, and Hiromitsu Kaneda (Tokyo: University of Tokyo Press, 1969), pp. 324–351.

[6] This assumption is based on observations of the results of a large number of comparative rice-yield tests used for the estimation of the k's in chapter 6, section 6–3.

[7] A survey of the Ministry of Agriculture and Forestry reported that the average increase in rice yield in the 23 districts improved by the projects under the Arable Land Replotment Law was 0.4 *koku* per *tan*, or by 29 percent. Taichi Uzaki estimated that 0.16 *koku* out of the 0.4 *koku* of yield increase was brought about by the increases in fertilizer inputs and the remaining 0.24 *koku* resulted from improvements in land infrastructure. Uzaki's estimates imply that the rate of increase in rice yield due to land-infrastructure improvements was 12 percent. Here we adopt 10 percent for the rate of yield increase, in order to avoid the possible overestimation of benefits produced from the land-infrastructure investments. See Ministry of Agriculture and Forestry, *Kochi Seiri Jigyo ni kansuru Keizai Chosa* (Economic Survey of the Arable Land Replotment Law Project), (Tokyo, 1931); and Taichi Uzaki, *Nogyo Doboki Gyosei* (Civil Engineering Administration in Agriculture), (Tokyo: Shozanbo, 1941), p. 34.

[8] The prices of rice and nitrogen are from Kazushi Ohkawa et al., eds., *Long-term Economic Statistics of Japan* (Tokyo, Toyokeizaishimposha), vol. 8 (1967), p. 170, and vol. 9 (1966), p. 203. The ratio of the cost of nitrogen in the total intermediate current-input cost is calculated from the data of rice-production cost surveys for 1934–1936, which are compiled in Yukio Ishibashi, *Teikoku Nokai Kome Seisanhi Chosa Shusei* (Compilation of Rice Production Cost Survey by the Imperial Agricultural Association), (Tokyo: National Research Institute of Agriculture, 1961), pp. 120–127.

[9] Based on Ministry of Agriculture and Forestry, *Kochi Seiri Jigyo ni kansuru Keizai Chosa.*

[10] "Agricultural income" used here is equivalent to "gross value added," because of the depreciation of farm capital.

[11] The costs of area expansion for cultivation are difficult to estimate conceptually as well as statistically. It is likely that the cost/benefit ratios for area expansion are substantially underestimated, because the cost data used in this study include only the direct costs of converting wild land into cultivated land and do not include the costs of immigration and settlement into new land.

[12] This is one of the major themes of the challenging book by Shigeru Ishikawa, *Economic Development in Asian Perspective* (Tokyo: Kinokuniya, 1967).

Part 4 Significance of Growth

Chapter 8

Implications of the Japanese
Experience

8-1　Summary of Findings

The major findings of our explorations into the sources of
agricultural growth in Japan may be summarized as follows:

1.　Over the period from the 1880's to the 1960's, which covers
nearly the whole period of modern economic growth in Japan,
agricultural output increased more than four times, at the annual
compound rate of 1.6 percent. Meanwhile, two primary inputs,
labor and land, remained relatively stable. Capital stock grew
rather slowly before World War II and began to rise at a dramatic
speed in the mid-1950's, corresponding to the progress in mechanization due to a reduction in the labor force in agriculture. The
rates of increases in current inputs, especially fertilizers, far exceeded those in other inputs. The rates of increase in the different
categories of inputs are inversely associated with the changes in
their prices relative to the price of farm products. Overall, the
rate of growth in the aggregate of conventional factor inputs was
only about one-half of that in output, implying that the other half
of the output growth resulted from an increase in total factor
productivity or, stated more correctly, is left unexplained by the
increase in conventional inputs.

2.　The rates of growth in agricultural output, inputs, and
productivities differ among periods. Output increased relatively
faster and at an accelerating rate from the 1880's to the 1910's;

then it slipped into stagnation until the 1930's. After the devastation of World War II, Japanese agriculture recovered quickly and
sustained rapid growth in output even after the recovery was
completed in the mid-1950's. Such distinct phases in agricultural-
output growth were not explained by changes in the rates of
increase in conventional inputs; large residuals, unexplained by
the growth in inputs, remained for the initial growth and the
postwar growth phases, and the interwar stagnation phase is
characterized by a small residual. In other words, the growth
phases of Japanese agriculture resulted primarily from changes in
the rate of growth in total factor productivity.

3.   Except for the recent decade, characterized by a rapid
reduction in the agricultural labor force, land has represented the
major limiting factor of agricultural production in Japan. Agricultural growth against the land-resource constraint was possible
by increasing the productivity of land. In fact, about 70 percent
of the growth in agricultural output per worker was brought about
by an increase in output per hectare of cultivated land area.
Parallel movements in total productivity and land productivity,
especially in the prewar period, suggest that the major growth
element in total factor productivity was technological progress
oriented toward saving land or increasing output per unit of land
area.

4.   It was hypothesized that the residual in agricultural output
growth or the increase in total factor productivity represents an
error due to: (a) the neglect of nonconventional factors, such as
rural education and agricultural research, that increase the
efficiency of farm producers and improve the technology applied
to agricultural production; and (b) the use of factor shares as
weights for the aggregation of conventional factor inputs, which do
not accurately reflect the contributions of those factors to output.
Attempts were made to include in the accounting of agricultural
output and productivity growth such nonconventional factors as
education of farm people, public expenditures on agricultural
research and extension, and improvements in land infrastructure.
Also, the production elasticities estimated from the cross-prefectural data were used as weights for aggregating both conventional and nonconventional inputs, in order to reduce the aggrega-
tional errors. By such attempts we were successful in reducing the

residual in the secular growth in output for the whole period or the whole prewar period to a negligible level. However, we were not successful in explaining the emergence of distinct growth phases; positive residuals remain for the initial growth and the postwar growth phases, while a negative residual emerges for the interwar stagnation phase.

5. The sources of the growth phases were explored in terms of the analysis of interregional diffusion of rice technology based on prefectural rice-yield data. The results of the analysis were consistent with the hypothesis that the rapid growth in productivity in the initial phase was supported by the backlog of technological potential accumulated during the feudal Tokugawa period, which was quickly exploited when the feudal constraints on farming innovations were removed after the Meiji Restoration. The major cause of the interwar stagnation was identified as the exhaustion of this backlog before the modern system of agricultural research and experiment began to supply new potential; and the spurt in agricultural productivity growth for the postwar period was explained by the backlog of new technological potential, gradually accumulated from the interwar to the war periods, which was dammed from diffusion due to the shortage of complementary inputs, such as fertilizers. The necessary condition for exploitation of the backlog of potential was identified as public investments in agricultural research and land infrastructure.

6. Agricultural research is an activity for producing technical information useful to agricultural production, which is typically endowed with attributes of the public goods, such as indivisibility, externality, and jointness in supply and utilization. An efficient supply of the agricultural-research product can hardly be expected if it is left to the private market mechanism, especially in agriculture characterized by a mass of small-scale farms, as is the case in Japan. Such "market failure" must be corrected by public support to agricultural-research and development activities. As a matter of fact, agricultural research in Japan has been dominated by public institutions, including both the national and the prefectural agricultural-experiment stations. The question arises as to whether government expenditures on agricultural research can be justified on the grounds of social benefits relative to social costs. The case study of rice-breeding research in the

history of Japan indicates that investment in agricultural research was indeed a lucrative investment opportunity to society in terms of the social rate of returns. Moreover, it was found that financing agricultural research out of tax revenue can be justified because the major gains from the research were captured by the consumers in the form of an increase in consumers' surplus or were used as fuel for overall economic development by contributing to foreign exchange. It appears that government investment in agricultural research in the course of modern economic growth in Japan was induced by such a high social pay-off. An interesting finding was that the social rate of returns to rice-breeding research was increased by the reorganization of the research system into a national-prefectural coordinated system, called the Assigned Experiment System, which aimed at solving the conflict between the scale economies in research and the location-specific nature of agricultural technology.

7.   Land infrastructure, such as irrigation and drainage facilities, represents another basic condition for the development and diffusion of location-specific agricultural technology. It is endowed with the attributes of the public goods, similar to the products of agricultural research. However, the public-goods characteristics are much weaker in the case of land infrastructure, and it is easier to exclude from the use of the irrigation and drainage systems those who do not share the costs. Therefore, group action of farm producers is equally or more important than government investments in land infrastructure. Improvement in land infrastructure played a critical role in Japanese agricultural development because of its inherent complementarity with the seed-fertilizer technology. In the growth-accounting analysis based on the assumption of independence and separability among various factors, the role of land-infrastructure improvement was underestimated. The rate of returns to the investment in land infrastructure becomes larger as we incorporate the complementarity aspects. We identified the basis of the development and diffusion of the seed-fertilizer technology in Japan from the early Meiji period as the relatively well developed irrigation system inherited from the feudal Tokugawa period. However, by the beginning of this century land infrastructure had become a major bottleneck for further progress in seed-fertilizer technology. In

order to solve the bottleneck, institutional innovation designed to facilitate the group action of farmers and landlords was developed in the form of the Arable Land Replotment Law. Group action for improvements in land infrastructure was also supported by government investments. The costs of land-infrastructure improvement rose sharply corresponding to the expansion of improved areas. Decline in the rate of returns to land-infrastructure investments, resulting from rising construction costs, was counteracted by the induced development of the seed-fertilizer technology. Government investments were effective in closing the gap between the private and the social rates of returns to investments in land infrastructure.

8-2 Resource Endowments and Technical Change

Perhaps the most significant aspect in the agricultural-development experience in Japan, relevant to the developing countries in Asia today, are the ways in which agricultural technology was developed in a manner consistent with the resource endowments of the economy.

From the beginning of modern economic growth at the Meiji Restoration, Japanese agriculture was characterized by a very unfavorable land/man ratio, even when compared with the densely populated areas of South and Southeast Asia (Table 1–2). Because the possibility of area expansion was limited, agricultural growth was brought about primarily by the increase in output per unit of cultivated land area through innovations of the land-saving type. The core of the land-saving innovations was the development of biological technology in the form of high-yielding varieties of major cereal crops, especially rice, complemented by improvement in land infrastructure, which facilitated the substitution of fertilizers for land in response to a rapid decline in fertilizer prices relative to land prices.

It was through such development in the seed-fertilizer technology that the productivity of Japanese agriculture grew at a rate sufficiently rapid to generate the agricultural surpluses that were used for financing industrialization and other modernization measures in the early stage of economic development. Overall, the requirements of the resources of high opportunity costs, such as capital and foreign exchange, for agricultural development in Japan seem relatively modest. Given the well-developed irrigation system inherited from the feudal Tokugawa period, the introduction of the seed-fertilizer technology at the farm level did not require large lump-sum investments. As a result, technical progress was neutral with respect to the scale of operation, or, rather, promoted the relative efficiency of the small-scale family farm, contributing, in turn, to the unimodal distribution of farm sizes.

Why is this experience of Japan relevant to the developing countries in Asia? These countries are now under an extremely strong population pressure against land. There exist wide variations in the relative endowments of land and labor among countries in Asia today. However, if the present rate of population growth, in the 2.5 to 3 percent range, is sustained, the population pressure in the rural sector will soon lead to a deterioration in the land/man ratio, at least in the short run, even in countries endowed with a relatively rich slack of unexploited land resources.

As the Ricardian model of economic growth and income distribution suggests, such a strong population pressure against limited land resources would lead to a rise in farm-product prices, resulting in a high cost of living for workers. This has the effect of pushing up the wage rate and lowering the rate of returns to industrial investments, thereby discouraging capital formation and economic growth.[1] The stagnation of the economy would then become inevitable unless the constraint of land on agricultural production is mitigated by progress in technology.

The Japanese experience in overcoming the land-resource constraint by developing a land-saving technology should be highly relevant, considering the present trends in relative resource endowments in the countries of Asia. Indeed, the Japanese experience in attaining a secular rise in the yields of staple cereal crops in a monsoon climate should be considered a forerunner of the recent development in the seed-fertilizer technology in tropical Asia heralded as the " green revolution."[2]

However, several critical differences between the historical experience of Japan and the present situation in Asia must not be

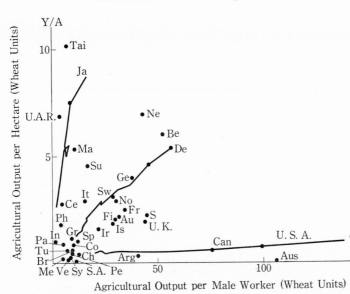

Figure 8-1. Historical growth paths of agricultural output per male farm worker and agricultural output per hectare of agricultural land area in Japan, Denmark, and the U.S.A. (1880–1965), in terms of quinquennial data, compared with intercountry cross-section data of 1960 (1957–1962 averages).

Key to symbols:

Argentina	Arg	Mauritius	Ma
Australia	Arg	Mexico	Me
Austria	Au	Netherlands	Ne
Belgium (and Luxemburg)	Be	New Zealand	N.Z.
Brazil	Br	Norway	No.
Canada	Can	Peru	Pe
Ceylon	Ce	South Africa	S.A.
Chile	Ch	Spain	Sp
Colombia	Co	Sweden	S
Denmark	De	Switzerland	Sw
Finland	Fi	Syria	Sy
France	Fr	Taiwan	Tai
Germany	Ge	Turkey	Tu
Greece	Gr	United Arab Republic	U.A.R.
India	In	United Kingdom	U.K.
Ireland	Ir	United States	U.S.A.
Italy	It	Venezuela	Ve
Japan	Ja		

SOURCE: Yujiro Hayami and V. W. Ruttan, *Agricultural Development: An International Perspective* (Baltimore and London: Johns Hopkins University Press, 1971), pp. 70 and 327–329. Japan's time series are revised according to the revised data in the appendix of this book.

overshadowed by an emphasis on the relevance of the Japanese experience. Viewed from the broad international perspective, the predominant contribution of agricultural growth in Japan was the increase in land productivity. As is clear from Figure 8–1, which compares the historical paths of agricultural productivity growth in Japan, Denmark, and the United States with the intercountry cross-section data for 1960 (1957–1962 averages), the Japanese growth path is indeed characterized by an extremely large gain in land productivity (Y/A) relative to the gain in labor productivity (Y/L). The Japanese experience represents a sharp contrast to the experience of U.S. agriculture, in which the increase in labor productivity (Y/L) was primarily brought about by an improvement in the land/man ratio (A/L) rather than by an increase in land productivity (Y/A).

It should be clear in terms of resource-endowment considerations that the Japanese experience is more relevant to Asia than to the United States or Denmark. Yet, it must be recognized that within the Asian perspective the Japanese experience is not typical, but rather unique. Figure 8–2 compares the agricultural-growth path of Japan with those of Taiwan, Korea, and the Philippines. While Japan's agricultural growth was accompanied by gradual improvements in the land/man ratio, Taiwan's growth was realized in spite of the constant or slightly deteriorating land/man ratio. Korea's growth path is more vertical than Taiwan's, implying a sharp decline in the land/man ratio.

The possibility of expanding the cultivation frontier was relatively great in Taiwan but was exhausted by the end of the 1920's. Given the limitation of area expansion the contrasting growth paths among the three countries resulted from differences in (a) population-growth rate and (b) the rate of labor-absorption in nonagriculture. Throughout the modern history of Japan the population-growth rate remained at a level of 1 percent per annum. In Taiwan it accelerated from 1 percent in the 1910's and the 1920's, to 2.5 percent in the 1930's, and 3 percent in the postwar period. In Korea it also began at 1 percent in the 1920's, increased to 2 percent in the 1930's, and jumped to the 3 percent level in the postwar period.

The progress of industrialization in Japan was sufficient to provide nonfarm employment for the increase in the total popula-

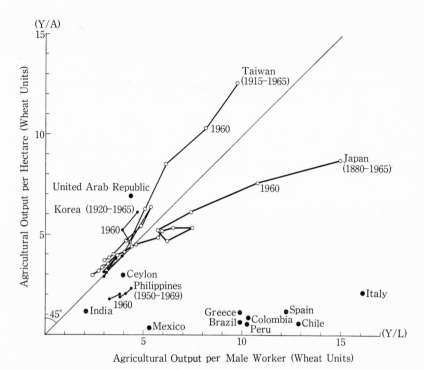

Figure 8–2. Historical growth paths of agricultural output per male farm worker and agricultural output per hectare of agricultural land in Japan, Taiwan, and Korea in terms of quinquennial time series data, compared with intercountry cross-section data of 1960 (1957–1962 averages).

SOURCE: Yujiro Hayami and V. W. Ruttan, "Agricultural Growth in Four Countries," in *Agricultural Growth in Japan, Taiwan, Korea and the Philippines*, eds. Yujiro Hayami, V. W. Ruttan, and Herman Southworth (Honolulu: University of Hawaii Press, 1975).

tion, with the result that the agricultural labor population held nearly constant until the mid-1960's and then began to decline rapidly with the spurt of postwar economic growth. On the other hand, due to the lag in industrial development the expansion of nonfarm employment in Taiwan and Korea has until very recently been insufficient to absorb a labor force growing at an accelerating rate, with the consequence that there is increasing population pressure against land in the rural sector.

Under Japan's colonial rule, the land-saving technology developed in Japan since the early Meiji period was transplanted to Taiwan and Korea during the interwar period. This technology transfer was made feasible by (a) local adaptation and development of a technology of Japanese origin (embodied typically in improved seeds) and (b) investment in irrigation facilities as a prerequisite for the diffusion of the new technology.[3]

Continued efforts along this line have enabled Taiwan to move toward higher levels of agricultural output per worker, despite the growing population pressure against land in the rural sector. Through technological progress, as well as through the development of irrigation infrastructure, both the utilization of arable land and the yield per unit of crop area have increased.

As Figure 8–2 shows, the rate of growth in land productivity has been less dramatic and little gain has been achieved in labor productivity in Korea. The relatively poor growth performance of Korean agriculture may be explained by the lag in the construction of agricultural infrastructure both in irrigation facilities and in research and extension systems. For several reasons irrigation construction in Korea under Japanese rule lagged more than a decade behind that in Taiwan, and local research for high-yielding rice varieties was also late to start.[4] With the progress of irrigation construction in the 1920's high-yielding varieties were developed and began to be diffused. Thus, in the 1930's we see a spurt of agricultural growth in Korea. Unfortunately, within less than a decade the growth was interrupted by World War II. It is suspected that agricultural infrastructure in irrigation and in research and extension continued to lag in the postwar period, partly because of the devastation of the Korean War.

Until about 1960 Philippine agriculture was characterized by an elastic supply of land. The rapid growth in output could have been achieved at relatively little cost by expanding the cultivation frontier. This route of agricultural growth became increasingly costly as the slack of land resources was exploited, and the population continued to accumulate in the rural sector as the increase in urban nonfarm employment failed to keep up with an annual population-growth rate of 3 percent.

In this situation further growth in agricultural output and output per worker could not be possible without introducing the land-saving, yield-increasing technology that was developed in Japan and Taiwan. To introduce technology of this kind it was essential to establish agricultural infrastructure in (*a*) irrigation and water control and (*b*) research and extension for local adaptation and development.

It seems not a mere coincidence that the rate of government investment in irrigation systems accelerated in the Philippines by the end of the 1950's when the route of agricultural development via area expansion became costly.[5] It is also not coincidental that the higher-yielding varieties of rice developed at the International Rice Research Institute and the local experiment stations were diffused at a dramatic speed with progress in irrigation construction. As a result we see rapid growth in total and land productivities, and the Philippine agricultural-growth path moved toward a more vertical direction in the 1960's (see Figure 8–2). These are the sequences of agricultural development that Taiwan and Korea had experienced during the interwar period.

Wide variations in the relative endowments of land and labor exist among countries in Southeast Asia today. However, if the present rate of population growth, in the 2.5 to 3 percent range, is sustained, the population pressure in the rural sector will soon lead to a deterioration in the land/man ratio, at least in the short run, even in countries richly endowed with unexploited land resources. It would then be inevitable that these countries would follow the path of agricultural growth that the Philippines began to take in the 1960's.

Since the population pressure in the developing countries in Asia today is much stronger than in the history of modern economic growth in Japan, it is unlikely that their future growth paths will follow the historical path of Japanese agriculture (in terms of Figure 8–2). It is more likely that their paths will be even more vertical than those of Taiwan and Korea. There is even a danger that the increase in land productivity may not be able to compensate for the decrease in the land/man ratio, resulting in retrogression in agricultural output per worker. In order to avoid such a possibility, the rate by which the land-saving technology was developed in Japan is clearly insufficient. The efforts of developing technology have to be much more intensified in order to generate surpluses in agriculture that meet the requirements of the economy.

Agricultural growth in the Philippines and other developing countries in South and Southeast Asia does not seem likely to be "capital cheap" as it was in Japan, which inherited from the feudal period the well-developed irrigation system. Rather it appears that, because of stronger population pressures, these countries have to invest in irrigation on a larger scale and at a faster rate than Taiwan if they are to attain growth in agricultural output per capita of rural population via the more rapid increase in land productivity.

8-3 Feudal Heritage and Initial Conditions

The critical considerations in discussing the implications of the Japanese experience to developing countries today should be the differences in the initial conditions for modern economic growth.

The Tokugawa period preceding the Meiji Restoration was not "traditional" in the sense of the Rostovian stage classification, characterized by a stationary economy.[6] Rather it involved substantial dynamism and prepared the conditions for modern economic growth in terms of technology and institutions. Indeed, the feudal heritage was highly significant for the modern agricultural growth of Japan. The basic direction of technical progress toward land-saving by intensifying the application of labor and other forms of inputs had been established for the Tokugawa period. Selection of better seed varieties by panicle picking had been practiced among veteran farmers. The application of commercial fertilizers had begun in the districts of high population density and high land values. The improved techniques that diffused widely during the Meiji period, such as seed selection in salt water and oblong-shaped rice nursery-bed preparation, had already germinated in various localities. Above all, land infrastructure in the form of flood control and irrigation systems had been established at a level sufficient for the development and diffusion of the seed-fertilizer technology. It was on the basis of such a backlog that rapid rates of growth in agricultural output and productivity were realized during the Meiji period.[7]

Progress in agricultural technology during the Tokugawa period represents a response to the development of a market economy. Concurrently, the germ of modern market institutions, including the transactions of land properties, had been gradually developed against the feudal constraints. Because technical progress was of a nature that promoted the relative efficiency of small-scale family farms, the agrarian structure had also been induced to change from the dominance of large-scale farms to unimodal farm-size distribution. This process had been accompanied by development in the landlord-tenant relations, both through the dissolution of large farms and through the transaction of land properties. Such developments had prepared the institutional framework for Meiji agricultural development.[8]

Another important heritage was the organizational capacity of rural people. Highly stringent feudal rules on various facets of rural life, including the collection of feudal tax in kind, had been enforced through the village leaders, which had the effect of training local leadership. The organizational capacity of farmers had also been promoted by the need to cooperate in constructing and maintaining local infrastructures, above all, the irrigation system.

We cannot overemphasize the role of such feudal heritage in paving the way for the introduction of the modern system of institutions and technology after the Meiji Restoration. However, it would be dangerous if we forgot the critical role of institutional reforms and public investments in science and technology in exploiting the backlog of agricultural potential. Without such efforts the potential would have remained merely that, without contributing much to actual growth in agricultural productivity.

The conditions of agricultural development surrounding the countries in South and Southeast Asia today are certainly very different from those prevailing in Japan at the Meiji Restoration. These countries may not possess the backlog of indigenous technological potential and the organizational capacity of farm producers. The agrarian structure and the tenure institutions may be such that the introduction of new technology is difficult without causing serious instabilities or disruptions in the rural society.

On the other hand, the developing countries today are endowed with a huge backlog of potential in the form of the technology gap between the developed and the less-developed countries. By closing this gap these countries should be able to attain high rates of growth in agricultural output and productivity. The possibility of transferring agricultural technology from the developed countries in the temperate zone to the developing countries in the tropics has been suggested by the experience of the rice-technology transfer from Japan to Taiwan during the interwar period, as well as by the more recent experience of the " green revolution " in Asia. It requires (a) adaptation of foreign technology to the local environments by adaptive research and experiments, and (b) assimilation of environmental conditions to the environments where the technology was originated through investments in land infrastructure, for instance, irrigation.

The rate of growth in agricultural productivity that can be realized by the developing countries through successful technology transfer should be much higher than in Meiji Japan since the present backlog, in the form of the international technology gap, is extremely large. However, resource requirements for exploiting the backlog will be correspondingly larger. The adaptation of agricultural technology to an entirely different local ecology within a relatively short period will require a more sophisticated and systematic application of research resources than was required for exploiting the indigenous potential of similar environments within Japan. Also, the capital requirements for environmental modification or assimilation must also be extremely large in comparison to Japan, which inherited from the feudal period a relatively well developed irrigation infrastructure.

Moreover, the lack of capacity among the rural population to organize itself to build the necessary infrastructure will probably intensify the requirements of agricultural development for government funds, and may even exceed the limit that governments in the developing countries are able to mobilize with their present administrative capacity.

A more difficult problem that the developing countries are now facing is the adjustment of rural institutions in response to technical change. The adjustment of institutions usually involves a substantial time lag. If the change in technology is too rapid, there is a danger that the conflicts between technology and institutions increase cumulatively.

In this respect, it appears that Meiji Japan benefited from the gradual adjustments in rural institutions during the Tokugawa period in response to the very gradual progress in agricultural technology. The burden of technical change on the adjustments of rural institutions in the Meiji period appears relatively light, because the direction of technical progress in agriculture was essentially the extension of progress achieved in the Tokugawa period. Consequently, the acceleration in technical progress and productivity growth in agriculture did not require drastic changes in agrarian structure and institutions. The rural organization, based on small-scale family farms, which had gradually developed into the dominant mode of agricultural production during the Tokugawa period, was sustained or even strengthened during the Meiji period. In short, rapid growth in agricultural productivity in the initial phase of modern economic growth in Japan was not very inconsistent with the social stability of the rural sector.

It does not seem likely that the present and future impact of technical progress in agriculture on rural society in developing countries in Asia can be as modest as in Meiji Japan. The traditional pattern of agricultural growth in these countries has been to expand cultivation frontiers in response to expansion in world demand for tropical export crops and/or to the growth in population. The need for the development of a land-saving technology has emerged relatively recently with a rise in population growth, as discussed in the previous section with respect to the Philippines.

Consequently, the societies of these countries have not become accustomed to adjusting to such changes in technology. The rate of technical progress in agriculture must be much higher than in Meiji Japan in order for these countries to meet the requirements for agriculture consistent with the economic-development goal under much stronger population pressures; and the rate can be much higher because of the backlog of potentially borrowable technology.

It seems reasonable to expect that the conflict between agricultural technology and rural institutions will be greatly intensified if the rapid growth in productivity is realized through successful exploitation of the backlog. There is a real danger that the conflict might generate more social tension than the political structures of many developing economies in Asia are able to absorb.

8-4   In Search of Substitutes for Prerequisites

The discussions in previous sections lead us to a perspective on agricultural growth in modern Japan: (a) Japanese agriculture, given an initial level of labor productivity comparable to today's Asian countries together with a relatively high land productivity and a low land/man ratio, achieved growth at a rate sufficiently rapid to generate surpluses for supporting the development of the nonagricultural sector, concurrently with industrialization; (b) the growth in agricultural output and labor productivity was based primarily on the productivity of land by developing a land-saving technology that was designed to overcome the constraint of land resources on agricultural production; (c) the Japanese experience suggests a general direction for agriculture in the countries of South and Southeast Asia, which are now attempting to attain economic development under growing population pressure against land; (d) the Japanese experience, however, cannot be imitated or applied directly because of the differences in population pressures, the backlog of technology, and the initial conditions, especially of land infrastructure and rural institutions.

How does our perspective stand among various interpretations of the Japanese experience? Perhaps the most orthodox view (by, among others, Bruce Johnston, Kazushi Ohkawa, and Henry Rosovsky) has been to assume a unique model from the Japanese experience applicable to the development of traditional densely populated countries.[9] In their model, traditional peasant agriculture, without undergoing major structural changes comparable to the agricultural revolution in England and without an accompanying improvement in the land/man ratio, can grow rapidly in concurrence with the initial spurt of industrialization (or "take-off") and support it by contributing surpluses to the industrial sector.

The Johnston-Ohkawa-Rosovsky perspective was seriously challenged by James Nakamura.[10] He insisted that, by the beginning of modern economic growth, agricultural productivity in Japan had already reached a level considerably higher than that in today's Asian countries and that the creation of institutions able to exploit the already existing surpluses and/or the dispossession of the unproductive feudal ruling class made it possible to extract funds for industrialization. For Nakamura, a sufficiently high level of agricultural productivity was a prerequisite for industrialization in Japan as it was in the case of European nations, especially England in which there was an agricultural revolution and a subsequent rise in agricultural productivity for "take-off" or the initial spurt of industrialization. In this regard Japan was not "unique" and was no exception to the Marx-Rostow stage theory in following a determined order or sequence of economic development.

Our perspective is essentially along the line of the Johnston-Ohkawa-Rosovsky model. However, we question whether the Japanese experience represents a "unique" model readily applicable to today's developing countries. Although the empirical basis of the Nakamura hypothesis is subject to serious criticism, we share the perspective with him that the initial conditions of Japan's agricultural and economic development were critically different from today's Asia. In terms of population pressure and international technology gap, the conditions surrounding Japan at the take-off period may be more similar to the advanced countries in Europe for comparable periods. The concurrent growth of agriculture with industry may not be a unique experience in Japan.

How does the speed of agricultural growth in Europe compare with Japan for the take-off periods? In France, total farm output and output per male worker increased, respectively, by 1.3 and 1.0 percent per year from 1825–1834 to 1855–1864.[11] In Sweden, agricultural production rose by 1.7 percent and output per worker by 1.6 percent per annum from 1861–1865 to 1891–1895.[12] In Germany, agricultural production increased by 1.9 percent and output per worker by 1.3 percent per annum for 1816–1861.[13] The growth rate of agricultural output seems much higher in Russia, with crop production (including all grains) in the fifty provinces of European Russia increasing from 1885–1895 to 1905–1914 at the annual rate of 2.3 percent.[14] But, since the rural population in Russia increased from 81.6 million in 1897 to

102.7 million in 1916, the annual growth rate of labor productivity could well be less than 2 percent.[15] In Japan, the annual growth rates of total output and output per worker (male equivalent) were both 1.6 percent for 1880–1900, and they increased to 2.0 and 2.6 percent, respectively, for 1900–1920; the average growth rates for the initial growth phase from 1880 to 1920, which covers the initial stage of industrialization in Japan, were 1.8 percent for total output and 2.1 percent for labor productivity.

From the above comparisons, it can be observed that the later the start of industrialization the faster the increases in output and productivity in agriculture for the take-off periods. To offer a generalization based on limited evidence, the Japanese experience was only a specific case of the general pattern common to relative latecomers to industrialization. We recall the famous thesis of Alexander Gerschenkron that backward countries who do not possess certain " prerequisites " for industrialization can find their " substitutes."[16] At the beginning of modern economic growth Japan did not possess a sufficiently high level of agricultural productivity but found a substitute not recognized by Gerschenkron himself, namely, the concurrent growth of agricultural productivity with industrialization. The Japanese experience was not unique in this respect.

The unique aspect was that the growth in agricultural productivity was realized against the constraint of land resources, primarily by raising the yields of major cereal crops within a monsoon climate. This aspect makes the Japanese experience relevant to the developing countries in Asia. The rapid progress of land-saving and fertilizer-using technology in response to a decline in fertilizer prices relative to land prices, which was the key to the rapid increases in the crop yields per hectare, resulted from the exploitation of a backlog of technological potential. The conditions for the successful developments in land-saving technology have been identified as the relatively well developed irrigation systems and the agrarian institutions consistent with such technology, in addition to concurrent investments in agricultural research, experiments, and extension. To that extent, it would be difficult to apply the Japanese experience to the developing countries in Asia, as discussed in the previous section.

In this respect, our perspective is similar to Shigeru Ishikawa's.[17] Ishikawa has identified the irrigation infrastructure in monsoon Asia as the prerequisite for introducing the seed-fertilizer technology of the land-saving type. In his perspective, it is difficult to apply the Japanese experience of agricultural development to South and Southeast Asia. In the absence of necessary irrigation infrastructure there is little possibility of attaining sufficient gains in land productivity to produce agricultural surpluses at a rate consistent with the economic-development goal. Capital requirements for irrigation construction would be so large that the intersectoral resource transfer may have to be reversed in the direction of nonagriculture to agriculture.

We do not deny such a possibility. In fact, we see a real danger for the economies of South and Southeast Asia. In the future, they may be trapped in the Ricardian stagnation resulting from population pressures against limited land resources, because of the absence of the prerequisite in the form of irrigation infrastructure. However, we do not consider such a dark prospect as inevitable. It is true that recent technological breakthroughs in the production of major staple cereals have made the irrigation infrastructure a bottleneck more critical than ever for agricultural growth in South and Southeast Asia. However, the bottleneck implies a high social pay-off from irrigation investments, which can induce the allocation of resources to the construction of land infrastructure.

In Japan, the initial development of the seed-fertilizer technology was facilitated by the irrigation system inherited from the feudal regime. However, as the technology was propagated, the land infrastructure became the bottleneck. It appears reasonable to hypothesize that the enactment of the Arable Land Replotment Law and the subsequent spurt in public investments in land infrastructure represented a response to the increase in social pay-off.

In Taiwan, where it was attempted to transplant the Japanese rice technology during the interwar period, the irrigation system represented a major bottleneck. The Ponlai varieties were first diffused in the province of Taipei where the irrigation system was relatively well developed, and they were propagated to the southern and eastern provinces according to the progress in irrigation construction. It appears that the construction of the irrigation system in Taiwan was, to a large extent, induced by the

profitability of such investments which was increased by technological breakthrough in rice production. As the study of T. H. Lee
indicates, Taiwan experienced a net transfer of resources from
agriculture to nonagriculture during this period in spite of heavy
investments in irrigation construction.[18]

Although the lack of a prerequisite in terms of adequate irrigation infrastructure is a serious bottleneck in exploiting the technological potential in agriculture, those historical experiences
suggest that the very bottleneck represents a device for focusing
attention on the solution of the problem by inducing both public
and private investments. The recent experiences in South and
Southeast Asia do not seem inconsistent with this process. For
example, in the Philippines the development of new rice technology in the late 1960's was facilitated by an increase in the
government's irrigation investments since the late 1950's. However, as the diffusion of the high-yielding varieties has progressed,
the irrigation investments have further accelerated. This suggests a
process by which the inducement of public investments through
the dynamic interactions among technology and infrastructure
substitutes for the " missing prerequisite."

There is no doubt that the rates of growth in agricultural output
and productivity in the developing countries in Asia today, consistent with the economic-development goals under the present
population pressures, are much higher than in Meiji Japan. It
appears, however, that those countries are potentially capable of
attaining very high rates of agricultural growth if they are successful in exploiting the backlog in the form of the international
technology gap. The resources required for building the necessary
agricultural research and irrigation infrastructure seem so large,
however, that they may exceed the limits that the governments in
these countries are able to mobilize with their present institutional structures.

According to Gerschenkron's observations on the process of industrialization in Europe, the relative latecomers to industrialization could attain higher rates of industrial growth by exploiting
the technology gap between the advanced and the backward
countries. The " original capital accumulation," considered a
prerequisite for industrial development according to the experience of the industrial revolution in England, found a substitute in

the institutional innovations that were designed to mobilize surpluses in the society for industrial investments, such as the savings bank (Crédit Mobilier) in France and the industrial bank in Germany.

Considering the huge international gap in agricultural technology, there seems no reason to doubt that the developing countries in South and Southeast Asia today can attain agricultural growth at much higher rates than Meiji Japan, even if they do not possess the prerequisites at present. The necessary condition for success in agricultural growth should be the institutional innovations, both in the organization of mobilizing indigenous resources and in the form of international cooperation, which can substitute for the prerequisites. The critical consideration in this regard must be the promotion of participation and initiative by rural people, without which neither government program nor foreign aid can really be effective.

The lessons from the Japanese experience, if any, should be the process by which a unique pattern of agricultural and economic development was created in exploiting the available opportunities specific to Japan through a stream of technological and institutional innovations, in spite of the absence of several prerequisites for growth found in the Western economies. In designing a development strategy for South and Southeast Asia, a critical consideration must be to create a unique pattern of growth for each economy that is very different from the pattern in the history of Japan.

Notes to Chapter 8

[1]   David Ricardo, *On the Principles of Political Economy and Taxation*, 3d ed., ed. Piero Sraffa (Cambridge: Cambridge University Press, 1951).

[2]   See Yujiro Hayami, "Elements of Induced Innovation: A Historical Perspective for the Green Revolution," *Explorations in Economic History* 8 (Summer 1971): 445–472; and Yujiro Hayami and V. W. Ruttan, *Agricultural Development: An International Perspective* (Baltimore and London: Johns Hopkins University Press, 1971), pp. 192–235.

[3]   Ibid.

[4]   Ibid.

[5]   C. M. Crisostomo, W. H. Myers, T. B. Paris, Bart Duff, and Randolph Barker, "New Rice Technology and Labor Absorption in Philippine Agriculture," *Malayan Economic Review* 16 (October 1971): 117–158.

[6] W. W. Rostow, *The Stages of Economic Growth: A Non-Communist Manifesto* (Cambridge: Cambridge University Press, 1966).

[7] See chapter 3, sections 3.1. and 3.2.

[8] Ibid.

[9] See B. F. Johnston, "Agricultural Productivity and Economic Development in Japan," *Journal of Political Economy* 59 (December 1951): 498–513; and Kazushi Ohkawa and Henry Rosovsky, "The Role of Agriculture in Modern Japanese Economic Development," *Economic Development and Cultural Change* 9 (October 1960): 43–67.

[10] J. I. Nakamura, *Agricultural Production and the Economic Development of Japan* (Princeton: Princeton University Press, 1966).

[11] J. C. Toutain, *Le produit de l'agriculture française de 1700 à 1958: II. La croissance* (Paris: L'institut de science economique appliquée, 1961), pp. 126–127 and 207.

[12] Colin Clark, *The Conditions of Economic Progress*, 3d ed. (New York: Macmillan, 1957), p. 268.

[13] W. G. Hoffman, "The Take-off in Germany," in *Economics of Take-off into Sustained Growth*, ed. W. W. Rostow (New York: Macmillan, 1963), pp. 95–118.

[14] R. W. Goldsmith, " The Economics of Tsarist Russia, 1860–1913," *Economic Development and Cultural Change* 9 (April 1961): 369–386.

[15] V. P. Timoshenko, *Agricultural Russia and the Wheat Production* (Stanford: Food Research Institute, 1932), p. 26.

[16] Alexander Gerschenkron, *Economic Backwardness in Historical Perspective* (Cambridge: Harvard University Press, 1962), pp. 31–51.

[17] Shigeru Ishikawa, *Economic Development in Asian Perspective* (Tokyo: Kinokuniya, 1967).

[18] T. H. Lee, *Intersectoral Capital Flows in the Economic Development of Taiwan, 1895–1960* (Ithaca: Cornell University Press, 1971).

Appendix

Appendix

Basic Statistical Series

In principle the data are of Japan proper, including Okinawa before 1945 but not since 1945.

The following abbreviations are used in the explanations that follow:

LTES: Kazushi Ohkawa, Miyohei Shinohara, and Mataji Umemura, eds., *Long-term Economic Statistics of Japan since 1868*, 13 volumes (Tokyo: Toyo Keizai Shimposha, 1965-).

Social A/C: Ministry of Agriculture and Forestry, *Nogyo oyobi Noka no Shakai Kanjo* (Social Accounts of Agriculture and Farm Households), Tokyo, various issues.

Ag. Stat. Yearbook: Ministry of Agriculture and Forestry, *Norinsho Tokei Hyo* (Statistical Yearbook of the Ministry of Agriculture and Forestry), Tokyo, various issues.

Ja. Stat. Yearbook: Bureau of Statistics, Office of Prime Minister, *Nihon Tokei Nenkan* (Japan Statistical Yearbook), Tokyo, various issues.

Labor Force Survey: Bureau of Statistics, Office of Prime Minister, *Rodoryoku Chosa Hokoku* (Annual Report on the Labor Force Survey), various issues.

Arable Land E/I Report: Ministry of Agriculture, *Dai 16-Ji Kairyo Jigyo Yoran* (16th Report on Arable Land Expansion and Improvement Projects), Tokyo, 1941.

GRJA: Saburo Yamada and Yujiro Hayami, "Growth Rates of Japanese Agriculture, 1880–1970," in *Agricultural Growth in Japan, Taiwan, Korea and the Philippines*, eds. Yujiro Hayami, V. W. Ruttan, and Herman Southworth (Honolulu: University of Hawaii Press, 1975).

Survey P/W: Ministry of Agriculture and Forestry, *Noson Buka Chingin Hyo* (Survey on Prices and Wages in Farm Villages), Tokyo, various issues.

Table A-1.   Agricultural Production and Output, 1934–1936 Constant Prices

	Field Crops			Cocoon (4)	Livestock (5)
	Rice (1)	Other Crops (2)	Total (3) =(1)+(2)		
					million *yen*
1880	970	478	1,448	51	11
1885	1,025	555	1,580	50	19
1890	1,075	612	1,687	58	24
1895	1,035	660	1,695	86	32
1900	1,167	717	1,884	109	41
1905	1,266	767	2,033	128	49
1910	1,390	843	2,233	170	59
1915	1,518	965	2,483	218	71
1920	1,619	952	2,571	272	86
1925	1,594	921	2,515	327	116
1930	1,662	951	2,613	391	155
1935	1,725	1,061	2,786	351	196
1940	1,745	1,100	2,845	301	190
1945	1,657	904	2,561	118	89
1950	1,724	1,147	2,871	84	163
1955	1,909	1,402	3,311	112	403
1960	2,300	1,629	3,929	117	684
1965	2,383	1,656	4,038	109	1,144
1970	2,342	1,773	4,115	112	1,637

(1)–(6) Agricultural production: 1878–1963 data from *LTES*, vol. 9, Table 4, pp. 152–153, with the revisions of rice production explained in *GRJA*, Appendix A. Straw products are included in (2), "other crops." 1964–1972 data are extended by commodity groups from the 1963 data by the Index of Agricultural Production (1970=100) prepared by the Ministry of Agricultural and Forestry (*Ag. Stat. Yearbook*, 1972/1973, pp. 345–346).

(7) Agricultural intermediate products: Current inputs in agriculture produced within agricultural sector, including seeds, sericulture eggs, feed produced within domestic agriculture, green manure and forage crops, and others. 1878–1963 data from *LTES*, vol. 9, Table 16, column 6, pp. 186–187. For 1964–1972, total production (6) minus total output (8).

at Farm Gate, Five-year Averages Centering Years Shown

Total Production (6) =(3)+(4)+(5)	Agricultural Intermediate Products (7)	Total Output (8) =(6)−(7)	Gross Value-Added Ratio (9)	Gross Value-Added (10) =(8)×(9)
....			%	million *yen*
1,510	178	1,332	84.1	1,120
1,649	178	1,471	86.4	1,271
1,769	175	1,594	85.6	1,364
1,813	182	1,631	86.0	1,403
2,034	189	1,845	87.4	1,613
2,210	185	2,025	87.2	1,766
2,462	193	2,269	86.6	1,965
2,772	200	2,572	85.5	2,199
2,929	194	2,735	85.6	2,341
2,958	187	2,771	84.9	2,353
3,159	184	2,975	83.0	2,469
3,333	187	3,146	83.9	2,639
3,336	193	3,143	82.9	2,606
2,768	160	2,608	82.0	2,139
3,118	179	2,939	81.9	2,407
3,826	259	3,567	80.5	2,871
4,730	283	4,447	79.2	3,522
5,291	207	5,084	77.5	3,940
5,863	217	5,646	75.5	4,263

(8) Total output: For 1878–1963, total production (6) minus agricultural intermediate products (7). 1964–1971 data are extended from the 1963 data by the Index of Total Agricultural Output (1970=100) prepared by the Ministry of Agriculture and Forestry (*Ag. Stat. Yearbook*, 1971/1972, p. 330). 1972 data from the provisional manuscript of *Social A/C*, 1972.

(9) Gross value added ratio: Ratio of gross value added to total output at current prices; calculated from Table A-2 (8) and (10). 1940–1950 ratios are calculated from the data in Table A-2 with interpolations for 1941–1950.

(10) Gross value added: Total output (8) multiplied by gross value added ratio (9).

Table A-2. Agricultural Production and Output, Current Prices at Farm Gate,

	Field Crops			Cocoon (4)	Livestock (5)
	Rice (1)	Other Crops (2)	Total (3) =(1)+(2)		
					million *yen*
1880	286	163	449	42	4
1885	191	150	341	33	6
1890	243	183	426	39	10
1895	323	239	562	66	17
1900	501	327	828	95	25
1905	633	428	1,061	135	41
1910	790	550	1,340	155	48
1915	883	647	1,530	264	58
1920	2,140	1,343	3,483	575	146
1925	1,944	1,195	3,139	676	191
1930	1,297	927	2,224	439	181
1935	1,673	1,066	2,739	394	197
					billion *yen*
1955	724	563	1,287	48	153
1960	913	727	1,640	56	277
1965	1,416	1,097	2,513	88	604
1970	1,799	1,578	3,377	113	1,037

(1)–(6) Agricultural production: 1878–1963 data from *LTES*, vol. 9, Table 1, pp. 146–147 with the revisions of rice production explained in *GRJA*, Appendix A. 1964–1969 data from *Social A/C*, 1969, Table 17, pp. 40–41, excluding changes in plant and livestock inventory. 1970–1972 data from the provisional manuscript of *Social A/C*, 1972.

(7) Agricultural intermediate products: 1878–1963 data from *LTES*, vol. 9, Table 14, column 6, pp. 183–184. 1964–1969 data from *Social A/C*, 1969, Table 17, pp. 40–41. 1970–1972 data are estimated by multiplying total agricultural production by the ratio of intermediate products to total production in 1969.

Five-year Averages Centering Years Shown

Total Production (6) =(3)+(4)+(5)	Agricultural Intermediate Products (7)	Total Output (8) =(6)−(7)	Nonfarm Current Inputs (9)	Gross Value-Added (10) =(8)−(9)
495	60	435	69	366
380	42	338	46	292
475	51	424	61	363
645	66	579	81	498
948	94	854	108	746
1,237	115	1,122	144	978
1,543	123	1,420	190	1,230
1,852	135	1,717	249	1,468
4,204	275	3,929	567	3,362
4,006	229	3,777	569	3,208
2,844	174	2,670	454	2,216
3,330	192	3,138	505	2,633
1,488	83	1,405	274	1,131
1,973	92	1,881	391	1,490
3,205	120	3,085	692	2,393
4,527	138	4,389	1,093	3,296

(8) Total output: Total production (6) minus agricultural intermediate products (7).

(9) Nonfarm current inputs: Current inputs in agriculture supplied from nonagricultural sector. 1878–1963 data from *LTES*, vol. 9, Table 14, column 12, pp. 183–184. 1964–1972 data are the total of the inputs of fertilizers, agricultural chemicals, fuels, feeds, and miscellaneous items in the provisional manuscript of *Social A/C*, 1972.

(10) Gross value added: Total output (8) minus nonfarm current inputs (9).

Table A-3.   Numbers of Workers and Workdays in Agriculture, Five-year
Averages Centering Years Shown

	Number of Workers				Number of Workdays		
			Total			Per Worker	
	Male (1)	Female (2)	Simple Sum (3)=(1)+(2)	Male Equivalent (4)	Total (5)	(5)/(3)	(5)/(4)
	⋯⋯⋯⋯⋯⋯⋯1,000 workers⋯⋯⋯⋯⋯⋯				million days	days	days
1880	8,332	7,256	15,588	13,556	1,776	113	131
1885	8,339	7,264	15,603	13,569	1,830	117	135
1890	8,354	7,275	15,629	13,592	1,921	123	141
1895	8,390	7,295	15,685	13,642	2,002	128	147
1900	8,475	7,355	15,830	13,771	2,067	131	150
1905	8,529	7,400	15,929	13,857	2,103	132	152
1910	8,527	7,348	15,875	13,818	2,208	139	160
1915	8,391	6,921	15,312	13,374	2,276	149	170
1920	7,626	6,375	14,001	12,216	2,283	163	187
1925	7,386	6,150	13,536	11,814	2,157	159	183
1930	7,631	6,340	13,971	12,196	2,113	151	173
1935	7,458	6,318	13,776	12,007	2,200	160	183
1940	6,263	7,122	13,385	11,391	2,186	163	192
1945	6,260	7,674	13,934	11,785	2,012	144	171
1950	7,692	8,194	15,886	13,592	2,262	142	166
1955	7,268	7,904	15,172	12,959	2,282	150	176
1960	6,232	7,166	13,398	11,392	2,080	155	183
1965	5,090	6,144	11,234	9,514	1,740	155	183
1970	4,267	4,893	9,160	7,790	1,346	147	173

(1)–(3)   Number of gainful workers in agriculture: male, female, and
total. 1878–1920 data are Mataji Umemura's estimates of the number of
gainful workers in agriculture and forestry (prepared for *LTES*, vol. 2)
multiplied by the ratio of the number of workers in agriculture to the
number in agriculture and forestry in the 1920 population census. 1921–
1940 data are estimated by multiplying the Umemura series by the
ratios of the number of agricultural workers to the number of agricultural and forestry workers, which are estimated by interpolating the ratios
in 1920, 1930, and 1940 calculated from the population census data.
1941–1963 data from *LTES*, vol. 9, Table 33, columns 1–3, pp. 218–219.
1964–1967 data from *Labor Force Survey*, 1968, pp. 42 and 46, from which
1968–1972 data are extrapolated based on *Labor Force Survey*, 1972, pp.
45–47.
(4)   Total number of workers in terms of male equivalents: female
workers are converted into male equivalents by multiplying the ratio of

the male wage rate to the female wage rate (0.72 as the average for the whole period), and then are added to the number of male workers.

(5) Number of workdays applied to agricultural production: The number of workdays is calculated by aggregating the workdays for the production of various crops, sericulture, and livestock. The workdays applied for different products are estimated by multiplying crop areas and numbers of livestock animals by the numbers of workdays per hectare or per animal. For detail, see Masahiko Shintani, "Nogyo Bumon ni okeru Toka Rodo Nissu no Suikei" (Estimation of Labor Input in Agriculture since 1874), *Keizai Kenkyu* 25 (July 1974): 264–271.

Table A-4.   Land Resource and Utilization in Agriculture, Five-year Averages

	Paddy Field (1)	Upland Field (2)	Simple Sum (3)=(1)+(2)	Paddy-Field Equivalent (4)
			Cultivated Land Area	
			Total	
				·······1,000 hectares
1880	2,790	1,945	4,735	3,626
1885	2,825	1,996	4,821	3,683
1890	2,857	2,067	4,924	3,746
1895	2,875	2,158	5,033	3,803
1900	2,904	2,289	5,193	3,888
1905	2,936	2,371	5,307	3,956
1910	3,006	2,568	5,574	4,110
1915	3,073	2,711	5,784	4,239
1920	3,133	2,850	5,983	4,359
1925	3,199	2,728	5,927	4,372
1930	3,271	2,704	5,975	4,434
1935	3,291	2,817	6,108	4,502
1940	3,277	2,833	6,110	4,495
1945	3,200	2,661	5,861	4,344
1950	3,230	2,625	5,855	4,359
1955	3,302	2,675	5,977	4,452
1960	3,375	2,701	6,076	4,536
1965	3,399	2,610	6,009	4,521
1970	3,393	2,400	5,793	4,425

(1)–(3)   Cultivated land area: paddy field, upland field, and total area. 1878–1963 data from *LTES*, vol. 9, Table 32, columns 13–14, pp. 216–217. 1964–1972 data from *Ag. Stat. Yearbook*.

(4)   Total cultivated land area in paddy-field equivalents: Upland-field areas are converted into paddy-field equivalents by multiplying the ratio

Centering Years Shown

Crop Area			Land-Utilization Rate	
Rice (5)	Other Crops (6)	Total (7)=(5)+(6)	(7)/(3)	(7)/(4)
....			.........hectares.........	
2,639	3,643	6,282	1.33	1.73
2,657	3,968	6,625	1.37	1.80
2,723	4,306	7,029	1.43	1.88
2,752	4,531	7,283	1.45	1.92
2,813	4,698	7,511	1.45	1.93
2,862	4,807	7,669	1.45	1.94
2,933	5,008	7,941	1.42	1.93
3,030	5,191	8,221	1.42	1.94
3,094	5,181	8,275	1.38	1.90
3,129	4,771	7,900	1.33	1.81
3,203	4,695	7,898	1.32	1.78
3,169	4,893	8,062	1.32	1.79
3,161	5,051	8,212	1.34	1.83
2,915	4,322	7,237	1.23	1.67
2,996	4,572	7,568	1.29	1.74
3,154	4,828	7,982	1.34	1.79
3,287	4,791	8,078	1.33	1.78
3,261	4,201	7,462	1.24	1.65
2,962	3,291	6,253	1.08	1.41

of the price of upland fields to the price of paddy fields (0.43 as the average for the whole period), and adding to the area of paddy fields. (5)–(7) Crop area: rice, other crops, and total. Data from *Ag. Stat. Yearbook*, various issues.

Table A-5. Indices of Land and Labor Productivities, and Land/Labor Ratios in Agriculture, 1880=100, Five-year Averages Centering Years Shown

	Labor Productivity		Land Productivity		Land/Labor Ratio	
	Per Male Equivalent (1)	Per Workday (2)	Per Paddy-Field Equivalent (3)	Per Hectare of Crop Area (4)	Paddy Field per Male Equivalent (1)/(3)	Crop Area per Workday (2)/(4)
1880	100	100	100	100	100	100
1885	111	107	109	105	102	102
1890	119	110	116	107	103	103
1895	122	108	117	106	105	102
1900	136	119	129	116	106	103
1905	149	128	139	125	107	102
1910	167	137	151	135	111	101
1915	196	150	165	148	119	101
1920	228	159	171	156	134	102
1925	239	171	173	166	139	103
1930	248	187	183	178	136	105
1935	267	190	190	184	140	103
1940	281	191	191	181	148	106
1945	225	173	164	171	138	101
1950	220	173	184	183	120	95
1955	280	208	218	211	129	99
1960	398	285	267	260	149	110
1965	544	390	306	321	178	121
1970	738	559	347	426	213	131

(1) Labor-productivity index in male equivalent terms: Index of total output in Table A-1 (8) divided by the number of workers in male equivalents in Table A-3 (4).

(2) Labor-productivity index in workday terms: Index of total output in Table A-1 (8) divided by the number of workdays in Table A-3 (5).

(3) Land-productivity index in paddy-field equivalent terms: Index of total output in Table A-1 (8) divided by cultivated land area in paddy-field equivalents in Table A-4 (4).

(4) Land-productivity index in crop area terms: Index of total output in Table A-1 (8) divided by crop area in Table A-4 (7).

Table A-6.   Fixed Capital and Current Inputs in Agriculture, 1934–1936
Prices, Five-year Averages Centering Years Shown

	Fixed Capital				Nonfarm Current Input		
	Machinery and Imple- ments (1)	Live- stock and Plants (2)	Build- ings and Struc- tures (3)	Total (4) = (1)+ (2)+(3)	Fertiliz- ers (5)	Other (6)	Total (7) = (5)+(6)
				million *yen*			
1880	561	811	1,542	2,914	29	57	86
1885	582	845	1,568	2,995	28	63	91
1890	603	906	1,607	3,116	28	66	94
1895	627	1,015	1,672	3,314	32	74	106
1900	655	1,089	1,720	3,464	40	82	122
1905	713	1,184	1,787	3,684	57	87	144
1910	798	1,358	1,898	4,054	101	103	204
1915	884	1,444	1,961	4,289	131	115	246
1920	968	1,492	2,013	4,473	177	128	305
1925	1,054	1,540	2,070	4,664	217	159	376
1930	1,164	1,639	2,147	4,950	266	177	443
1935	1,269	1,663	2,194	5,126	293	193	486
1940	1,324	1,664	2,222	5,210	342	179	521
1945	1,242	1,199	2,015	4,456	177	68	245
1950	1,364	1,165	2,076	4,605	373	163	536
1955	1,675	1,400	2,356	5,431	626	363	989
1960	2,555	1,871	2,806	7,232	733	674	1,407
1965	4,994	2,573	3,929	11,496	895	1,351	2,246
1970	8,066	3,476	4,588	16,130	952	2,394	3,346

(1)–(4)   Fixed capital: 1878–1962 data from *LTES*, vol. 9, Table 28, pp. 210–11, columns 1 and 2 for (2) livestock and plants, and column 5 for (1) farm machinery and implements; data for (3) farm buildings are the revised estimates from the estimates in column 7 of Table 28, *LTES*, vol. 9 by Kazushi Ohkawa and Nobukiyo Takamatsu for *LETS*, vol. 1. 1963– 1971 data are obtained by deflating the current values of fixed capital by items (*Social A/C*, 1971, pp. 76, 77, 92, 93), which are spliced to the *LTES* series at 1960–1962. 1972 data are extrapolated from data in the provisional manuscript of *Social A/C*, 1972.

(5)–(7)   Nonfarm current inputs: 1878–1963 data from *LTES*, vol. 9, Table 16, column 12, pp. 186–187. 1964–1971 data are the nonfarm current inputs in current prices in Table A-2 (9) deflated by a price index calculated from the data prepared for the Price Index for Agricultural Production Goods of the Ministry of Agriculture and Forestry (*Ag. Stat. Yearbook*, 1971/1972, pp. 144–145), which are spliced with the *LTES* series at 1961–1963. 1972 data are extrapolated from data in the provisional manuscript of *Social A/C*, 1972.

Table A-7. Indices of Factor Inputs in Agriculture, 1880=100, Five-year Averages Centering Years Shown

	Labor (Male equivalents) (1)	Land (Paddy-field equivalents) (2)	Capital		Nonfarm Current Input	
			Machinery and Implements (3)	Total (4)	Fertilizers (5)	Total (6)
1880	100	100	100	100	100	100
1885	100	102	104	103	97	106
1890	100	103	108	107	97	109
1895	101	105	112	114	110	123
1900	102	107	117	119	138	142
1905	102	109	127	126	197	167
1910	102	113	142	139	348	238
1915	99	117	158	147	452	286
1920	90	120	173	154	610	355
1925	87	121	188	160	748	437
1930	90	122	208	170	917	515
1935	89	124	226	176	1,010	565
1940	84	124	236	179	1,179	606
1945	87	120	221	153	610	285
1950	100	120	243	158	1,286	623
1955	96	123	299	186	2,159	1,150
1960	84	125	455	248	2,528	1,636
1965	70	125	890	395	3,086	2,612
1970	57	122	1,438	554	3,283	3,891

(1) Index of the number of farm workers in terms of male equivalents in Table A-3 (4).
(2) Index of cultivated land area in terms of paddy-field equivalents in Table A-4 (4).
(3) Index of farm machinery and implements in Table A-6 (1).
(4) Index of total fixed capital in agriculture in Table A-6 (4).
(5) Index of fertilizer inputs in Table A-6 (5).
(6) Index of nonfarm current inputs in agriculture in Table A-6 (7).

Table A-8.   Agricultural Product and Factor Prices (indices with 1934–1936

| | Price Index of Agricultural Products (1) | Farm Wage Rates | | Cultivated Land |
		Yen per Day (2)	Index (3)	*Yen* per Hectare (4)
1880	34.0	n.a.	n.a.	n.a.
1885	23.8	n.a.	n.a.	n.a.
1890	27.3	0.183	21.2	343
1895	36.1	0.268	31.2	635
1900	47.8	0.371	43.2	968
1905	57.0	0.403	46.9	1,049
1910	63.6	0.469	54.5	1,613
1915	66.9	0.550	64.0	1,815
1920	146.3	1.472	171.2	3,882
1925	137.4	1.424	165.6	3,822
1930	90.5	1.098	127.7	3,206
1935	100.7	0.878	102.1	2,833
1955	40,049	352	40,976	686,178
1960	42,883	484	56,279	1,429,528
1965	60,804	966	112,325	1,585,728
1970	79,239	1,794	208,588	2,358,431

(1)   Price index of agricultural products: 1878–1963 data from *LTES*, vol. 9, Table 10, column 5, p. 164. 1964–1972 data are extended from the 1961–1963 average by the index of agricultural prices in *Survey P/W*, various issues.

(2)   Daily wage rates of male farm workers: 1888–1963 data from *LTES*, vol. 9, Table 34, column 3, pp. 220–221. 1964–1972 data from *Survey P/W*, various issues.

(3)   Index of (2).

(4)   Cultivated land prices: Weighted average of upland and paddy-field prices. 1878–1963 data from *LTES*, vol. 9, Table 34, column 9–10, pp. 220–221. For 1964–1967 the prefectural land-price data from Nihon Fudosan Kenkyujo (Japan Real Property Research Institute), *Denbata oyobi Kosakuryo Shirabe* (Survey on the Prices and Rents of Paddy and Upland Fields), (Tokyo, 1970), are agregated by using as weights arable paddy and upland fields in 1955. 1968–1972 data are extrapolated by the national average cultivated land prices from *Denbata oyobi Kosakuryo Shirabe*, 1972.

=100), Five-year Averages Centering Years Shown

Price	Indices of Fixed Capital Prices		Indices of Current Input Prices	
Index (5)	Machinery and Implements (6)	Total (7)	Fertilizer (8)	Total (9)
n.a.	52.7	29.7	102.1	89.50
n.a.	42.4	27.8	67.8	58.46
12.5	47.6	30.4	93.5	75.71
22.9	50.4	37.6	100.7	87.55
35.0	60.8	49.6	113.0	99.80
37.7	69.8	56.3	122.5	109.73
58.0	69.8	61.7	105.3	96.60
65.5	92.6	67.9	117.0	104.86
140.0	148.3	146.2	199.4	185.58
137.6	122.3	140.4	159.5	152.48
115.6	94.6	103.2	104.3	101.86
102.2	107.2	103.0	102.9	102.62
24,718	33,722	47,375	23,000	35,477
51,497	36,562	50,885	20,760	32,142
57,123	37,347	65,789	20,793	33,916
84,904	32,483	84,221	22,041	35,487

(5)   Index of (4).
(6)   Price index of farm machinery and implements: 1878–1963 data from *LTES*, vol. 9, Table 31, column 4, p. 215. 1964–1972 data are extrapolated from the 1961–1963 average by the price index of farm machinery and implements in *Survey P/W*, various issues.
(7)   Price index of total fixed capital in agriculture: 1878–1963 data from *LTES*, vol. 9, Table 31, column 6, p. 215. 1964–1972 data are extrapolated from the 1961–1963 average by the price deflator of fixed capital investment in the provisional manuscript of *Social A/C*, 1972.
(8)   Price index of fertilizers: 1878–1963 data from *LTES*, vol. 9, Table 18, column 6, pp. 192–223. 1964–1972 data are extrapolated from the 1961–1963 average by the price index of fertilizers in *Survey P/W*, various issues.
(9)   Price index of nonfarm current inputs: 1878–1963 data from *LTES*, vol. 9, Table 17, column 10, pp. 188–191. 1964–1972 data are extrapolated from the 1961–1963 average by the price index of nonfarm current inputs in *Survey P/W*, various issues.

Table A-9.   Indices of Total Output, Total Input, and Total Productivity
in Agriculture, 1880=100, Five-year Averages Centering Years Shown

	Total Output (1)	Total Input		Total Productivity	
		Stock Terms (2)	Flow Terms (3)	Stock Terms (4)	Flow Terms (5)
1880	100	100	100	100	100
1885	111	101	104	110	107
1890	120	103	110	117	109
1895	123	105	115	117	106
1900	139	108	120	129	115
1905	152	111	124	137	122
1910	171	117	134	146	127
1915	193	119	142	162	135
1920	206	119	147	173	140
1925	208	121	146	172	142
1930	223	126	148	177	150
1935	236	128	154	184	153
1940	236	126	156	187	151
1945	196	117	132	168	148
1950	221	145	164	152	134
1955	268	162	189	165	141
1960	334	167	198	200	168
1965	382	179	207	213	185
1970	424	186	205	231	210

(1)   Total output index: Index of total output in Table A-1 (8).

(2)   Total input index in stock terms: The indices of labor (male equivalents), land (paddy-field equivalents), fixed capital, and current inputs,
in Table A-7 are aggregated by the factor share weights in Table 2–11
using the chain-linked index formula (see discussion in main text).

(3)   Total input index in flow terms: The indices of labor (workdays)
in Table A-3 (5), land (crop area) in Table A-4 (7), and fixed capital
and current inputs in Table A-7, are aggregated by the factor share
weights in Table 2–11 using the chain-linked index formula.

(4)   Total productivity index in stock terms: Total output index (1)
divided by total input index in stock terms (2).

(5)   Total productivity index in flow terms: Total output index (1)
divided by total input index (3).

Table A-10.   Improvements in Land Infrastructure

Area Improved after Meiji Restoration

Area Irrigated by Water-Utilization Association		Area Covered by Projects under Arable Land Replotment Law (3)	Area Covered by Major Irrigation and Drainage Improvement Projects (4)	Total (5)	Total Improved Area (6)	Land Quality Index (7)
Reservoir (1)	River (2)					
		1,000 hectares				1880=100
1880 — 22	166			188	1,814	100.0
1885 — 30	235			265	1,891	100.2
1890 — 37	270			307	1,933	100.3
1895 — 44	291			335	1,961	100.3
1900 — 50	311			361	1,987	100.4
1905 — 57	330	5		392	2,018	100.4
1910 — 64	357	43		464	2,090	100.4
1915 — 74	376	150		600	2,226	100.5
1920 — 84	397	258		739	2,365	100.6
1925 — 94	418	354	45	911	2,537	101.0
1930 — 105	427	480	197	1,209	2,835	101.5
1935 — 119	434	603	330	1,486	3,112	102.0
1940 — 133	441	700	518	1,792	3,418	103.0

Area Improved after World War II

	Irrigation and Drainage (8)	Land Replotment (9)	Other (10)	Total (11)			
		1,000 hectares					
1950	474	88		562	2,354	3,980	104.0
1955	1,023	344	7	1,374	3,166	4,790	105.6
1960	1,464	595	14	2,073	3,865	5,491	106.9
1965	1,960	803	22	2,785	4,577	6,203	109.0

(1)–(2)   Area irrigated by water-utilization associations: Areas irrigated by water-utilization associations, using reservoirs and rivers as the sources of water, are estimated by multiplying total areas irrigated from reservoirs and rivers by the ratios of areas irrigated by water-utilization associations from the respective water sources. The data of total areas irrigated from the sources of reservoirs and rivers are from the Imperial Agricultural Association, *Suiri Chosa* (Survey on Water Utilization), (Tokyo, 1942), pp. 15–19. The data on the ratios of areas irrigated by water-utilization associations to total area irrigated from reservoirs and rivers are based on sample surveys by the Ministry of Agriculture and Forestry, *Tameike Tokei* (Statistics on Reservoirs), (Tokyo, 1957), pp. 18–20, and by the Ministry of Construction, *Showa 42/43 Nendo Kanko Suiriken Chosa* (Survey on the Customary Water Utilization Rights), (Tokyo, 1967/1968), pp. 64–170.

(3) Area covered by projects under the Arable Land Replotment Law: Data from *Arable Land E/I Report*, 1941, pp. 9–10.

(4) Area covered by the Major Irrigation and Drainage Improvement Projects: Data from *Arable Land E/I Report*, 1941, p. 71.

(5) Total area improved after the Meiji Restoration: Sum of (1), (2), (3), and (4).

(6) Total improved area: Area improved before the Meiji Restoration, estimated at 53 percent of the reservoir-irrigation area and 63 percent of the river-irrigation area in 1940, is added to the total area irrigated after the Meiji Restoration (5). These ratios of areas improved before the Meiji Restoration are based on the Ministry of Agriculture and Forestry, *Tameike Tokei*, pp. 18–20, and the Ministry of Construction, *Showa 42/43 Nendo Kanko Suiriken Chosa*, pp. 64–170.

(7) Land quality index: Assuming that the improved paddy field is 10 percent more productive than the unimproved area, this index is calculated as

$$(7) = \frac{0.1 \times (6) + \text{Table A-4 } (4)}{\text{Table A-4 } (4)}$$

See footnote 7 of chapter 7.

(8)–(11) Area improved after World War II: The 1946–1957 data are from the Ministry of Agriculture and Forestry, *Showa 33 Nendo Nochi Gyosei Hakusho* (1958 White Paper on Agricultural Land Policy), (Tokyo, 1958), Appendix Table 4, pp. 26–27. The 1958–1961 data are from the Ministry of Agriculture and Forestry, *Nochi no Kairyo oyobi Kanri ni kansuru Tokei* (Statistics on Cultivated Land Area Expansion and Improvement), (Tokyo, March 1962), pp. 22–23. The 1962–1965 data are from Norin Tokei Kyokai, *Pocket Norin Seisan Tokei* (Handbook of Agriculture, Forestry, and Fishery Statistics), (Tokyo, 1968), p. 93.

Table A-11.   Education, Research, and Extension, in Agriculture

	Average Years Formal Education per Farm Worker			Public Expenditure for Agricultural Research and Extension (1955 current prices)		
	Male (1)	Female (2)	Total (3)	Research (4)	Extension (5)	Total (6)
	·············years·············			···············million yen···············		
1880	n.a.	n.a.	n.a.	n.a.	n.a.	n.a.
1885	1.25	0.46	0.86	98	159	257
1850	1.42	0.57	1.01	27	289	316
1895	1.59	0.68	1.16	269	99	368
1900	1.97	0.85	1.37	455	144	599
1905	2.12	1.14	1.65	786	836	1,622
1910	2.14	1.53	2.00	918	1,396	2,314
1915	3.00	2.17	2.60	951	1,592	2,543
1920	3.51	2.82	3.15	1,283	1,241	2,524
1925	4.09	3.45	3.74	1,748	2,791	4,539
1930	4.97	4.09	4.35	1,414	3,035	4,449
1935	5.31	4.71	4.99	1,943	3,856	5,799
1940				2,350	7,179	9,529
1950	9.5	8.7	9.1	2,176	21,059	23,235
1955	9.8	9.0	9.4	4,783	24,396	29,179
1960	10.0	9.3	9.7	7,469	24,666	32,135
1965	10.1	9.5	9.8	n.a.	n.a.	n.a.

(1)–(3)   Average years of formal education per farm worker: The 1885–1935 data are estimated by the following formula:

$$E_t = \sum_{i=1}^{12} e_1 p_1(i, t)h_i + \sum_{i=1}^{12} (e_2 - e_1)p_2(i, t)h_i + \sum_{i=1}^{12} (e_3 - e_1)p_3(i, t)h_i$$

where E_t is the average number of school years of a farm worker at year t; e_j is the average number of school years of a worker who completed the i-th level of education; $j=1$ stands for the primary education (4 years before 1907, and 6 years since then); $j=2$ stands for the semi-secondary education including various kinds of subsidiary vocational schools (7 years before 1907, and 9 years since then); and $j=3$ stands for the secondary level of education (9 years). P_j (i, t) is the ratio of the farm workers of the i-th age bracket) 5 years each, who completed the j-th level of education, to the total number of farm workers who belong to the i-th age bracket at year t. h_1 is the ratio of the farm workers who are in the i-th age bracket to the total number of farm workers gainfully occupied. For more detail, see Masakatsu Akino, " Heikin Shugaku Nensu no Suikei, 1885–1935 " (Estimation of Average Years of Formal Education), *Nogyo Sogo Kenkyu*, 26 (July 1972): 193–203. The 1950–1965 data are from the Economic Planning Agency Institute for Economic Research, *Nibumon Seicho Model ni yoru Keizai Seichoryoku no Sokutei* (Estimates of the Economic Growth Potential by Two-Sector Model), (Tokyo, 1970), p. 130.

(4)–(6)   Public expenditure for agricultural research and extension: Sum of expenditures for agricultural research and extension by both national and prefectural governments at current prices is deflated by the cost-of-living index. For details, see Saburo Yamada, " Changes in Output and in Conventional and Nonconventional Inputs in Japanese Agriculture since 1880," *Food Research Institute Studies* 7 (1967): 371–413. In this appendix the original Yamada estimates are adjusted for different time intervals by interpolations.

Index

1. Subject

for measuring input and productivity, 37–38; stock, and measurement of agricultural productivity, 38; time-series, 15

depression: agriculture during, 62

double cropping: effect of, on labor utilization, 39, 58; effect of land improvements on, 184; effects of, on land-utilization rate, 28

economic growth, Japanese: dependence of, on food supplies, 7; and land utilization, 28

education: character of, 129; contribution of, to output growth, 107; contribution of, to technological progress, 128; measurement of, in production function, 93; in Meiji period, 46; role of, in agricultural productivity, 46, 101, 196; role of, in Asian agricultural development, 129; trends in production elasticity of, 101–102

Evenson, Robert: and character of agricultural research, 90; estimation of U.S. scale economies by, 91

Ever-Normal Granary Plan, 62

Europe: as model for Japanese agricultural development, 49

Experiment Farm for Staple Cereals and Vegetables, 50, 51

experiment stations: crossbreeding research in, 65; early development of, 49, 51; effect of, on agricultural production function, 115; growth of, on local level, 64; and local application of rice research, 145; relation of, to extension services, 69; role of, in development of agriculture, 52, 61; and rōnō techniques, 54

exports, Japanese: 1950's nature of, 74

extension services; in post-World War II period, 69

factor inputs: relation of, to factor prices, 33

factor prices: effects of, on inputs, 33

factor shares: estimates of, in pre- and postwar periods, 97

farm efficiency: 1950's attempts to improve, 73

farmers: benefits to, of agricultural cooperatives, 54; benefits to, of post-

World War II land reforms, 68; decline in living standards of, 63; effects of Land Tax Revision on, 47; legislation affecting, 46, 54, 56; restrictions on, in Tokugawa period, 44, 115; role of, in development of market economy, 44, 45

farm income, 75; determinants of, 28

Farmland Adjustment Law: post-World War II amendment of, 67

Farmland Development Corporation: land improvement projects of, 174

Farmland Price Control Order, 67

farm prices: action for government support of, 74

farm size: and character of agricultural production, 45; in Japan, 48; relation of, to use of farm machinery, 72

Fertilizer Control Law, 56

fertilizers: adoption of, by farmers, 55–56; development in, 45, 55–56, 66; disequilibria in input of, 98; effect of land infrastructure on use of, 56–57; effect of, on land productivity, 42; effects of, on rice yields, 182; government control of development of, 56; interregional differences in input of, 92; interregional differences in price and demand of, 92; marketing of, 69; measurement of, in production function, 93; and need for pesticides, 71; and nitrogen-response function, 182; as nonfarm current input, 15; production elasticity of, 89, 91; rate of growth of, 32, 195; as substitute for land, 33, 55; in Tokugawa period, 55; trends in price of, 33; trends in production elasticity of, 98

fertilizer-responsive agriculture: conditions for development of, 92

feudalism: decay of, 46

flow data: limitations of, 23, 24

flow terms: and land and labor productivities, 30

food: contribution of, to economic growth, 7; and living costs of urban workers, 7; as principal wage good, 7. SEE ALSO rice

Food Control Special Account, 74

Gerschenkron, Alexander: and substitutes for agricultural growth, 212, 214

2. Authors Cited in Notes

Akino, Masakatsu: 110, 111, 167, 235
Ayer, H. W.: 169
Barker, Randolph: 215
Barletta, L. A.: 169
Clark, Colin: 43, 216
Crisostonio, C. M.: 215
Dore, Ronald P.: 83

Duff, Bart: 215
Evenson, R.E.: 110, 168
Fei, J. C. H.: 12
Fishel, W. L.: 168
Fukushima, Masao: 81
Furushima, Toshio: 80, 81, 82
Gerschenkron, Alexander: 216